HOW TO WRITE A SCREENPLAY IN 3-DAYS

HOW TO WRITE A SCREENPLAY IN 3 DAYS:

The Marathon Method

HOW TO WRITE A SCREENPLAY IN 3 DAYS

The Marathon Method

YOUNG FILMS & PUBLISHING LLC
www.readamovie.com

Copyright © 2008 by Young Films & Publishing LLC.
All rights reserved.

This book is a work of nonfiction.
All rights reserved, including the right of
reproduction in whole or in part in any form.

Edited by Jill Pomerantz

Book cover design by Jackie Young

Authored by Jackie Young

ISBN-10: 0-9774328-7-4
ISBN-13: 978-0-9774328-7-5

Printed in the United States of America
10 9 8 7 6 5 4 3 2 1

HOW TO WRITE A SCREENPLAY IN 3-DAYS

To those with a story to tell that belongs on the silver screen...

A SPECIAL THANKS TO

My parents, Lester & Edna Young, and my family for always encouraging my creativity.

CONTENTS

PREFACE	1
INTRO	3
SCREENPLAY FORMAT	13
SCREENPLAY STRUCTURE	19
STORY DEVELOPMENT	23
CHARACTER DEVELOPMENT	31
SCENES AND DIALOGUE	45
THE INSANITY OF IT ALL	49
PREPARING FOR THE MARATHON	171
THE MARATHON	173
POLISHING/REWRITES	179
SELLING YOUR SCREENPLAY	181
PROTECTING YOUR SCREENPLAY	185
RESOURCES	187
RECOMMENDED SCREENPLAYS/FILMS	189
SCREENPLAY EXAMPLE	191
FINAL NOTE	299
AUTHOR BIO	301

HOW TO WRITE A SCREENPLAY IN 3 DAYS:

The Marathon Method

PREFACE

My family, which consisted of seven brothers and sisters, moved to Rockford, Illinois from Missouri during the 1950s and although both my parents worked hard, there wasn't much of a future for me in an industrial town. A high school diploma was more than what was expected for most jobs. The discussion of a higher education never came up and even if it did, how would they afford it? My parents encouraged my creativity as a child and I never quit dreaming of great adventures and letting my imagination run wild. I loved movies, because, like everyone else, it was my great escape.

At home, my brothers and I used to stay up late to watch late night horror movies. And when spending the summer at Grandma's, we'd quietly sneak out of our rooms to watch great *Twilight Zone* and *Outer Limits* episodes. Those wonderful and imaginative shows still carry their influence with me today. However, when I joined the military, the war took me away from all of that and offered opportunities far beyond my wildest imagination. I was able to see cultures and peoples that have influenced me for a lifetime.

Along the way, I have had great luck and opportunity in my career and education, but I have never forgotten my roots back in Missouri and Rockford and the beginning of my creative expression. If I've learned only one thing in my life, it's that the things we learn early in life never leave us and are burned in at our core. Parents reading this please encourage your children in the arts and nurture every creative possibility that comes to them. Creativity lets us dream…and share that dream with others. That said, please enjoy the book and if I teach you only one thing, then I have completed my mission.

INTRO

WELCOME TO OUR book on screenwriting! Because you are reading this, I assume that you are probably interested in writing your first screenplay. In our book, we will try to have a little fun as you learn the process of screenwriting and how to write your first screenplay.

Screenplays are merely a way for storytellers to express their tales using the visual medium, film. Storytellers have existed since the dawn of man, with early cave dwellers scribing their accounts on cave walls. A few believe that only the most creative of us are capable of telling a story or writing a screenplay. I believe that any of us can do this if we have a story inside desperate to be told. Telling a story in screenplay format is like any other process. It requires an understanding of the basic elements, access to resources to complete it, and a plan of action to follow it through until the end. Each screenwriter approaches their screenplay differently and hones their craft in their own individual and distinct way. Each screenwriter is as different as the stories that they tell. Yet, screenwriters all have one thing in common; the need to convey the story for film in the screenplay format. Otherwise known as the screenwriter's language.

This book will help you to understand the screenwriter's language, including format, and some of the other basic elements that are essential for its composition. The beginning screenwriter should also study screenplays of their favorite films to see the blueprint that drove the film and how it translated from screenplay to film. Once I have introduced you to the basic elements, I invite you to schedule an uninterrupted 3-day creative writing marathon, with the goal being a complete first draft of your screenplay.

I began writing screenplays over fifteen years ago when I took a course at a local college in Nebraska. I then joined a writing group to learn more about the screenwriting process. The group, *Nebraska Writers*, was coordinated by a protégé of Lew Hunter. Her name was Sally Walker. I attended the writing group for over five years before spinning off my own group called *Nebraskans for Film*. I coordinated that group for more than four years, working with screenwriters to develop their screenplays and work out problems with their projects. During that period, I started my own film company, Young Films LLC, and shot a short film in 1997, titled *Manimals,* which starred an unknown Chris Klein. In 2001, I wrote and executive produced a romantic comedy in Canada, called *Love Wine*. You can get more information about me and our company on our www.readamovie.com website.

Several years ago, our company, along with my brother Dan, created the *Read-A-Movie* book series, which prints short stories adapted from screenplays. Since then, I have had the opportunity to read many screenplays. Our first book, *Movies That Hollywood Didn't Make* was released in 2006, followed by our genre book, *Family Movies Hollywood Didn't Make But Should,* released in July of 2008, by Easton Studio Press. We are finishing production of *Romantic Comedies Hollywood Didn't Make But Should* for release in September of 2008. During one of my first years writing screenplays, I wrote fourteen while working full time as a Logistics Support Engineer for a large government contractor that develops weather data processing systems. I have also written another twenty screenplays since. Most of the screenplays that I wrote during that year, were done in 3-day marathons. I got quite good at churning out scripts in short periods. I was able to leverage 3-day weekends by working an extra hour a day in order to get a 3-day weekend every other week. Three of the screenplays that I wrote that year appear in *Movies Hollywood Didn't Make* in short-story form. Another one appears in *Family Movies Hollywood Didn't Make But Should.*

Getting a screenplay made into a movie is not a simple feat. My agent once told me that putting words on a hundred pieces of paper and convincing a studio to spend their money to put it on the big screen would be one of the hardest things I would ever try in my life. He's right.

It's difficult, but not impossible. To begin with, you'll need the screenplay. In the old days, screenplays were written on typewriters and it was a tedious and a very time-consuming venture. I used one very early in my career when I first began writing fiction. Errors have to be manually corrected and, well, let's not go there. Anyway, with today's computers, writing is a snap and anybody with a PC and some word processing software can do a screenplay. There is also software on the market that streamlines the process by providing templates for automatic formatting. Personally, I use Word and do everything manually. So, most people are already equipped to start a screenplay. Later on, once you have written several, you may want to look at software applications that simplify things. Nevertheless, right now we'll focus on the process.

This book's intention is to prepare the beginning screenwriter for a 3-day screenwriting marathon, during which, they will write a draft screenplay. For excellent and authoritative advice on screenwriting, there are several must-read books in the marketplace by Syd Field, Lew Hunter, and Linda Segar, among others. This book is my perspective on the screenwriting process as it relates to my own experiences. It is a supplement to the books by the authors mentioned above, and a process to complete your first draft of a screenplay. Many writers get stuck and never finish their screenplays, or they spend years on a single screenplay. Writing them using the marathon method provides continuity throughout the process and creates an environment for the successful creation of a first draft in three days.

I talked with my brother, Dan, who brought up a good point about the creative advantage of doing a screenplay in a marathon session. Dan had worked on a couple of screenplays of his own, and had provided advice and ideas on dozens of mine as well. So, as he went through the writing process, he realized that once the creativity is flowing, it isn't like a switch that can just be turned off. After a day of writing, the brain is still trying to generate ideas. He remembered ideas swirling around in his mind after he went to bed. He said he dreaded going to work the next day because the creative juices were still flowing. I had experienced the same myself. This is the continuity that is so necessary when writing in a 3-day marathon. The next morning when you jump out of bed, it is easier to get back into the creative mode. If you work the screenplay only when you get time, then where is the continuity of thought, tone, or tempo that you had set that first day of writing? It's gone and you have to find a new one, or just plod ahead anyway. Creativity breeds creativity, and ideas breed ideas.

Let's talk about creativity for a second. Creativity is at the heart of storytelling. I once had a friend who was the analytical type – one of those 4.0 students in college. He asked me one day how an artist creates something from nothing. If I could answer that, I would probably be teaching philosophy at a university. Naturally, I couldn't answer anything more than, "I don't know. It just comes to me." After years of creating stories and characters, that question has always been in the back of my mind. I still can't answer it, but I can give you some insight into how it works for me. For me, it doesn't seem to operate at the conscious level. Because, as I mentioned before, the harder I deliberately try to come up with ideas, the less I actually have. Ideas, for me, work at a subconscious level.

Collaboration is another alternative to consider. Have you ever noticed a screenplay with several writers credited? You bet. That's collaboration! I've collaborated on several of my screenplays and it can be great. One writer, who had never written a screenplay, worked with me on one called *Desperate in Hollywood,* and later went on to write his own screenplay that is currently a finalist in a screenplay contest. Way to go, Jeff! We all win when we collaborate. Choose other writers or friends that you get along with and who have some creativity. You can also team up with other writers today via the Internet. It works. I've done it. So shop around for a good writing partner and see how collaboration works for you!

A screenplay is a creative process, but it needs to have a structure. Remember that films are a collaborative medium, like television. It takes many professionals such as producers, directors, directors of photography, editors, and so on to get a film made. Standards in format and structure allow the screenwriter to communicate their concept efficiently to others. Therefore, it is a twofold process. Yes, it has to be creative. However, it also has to be mechanically sound in many aspects. So, how do we move from a creative process to a sound mechanical product? The following paragraphs hit highlights of the model. I will cover the elements in more detail later in the book.

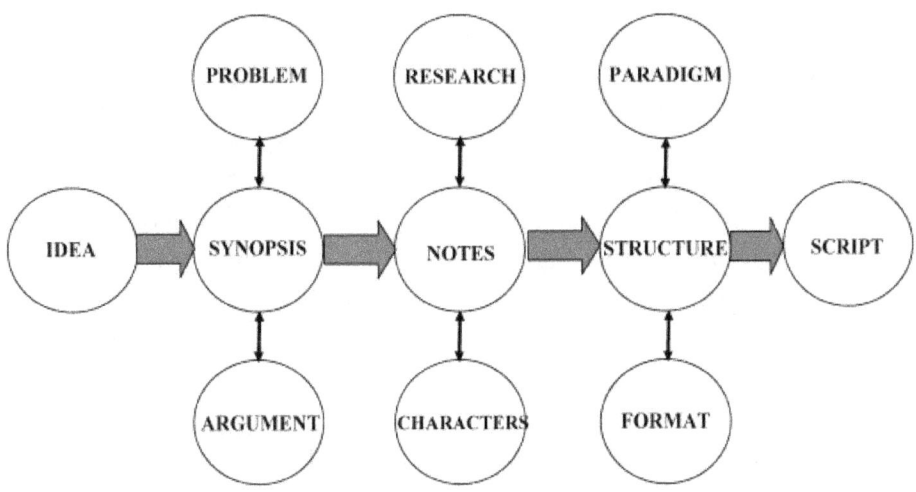

Screenplay Creative/Technical Model

It begins with a general idea. This could be as simple as a story about teen pregnancy as in the movie *Juno,* or as complex as the life and times of Howard Hughes in the movie *The Aviator.* It may begin with a simple question. One day, I was following close behind a cattle truck when I asked myself, "What if cows could talk?" That question generated ideas for a story. When people tell me, "I have this idea, but I don't know how to start," I say great! You start with an idea and you move forward from there. The idea is the starting point, as shown in the model above.

The idea can be a problem or an argument. When you are dealing with social issues, believe it or not, you are making an argument, because it has to be told from some perspective. Even the Mel Gibson film about Christ became an argument. Once we have an idea, argument, or problem we want to address, we move on to developing the idea into a synopsis. The synopsis will then expand on your general idea and present our character's problem. It should lay out the beginning, the middle, and the end of your story. You'll need a solid one-page synopsis that defines your main character, what they are trying to accomplish, and what conflict they face. I know that when I'm working on a new screenplay, the title really helps. When I decide on a title early on, it sets the tone of the project. Titles are a very important part of the process, because it says that I have decided on an idea and I am committed. A good title says a lot about the project. Think about some of the great movies with titles that capture what the film's essence. The title, *True Grit*, is a great title for a one-eyed U.S. marshal that is stubborn and set in his ways. Other titles like *Jurassic Park, Alien, Predator, War of the Worlds, Indiana Jones and the Temple of Doom* and *Halloween* all tell us in a few words what kind of movie they are. Once you get an idea for a screenplay, spend some time coming up with a good title. It will help provide direction for where you are going.

In industry terms, the idea for the screenplay or film is summed up in a logline. Below is the logline for *In Your Dreams*.

In Your Dreams: When a daydreaming dogcatcher in a small town discovers that he can see and interact with people's dreams, he sets out to make their dreams come true. In the process, he also makes his own dream come true.

A synopsis expands on this logline, or main idea, to include the characters and what will happen in Act I through Act III. Below is the synopsis for *In Your Dreams*.

Morris Hill, our main character of the story, lives in a small Midwestern town where his family has a long tradition of lawmen. As far back as recorded history, a Hill has been the elected police chief. That is until Morris came on the scene. Morris is a daydreamer. He lives out his life through his very real and vivid daydreams to the point that the line between real and imagined has become blurred and has made him a failure in the eyes of everyone (especially his father). So Morris settled for becoming the town's dogcatcher. And that's all right for Morris because he loves animals and has a special relationship with them.

Then, one day on a trip to a nearby town to pick up some strays, he picks up some hitchhikers, an Indian shaman and his son. The shaman sees Morris' problem — he's not living but dreaming his life away. He performs a ceremony to help Morris. Morris finds that he cannot daydream anymore, but instead finds himself in other people's dreams and is able to interact with them!

As he experiences the dreams of the town and his parents (Morris still lives at home) he begins to understand that so many of the people that he's been surrounded by his whole life have unfulfilled dreams and have really lost all hope. When he discovers that he can interact with the dreamers, he starts to help their dreams come true. So during Morris' daily dogcatcher duties, he methodically works at a list of dreams to make them happen. However, when he's sucked into his father's dream of Morris accepting the office of sheriff, Morris finds himself declining the job. When he sees that his father is distraught by the dream, he decides to move out of the house. He moves into an apartment above the waitress of a local café who he's secretly in love with (Jenny). Oddly enough, she doesn't have dreams at all. As Morris and Jenny become closer, he discovers that she has resolved herself to a life without dreams or hope. Jenny is also considering marrying the sheriff (Ben), who has been Morris' lifelong adversary and instigated an embarrassing event in high school that changed Morris' life forever.

As the town begins to change, due to some strange facility to achieve their dreams, their attitude about Ben, who's running for reelection even though there's no one running against him, changes as well. The town wants someone better, but what choice do they have? At this point, Morris finally realizes his dream, that of becoming the next sheriff. Really, something that he's wanted since childhood but was just afraid to go after. When Morris decides to run against Ben, he discovers that he needs the required signatures to run by the following Monday. Yet, Morris had already scheduled a pick-up of strays and cannot get out of it. Morris feels that he has failed again so he departs town without registering. While he is gone, the word soon spreads that he had made the effort to file for the sheriff's job. As Jenny and others work to collect the required signatures during the weekend, a couple of no-good cons escape from a prison detail and are making their way toward Hopeville to rob the bank. While on the road with his dog, Morris realizes how much he's in love with Jenny and is provided relief when his dog shares his dream of her with him.

Morris arrives back in town and stops at the local café just as the convicts are staging their robbery of the bank. When the bank alarm test doesn't go off at 8:00, like it does every Monday, the sheriff (Ben) and the town's citizens become concerned. As Ben exits to check on the bank, the robbers exit and fire at him. Ben is wounded as the robbers make their break in a car. Without thinking, Morris reacts (like he had in his daydream every Monday at 8:00, but this time it's real). He bravely intervenes, defeating the bank robbers. Despite being wounded in the battle, he leaves the hospital with the help of his parents and friends, to go to the courthouse to file the paperwork for the election. He's met by supporters and Ben who wishes him luck.

I dread writing a synopsis, but some studios still request it. You can do as I did or you can do as many writers do — divide their synopsis into paragraphs dedicated to each act. For instance, paragraph one for Act I, paragraph two for Act II, and finally, paragraph three for Act III. I usually try to capture key events throughout the story from beginning to end.

The next phase develops the synopsis further into Notes on scenes or sequences that will be used in the structure of the screenplay. An idea for a scene could be as simple as a note to yourself that your character stops at a local bar to have a drink with his buddies. A sequence idea would be a note that you need to show how crappy your character's life is today. The sequence ideas are the main themes that form the story. They could end up being anywhere from several scenes to a dozen major scenes. In some screenwriting circles, using sequences rather than the three-act structure to roadmap the screenplay is preferred. Although I don't adhere to a strict sequence structure, I think screenwriters do think in terms of sequences when contemplating the scenes necessary to tell their story.

Before you sit down to begin the 3-day marathon, you'll be brainstorming your idea to make sure it is complete with details about characters and locations. This process could take anywhere from a week to four weeks of thought, research, and notes. In the, section entitled, The Insanity of it All, I show you my notes that I developed and how they formed into the screenplay. These are the kind of notes you will be developing. You may also be doing research on the subject until you have enough notes to feel confident.

The next phase is the technical or STRUCTURE phase, where you will be translating what you have done so far into an ordered whole. You will be taking your ideas and research that you've done and applying them to a structure, like the three-act structure mentioned earlier. You will begin reorganizing those notes so that they fit sequentially (or not, if you're doing something like *Pulp Fiction* or *Memento*) into the screenplay structure. Each of the scenes from your notes will drive the next scene and that will drive the next scene and so on. As mentioned in the model, you will be putting these in following the correct screenplay outline, and the events that unravel will fit into a paradigm. Dramatic events that either move the story forward, or provide turning points to keep the story alive and interesting to the audience are called Plot Points. The final product is the result of your creative ideas organized into a structure that follows an accepted format. For additional information on structure, see my reference section for great books to read on this subject.

THINKING OUTSIDE OF YOURSELF

Conan O'Brien once said, (paraphrasing here) that you give your best performance when you work outside of yourself. I think he meant that if you are aware that you are doing something, then you can't do your best. For instance, if you are aware that you are acting, then you aren't doing your best acting. You must forget yourself and get lost in what you are doing. Many times, I get lost in the story that I am writing. Once, I totally forgot that I was writing a story and for a split second found myself in the scene as a spectator taking notes. This is the ultimate writing experience when you, the writer, are swept away by the story!

Find a quiet area to concentrate on the work, tap into the creative forces in your subconscious, work outside yourself, and hang on as your creativity unveils the story at your fingertips!

SCREENPLAY FORMAT

SCREENPLAY FORMAT IS probably the single aspect of screenplays that can hurt the screenwriter the most. Our company receives numerous screenplays that are not even close to being the correct format. It is extremely important! Structure is also critical, but we'll discuss that later. Format is the basic blueprint that must be followed, or the reader or person who first sees your screenplay at a studio will immediately smell an amateur. If the format is anything but standard, you are done. Once you understand the format and follow it, this will allow the reader to focus on the story you are telling. If they don't get past the format, it is most likely they will not care what kind of story you are telling.

What is the format? Just as with any form of writing or prose, screenplays follow a format for their construction. Everyone has had an English composition class where the format for a letter or paper was discussed and the instructor explained where the elements, such as heading, salutation, and body, were positioned. A screenplay is similar. There are specific elements that appear in every screenplay. These are defined below:

- Scene Description Heading
- Action or Description
- Character Name
- Dialogue

Below is a typical scene with all elements tagged for clarity:

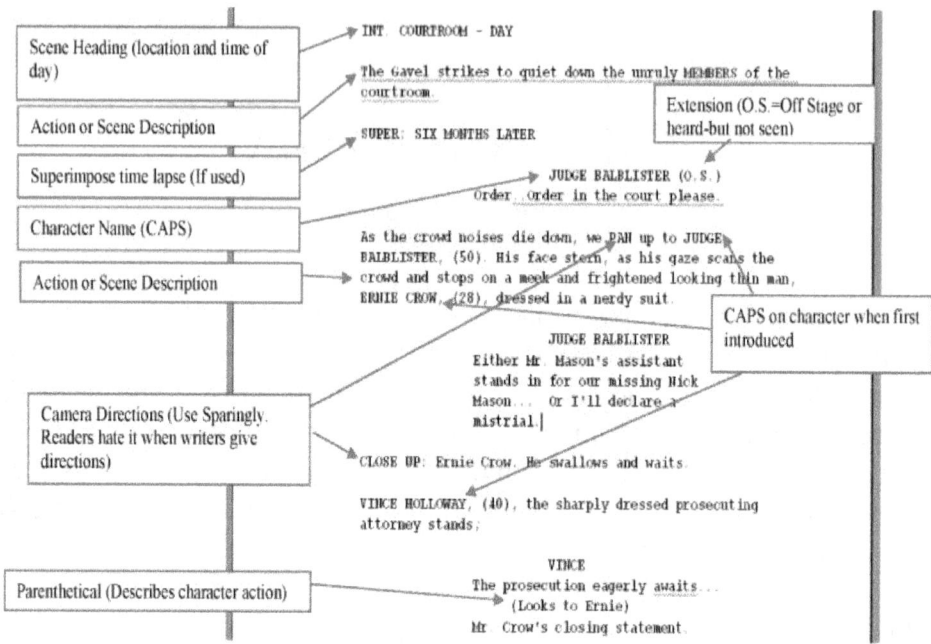

There are guidelines for where the elements are placed. Usually, the page should be formatted with a 1½- inch left margin and a 1-inch right margin. The font should be Courier set to 12-point font size. To accurately place the actor's name or dialogue, use the tab key. This is the simplest method without using software. Here are the tabs for each of the elements:

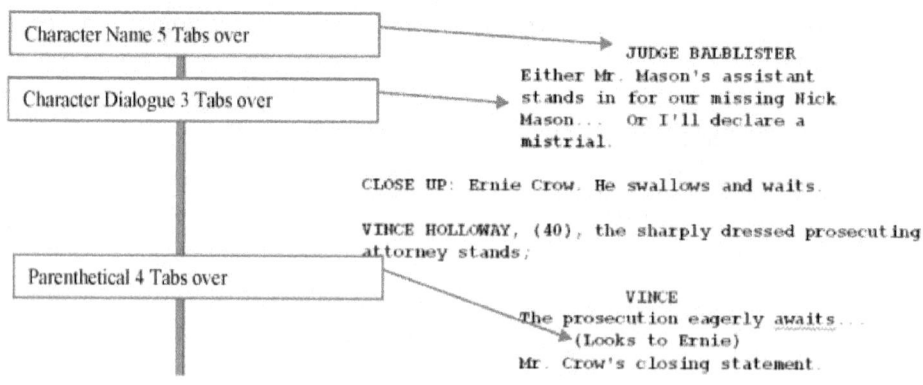

There are also variations of use for scene headings. For a series of short scenes, the writer may choose to title the section "SERIES OF SCENES" or for a scene happening at the same time, may use "- SAME TIME" and

HOW TO WRITE A SCREENPLAY IN 3-DAYS

for the time of day at the end of the tag line. Most writers use general descriptions such as "- DAY", "- MORNING", "- NIGHT", "- EVENING" or "- AFTERNOON" at the end of the tagline.

The FADE IN: title is used at the beginning of the screenplay and the FADE OUT: is used at the end. Both of these suggest that we're either fading from black (FADE IN) or fading to black (FADE OUT). When a scene has long dialogue and is split across two pages, the "MORE" extension is used and is complemented by the "Cont'd" extension following the character's name on the following page. See example below:

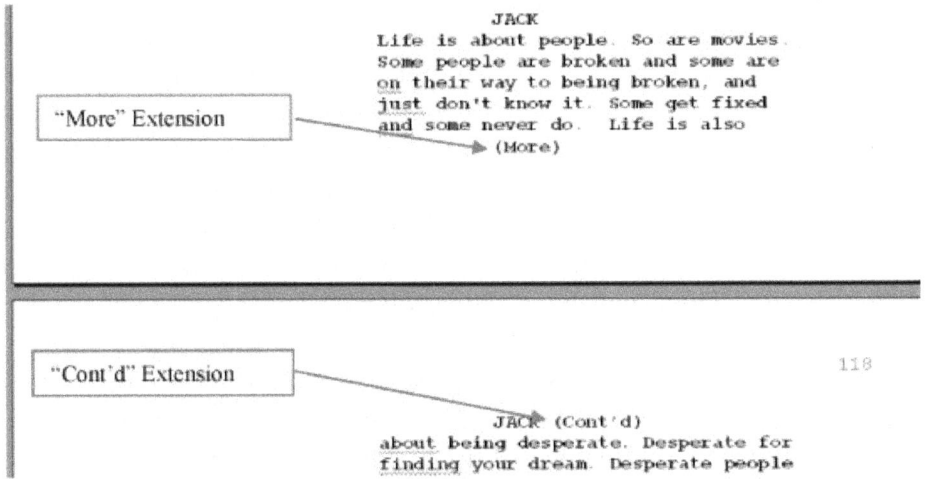

The screenwriter should also capitalize other specific elements of the screenplay, such as the scene heading, character's name when first introduced, and the character's name before the dialogue.

When an actor is speaking, but not on camera or seen, use the Off Stage extension in the following format: (O.S.)

When an actor is speaking off the set, like on a telephone, or providing narrative for the film use the Voice Over extension in the following format: (V.O.)

                JOE (V.O.)
Honey, I'll be working late. I'll call
you when I leave work.

15

                                CINDY
                       Okay, dear. See you then.

Cindy is on the phone and in the current scene. She doesn't need a V.O. However, her husband, Joe, is at work and not physically in the scene. Therefore, his dialogue would be V.O. Remember that we use Offstage (O.S.) when the person is physically in the scene but not seen or visible.

Voiceover can also be used, as I mentioned, for narration over the story. This kind of narration is used to provide additional information to the audience about what's going on in the scene or story. Narration should always provide information that the audience can't get from the characters' dialogue. If the narration simply said the same thing that the character was saying, it would be pointless. Use it sparingly. The film audience doesn't want narration in every scene. They want to get into the story. Too much narration can be distracting.

Use two hard returns between scenes and try to keep dialogue to a maximum of six lines and about 3½ inches wide. It should not extend to the right column of the page. I use a manual return to size the lines of dialogue. Make sure that you have the ruler turned on at the top of the page so you can check your settings. See the example below:

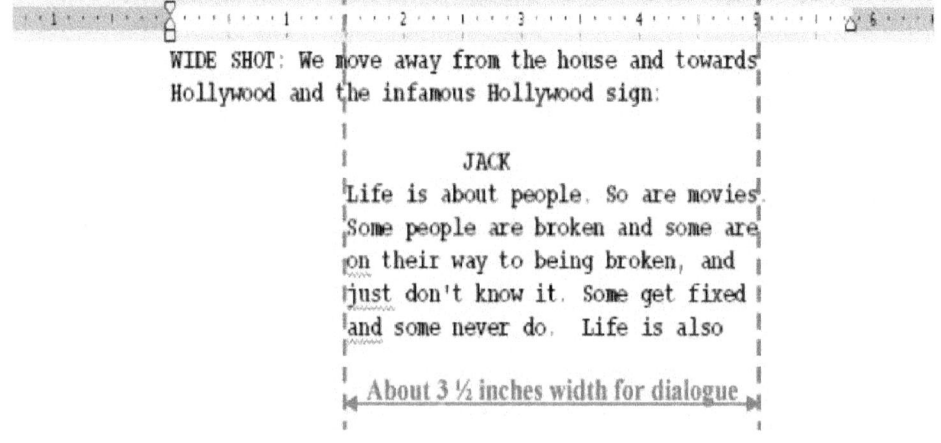

The screenplay should be an equal balance of action and dialogue. Readers will thumb through the pages looking for dialogue that runs extensively. I've seen screenplays that have full pages of nothing but dialogue. This is symptomatic of a talking head film. You want characters interacting with other actors and their environment, not just talking to each other.

At the end of the screenplay, use the words "The End" centered then the FADE OUT: slug line to fade to black. Do NOT use "Continued" or other directions in the header or footer of the screenplay. This has been discontinued and is no longer used in screenplays. You don't want anything that slows down the reading of a screenplay or distracts the reader.

On the title page of the screenplay, simply put the title in a normal font followed by "Screenplay by" and your name. When you use fancy or colorful fonts, it screams amateur. The cover page should NOT have a page number. Consult your word processing help file to see how to number a document and exclude the first page. In Word this is done using section breaks and disconnecting the page headers. See the example below:

|

"Desperate In Hollywood"

Screenplay by Jack L. Young

The page number is placed in the right-hand corner of the header of the document. Some writers use a hyphen before the page number. See example below:

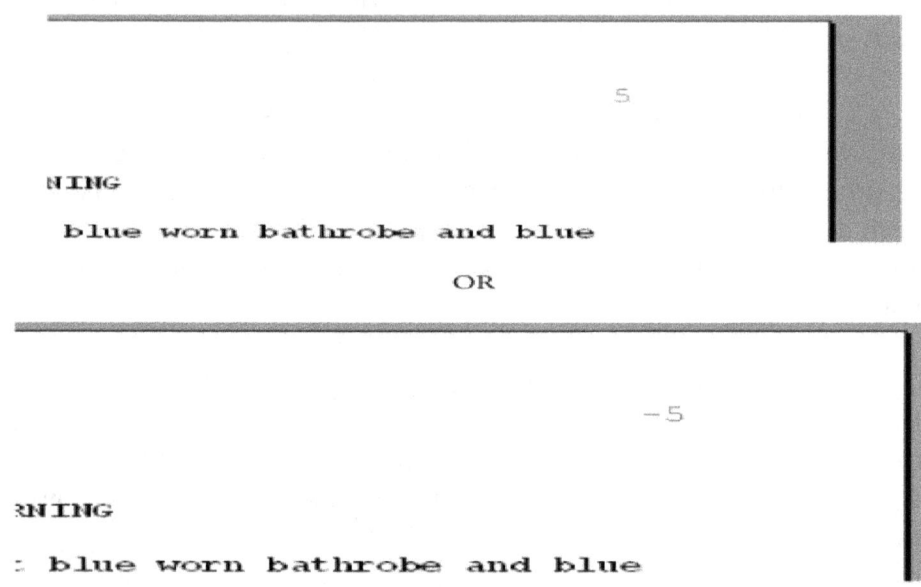

When you have completed the screenplay, three-hole punch the screenplay including the front cover and back cover. A three-hole punch can be easily purchased from an office supply store. The paper that the screenplay is printed on should be standard white 50lb. bond paper. The front and back covers should be plain/neutral cover stock such as white or beige. Brass plated fasteners or brass brads should be used to bind the screenplay together. DO NOT have a printing service do a special printing job and fasten the screenplay with spiral or other binding. All of the items listed above are available at any office supply store. Do not print the name of the screenplay or other information on the cover stock. It is not required and, again, sends the message that you are an amateur.

SCREENPLAY STRUCTURE

As I mentioned earlier, the structure of the screenplay is critical. Although you now understand the format and know how to make it look like a standard screenplay, once the reader begins, they will quickly know whether you understand structure. Since film is a linear medium of visual storytelling, the story must also be linear and have a beginning, middle, and end.

You will soon discover that there are different beliefs among working screenwriters about the best paradigm for story structure. Some still believe in the classic three-act paradigm, while others believe it is too restrictive for contemporary or sophisticated storytelling. Most of what I write loosely follows the three-act structure, because that is how I learned to write screenplays. However, I am one for breaking rules and following your gut.

Unfortunately, readers will have expectations for structure and unless your screenplay is spectacular and groundbreaking, you will lose them. That said, tell the best visual story possible, keeping the reader or audience glued to every scene in anticipation. If you can do that, to hell with following structure. However, since you are just beginning, let's start off using the three-act structure. The only way you'll discover what works best for you is to write screenplays. Later, if you find that you prefer a different structure for writing, go for it.

Let's divide the screenplay into three sections or three acts. Act I introduces the main characters and must let the reader know before page 10 why they should spend their time watching the movie. If they don't understand the main character's dilemma early on in the film, they will lose interest. This all must be achieved in the first act. Act II provides the confrontation to our character's journey and Act III provides the resolution to our character's dilemma. Act I can be anywhere from twenty to thirty pages, ACT II should be around sixty pages, and Act III should be around twenty to thirty pages. The screenplay should be between 105 and 120 pages. Each page of the screenplay equals one minute of film time. Each time you create a scene heading, you should realize that each scene must also have a beginning middle and end. Each of the scenes must move the story forward and be essential to understanding the story. If the scene can be removed without affecting the story, then it wasn't needed after all and is extraneous.

Simply put:

>   Beginning = Setup = Act I
>   Middle = Conflict = Act II
>   End = Resolution = Act III

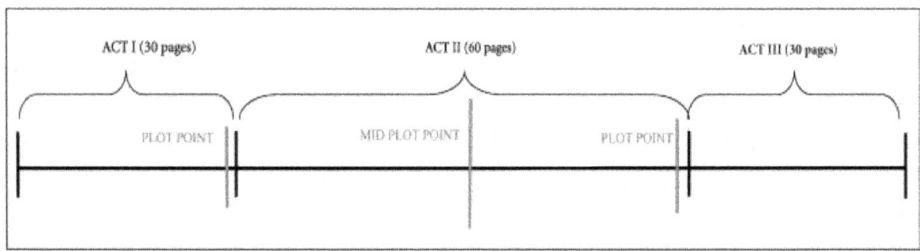

Each act also has what are called Plot Points. There is a plot point near the end of the first act, one in the middle of the second act and one near the end of the third act. Plot points are pivotal turning points in the story. It is where an important piece of information is revealed to the audience that changes the course of the story and the actions of the characters in the story. Readers will expect to see these plot points and although they can vary by a few pages, they should not be forgotten.

I use a technique that seems to work well for me on mapping out my structure. Although I don't use index cards, I do write down all of my scenes in a notebook. I start with a fresh notebook and with my main concept for the story. Let's say we have a story of a straight-laced female police officer who falls in love with a drug dealer. We'll call it "Fall from Grace." We already know just from the title where this story could lead.

Let's play with it some. In Act I, we will show her as a perfect cop, by the book, and highly respected in the precinct. Therefore, by the end of Act I we will have shown this, maybe her involvement in some arrests and possibly another cop who has a crush on her. We'll also show her love interest who might be a drug dealer doing what he does, maybe even violent in nature. We will end the act with her meeting the drug dealer and something happening between them where an attraction for each other is kindled (the first plot point). In Act II, we could show them meeting secretly, passionate about each other. As their love affair grows, the different worlds that they live in begin to creep into their relationship and this is where Act II could climax (another plot point) with her making a decision to leak information to her lover about a sting operation with him as the target. You see where this could go.

Anyway, as we expand our original concept, we begin to think of scenes that make up the structure. We know from our discussion that we're going to have a scene where she's on the job and proving that she's a loyal and trustworthy cop. We also know that we need to have a scene where she meets the drug dealer. As you expand the story, write down the scenes in the notebook, or on index cards. Think about how many pages you would estimate for each of the scenes. You should have a card for each scene description. For a 120-page screenplay, you could have as many as two hundred index cards. Although most screenwriting authors don't recommend this, I also jot down dialogue that comes to mind as well. I will write down anything that comes to mind related to the screenplay in the notebook. You can choose to use it or not later.

STORY DEVELOPMENT

THE STORY, FOR ME, is the hardest part of the screenplay. Is it unique, interesting, or original? For me, story ideas seem to come from left field. My wife once asked me while we were watching one of the franchise horror movies (*Nightmare on Elm Street*) why I didn't come up with the next horror franchise. When I sat to think of a new one, it seemed the harder I tried, the less that came out. It's hard to spit out a work of genius on demand. I don't know about most writers, but I don't work that way. Inspiration for a story idea seems to fall in my lap and can come from the strangest places. Two story ideas for screenplays that I wrote came from the same source. *Manimals* popped into my head as I followed that cattle truck I mentioned earlier and wondered what they would say if they could talk, and that sparked the screenplay. DreamWorks had four meetings about the story idea, but eventually passed. Ouch! Later, during an attempted rewrite of *Manimals*, I developed an original animation screenplay called *Animal Revolution*. All of that from just following a cattle truck.

Sometimes story ideas can grow out your own frustration. *Desperate In Hollywood* grew out of my frustration with trying to break down the doors of Hollywood. I was determined to break into Hollywood and couldn't stop thinking about it. That's when it struck me that there had to be a story in there somewhere. Then the idea came to me. Write the story of a desperate writer trying to break into Hollywood. Sometimes the story idea is sitting in front of us and we can't see it. Maybe we try too hard and miss the obvious. The short story adaptation appears in the upcoming book, *Romantic Comedies Hollywood Didn't Make But Should*.

The idea for another screenplay I wrote, *Mister Christmas,* came from an article I read about a man in Chicago that started a Christmas tree decorating service. I also wrote two true-life drama screenplays based on people's lives that touched me. The first, *The Gray Mare*, came from the true story of a Hispanic man that went from being a hardened criminal in prison to a model citizen. The story centers around his trip he takes in his seventies to visit the retired warden for one last time before they both die. His grandchildren learn of his unsavory past while he is away, but they have mixed reactions. The other story, *Heart Catcher*, is a true-life drama that I wrote with a writing partner about a young local girl who died from cancer. I discovered the story accidentally while reading the obituary page, which I don't usually make a habit of. I was so touched by what I read that I contacted the mother for permission to write the story. If you keep your mind open to the world around you, and are constantly asking yourself, "what if?" you will get so many ideas that you will be, like myself, backlogged with story ideas.

    Your preferences for movie genres will also have a big influence. I know, growing up loving sci-fi and big action movies drove my original choices for screenplays when I first began writing. Now, if you love these genres, I don't want to sway you away from them, because you should write what you love, but be aware that with film budgets rocketing for big sci-fi and action films, be creative in what projects you choose. Selling a big budget screenplay to a Hollywood studio as an unknown is near impossible without knowing someone or having a past track record. A smarter choice for new screenwriters are character driven stories that cost less to produce. This also gives you the option of pitching to independent film producers as well. But, like I said, write what you love and are passionate about. I grew up watching Saturday afternoon cowboy shows (now I'm dating myself) and always loved them. I called the son of Roy Rogers (you may want to look him up since he's a 1950s icon) and pitched to them about writing the Roy Rogers story. The son said that something was already in development and passed. I didn't give up. I wrote my own take on the Saturday afternoon cowboy star in the screenplay *Tex and Kate*, a story in our first book, *Movies That Hollywood Didn't Make*.

    Newspapers and magazines are great places to shop for ideas. Many times, if you catch the article fresh, you can contact the person associated with the story and most are open to having their story on the silver screen. Be sure to draw up a simple contract with the person allowing you to do their story, otherwise your time might be wasted. Be sure to word the contract to allow you the permission for literary freedom to dramatize or even add additional scenes as needed. Although real-life stories on the surface seem solid, you'll quickly find that without improvising, the story may be lacking in drama or other required elements. Television broadcasting promotes a lot of true-life, or stories based on true-life, made for television movies. Look at the Lifetime Channel, for example. Be wary of people who approach you with "my life would make a good movie" pitch. Most people's lives wouldn't be interesting enough to hold a TV audience, much less a movie audience. If everybody's life were that entertaining, they would never have to go to the movies! The truth is sometimes painful.

You can pursue books in print as well. Did you know that Frank Darabont, the screenwriter/producer who wrote the *Green Mile* screenplay and other Stephen King adaptations, bought one of the screenplay rights from Stephen King for one dollar? Never be afraid to approach an author for adaptations. If you find an interesting book and think that you're the only one who really gets it, approach the author and let them know. What do you have to lose? If Stephen King can be open to it, who knows? I'd suggest getting some screenplays under your belt first, because that's the first thing they'll ask, "What have you written?"

Nightlings, which was renamed from *Darklings* because of several other films with the same name, started out as just a name that I found in the dictionary. Surprisingly enough, sometimes just a name is enough to spark creativity. As soon as I saw the name, the story began to develop. Creatures of the dark, hmmm. Let's set it in a small isolated town and put the creatures underground, hmmm. And let's have the creatures multiply like rabbits, capable of growing to the size of a man, and let's make light their only weakness. And finally, let's make the heroes college students who are home on break, and they're the only ones who can figure out what's going on and what to do about it. Try browsing the dictionary to see if something sparks your imagination.

Heaven's Door, one of my favorite short screenplays, started with a question, just as *Manimals* had. I thought to myself, with all the different forms of communication we have today, what would happen if man finally figured out how to communicate with the other side—Heaven? What would happen? How could man possibly screw that up? It's interesting where a question like that can lead you. I loved the premise and it took me where I had never been before.

Another screenplay that I wrote asked a completely different question. Because I worked for a government contractor that designed weather data systems, I had seen first hand how systems were built and tested. At that time, there were discussions about a Space Defense Initiative (SDI) for defending the United States from space. The idea intrigued me, but I wanted to add another concept to the mix. Computers. Throughout the years, there has been research with neural networks and computers that simulate the human brain. I took it one-step further. What if science found a way to reuse brains as CPUs. Instead of simulating the brain, they could use a pool of brains to run an SDI system. So, the story premise is a space defense system with access to nuclear weapons that is designed using a brainpool (this is the title by the way). Gee, what could possibly go wrong? Anyway, part of the story idea came from my job experience and the rest came from questions like what would happen if we used human brains as computers, and what would happen if something went terribly wrong?

Another screenplay that I wrote, *Stream,* which appears in adapted short story form in *Movies That Hollywood Didn't Make*, tries to answer the question, What is after death? I love movies that take you out of your realm into entirely different worlds. Earlier in my life, while in the military, I had met a strange young enlistee who astral traveled. He taught me his technique and although I only tried it a few times, I did have out-of-body experiences. Years later, I stumbled onto a book about the subject and it brought back those memories and I knew that there had to be a story there. Shortly after, I wrote *Stream* and followed it up with the sequel, *Stream II.* So what am I getting at? Look at your personal experiences and ask "What if?"

So once you have the basic story idea, what do you do? For me, I'm lucky to have people around me that love to hear a good story. Using people around you as a backboard to bounce your idea off is extremely helpful. My brother, Dan, who is my business partner and screenwriter in his own right, has gotten very good at listening to pitches and helping me to develop the story line. Once you throw the idea out, your story buddy can help you to expand it and see where it goes. Although you won't know the exact path your characters will travel to reach their final destination, I like to have a fairly good idea where they are going before I start. Sometimes, characters will surprise you. This is a treat and is a testimonial to the fact that you've built fully functioning characters.

COINCIDENCE

Many times when a writer is working on a story, they realize that the only way to bring two story elements together is by sheer coincidence. Perhaps when two lovers first meet, it's by sheer coincidence or by accident. But later in the story when she just happens to be going to the same party as him and sees he has another love interest, or when she JUST HAPPENS to be going by the restaurant where he's having lunch with another love interest, and when she just happens to... Okay, okay, we get it. If I see more than one coincidence I get the feeling the writer wasn't using enough creativity to bring the elements of the story together and then I get irritated. I usually grumble something like, "oh, come on...." As a rule of thumb, if you must have a coincidence, because you're in a corner and can't figure it out without a coincidence, only do it once!

KILLING YOUR CHARACTER

Wait a minute. After I spent all of this time developing this great character and put him on this fantastic journey, you want me to kill him? Are you nuts? Now, hold on. Let me explain. The ultimate sacrifice that any hero can make is to sacrifice his life. Come on, you know that. In "*300*", the Spartans sacrificed their lives in what they believed. Sure it's a downer ending, but it is considered the ultimate price on the journey to wisdom, redemption, and truth. But there's a way of accomplishing the same thing without having to kill your character off. It is used a lot in movies, because it's the second best thing to killing them. Making it appear that they have been killed. When Ray, played by Tom Cruise, watches his son, Robbie, go over the hill in *War of the Worlds* to help fight the aliens, and we see the devastating explosion that follows, we assume he's dead. That strikes an emotion with us. But as you find out later, he survived. A pleasant surprise. Think about other movies where one of the main characters appears to have met their untimely death only to be resurrected later. It's one of those devices, like coincidence, that only works once in a film. Don't do it twice.

A WOMAN'S PERSPECTIVE

If you're not a woman and you are reading this, you're probably asking yourself, "What's this got to do with me?" Well, a lot, unless you never plan to write a female role or screenplay for a female lead. Okay, now I have your attention. Most of my first screenplays that I penned had male leads with some minor parts for women. That was fine. I could handle that. Then I had an idea for a screenplay that had females as the leads… five of them! I panicked. I'll never be able to do it, I thought. The story concept involved five young girls on a camping trip who are attacked and held hostage by a young serial killer. After one of the girls is raped, they kill him, toss the body in the river, and cover up the whole incident. Years later, when they have become adults, they are stalked and murdered one by one by someone who has knowledge of the murder from years earlier. I loved the idea, but dreaded writing five different female characters. I plodded ahead and because I belonged to a writer's group, where most of the writers were female. I was able to get the screenplay reviewed by the leader, who just happened to be an excellent, experienced writer. I was then able to get a take on the dialogue and the characters from a female perspective.

One thing you'll learn is that you can't learn to write in a vacuum. Writers need input and feedback from time to time. If you find yourself writing a female character, and you are a guy, ask a female writer or a female friend, to critique your character. Now, for girls writing male leads, the same applies to you. Just because you have the guy drinking beer, belching and grabbing his crotch, doesn't mean that you've mastered writing from the male perspective. Ask a male friend or writer to do the same, give you their feedback. After you've done this a couple of times and have made all of the mistakes, you'll have it mastered and be able to do it on your own and make it believable.

THE TICKING CLOCK

The Merriam/Webster Dictionary defines tension as *"a state of latent hostility or opposition between individuals or groups."* Tension is good, well, for films anyway. Without conflict and tension among the characters, it wouldn't be interesting. Screenplays need tension and the more, the better. Comedy might be an exception, but even then a little is good. A rollercoaster wouldn't be any fun if it just went up and never went down. The audience expects a rollercoaster ride. So, we agree that tension is a good element for screenplays.

One way to create additional tension is to use the "ticking clock" method of creating tension. One example of the ticking clock is when Snake, the main character in *Escape from New York*, played by Kurt Russell, goes into New York to rescue the President. They put a small explosive in his neck that will kill him at a specific time if he decides to run or not bring the President back. He's up against a ticking clock. I know this example is a little cheesy, but you get the idea. Get a character up against a timeline and then make something horrible happen if he doesn't make it. It gives additional tension to the story. To use the ticking clock though, you must make what's at risk worthy of the tension, like a human life. If you don't make it worthy of the audience's dread and anticipation, they will hate you when you reveal that the prize wasn't worthy of what you put them through. In *Ransom,* starring Mel Gibson, the ticking clock is the possible death of his young daughter. This is more realistic and used quite a bit in films. In *Man on Fire,* starring Denzel Washington, he's up against the same kind of clock. A young girl that he was hired to protect in Mexico City is kidnapped and faces a similar fate. If used right, it's a great tension device and will have the audience on the edge of their seat.

GENRES

Genres are categories of stories. There are varieties of genres that include:

Horror	Thriller/Suspense
Family	Comedy
Action	Children's
Adventure	Historical
Sci-Fi	True-Life
Romance	Fantasy
Romantic Comedy	Musical
Western	Drama

Your story should fit in one of these genres. There are also movies that mix the genres. What if you had a western story with a creature on the loose? Some genres do better at the box office and are hot. Right now, westerns aren't hot, while horror is hot at the video rental stores. Studios, like *Lion's Gate,* are always looking for independent horror films. Being able to put your film into a genre also helps you to market your screenplay. Many film studios will shop for genre films. You'll see solicitations like, "Looking for horror screenplays…"

CHARACTER DEVELOPMENT

THE BEST MODELS to use for developing characters are not the cliché characters we see in films but real people we know, see, or hear about. People are individuals and each of us is different from the next person. No two people will act the same in a given situation. Every person has something that distinguishes them from others. In the screenplay, *Desperate in Hollywood,* Jack Hollins is a screenwriter and in one of his scenes, he is found observing people at a Starbucks. The narrator notes that "*...being a writer and therefore a student of the human condition, it is practically Jack's job to notice.*" If you study humans, you'll see that people have quirks, habits, and even have favorite phrases and words they like to use. In the story *Southern Fried Yankees,* a story from our first book, *Movies That Hollywood Didn't Make But Should,* I based many of the characters on people I had known as a child. The name of the character "Smiley" was taken from a person I met in my teen years in Tennessee. I made him younger, however, and with missing teeth. It helped explain why everyone called him Smiley. It turned out that he didn't like to smile because of his missing teeth.

Each one of your characters will have a different take on events and must stand out as being different from the other characters. If not, all the characters will sound and act the same, and the person reading it will know that you didn't spend time developing them. Many actors suggest two things to get this right. First, develop a profile of each character. Decide if they went to college, if their parents were divorced, if they were ever arrested, etc. Secondly, for the main characters, figure out what they were doing during Act 0. Yes, I said Act 0. That act that takes place before the story starts. An imaginary act allows you to gain momentum prior to hitting Act I. If you do this, the first act will hit the ground running and the audience will sense the tension that already exists and be pulled into the story. They will want to know more. It will also prevent you from starting the story too early, and having to bore the reader as you build momentum. In *Sheriffs Incorporated*, from our second book, *Family Movies Hollywood Didn't Make But Should*, when we join the story, the three bungling and inept brothers are seated in a parlor for the reading of their father's will. He has already died before we started. We skipped his illness and death and jumped right to the reading of the will, which is the key to the whole story. So do a little thinking about the characters and run through a little pre-story for each. This will help you to understand the characters and what drives them. To me, I always think of the characters as autonomous. I build them, wind them up and let them go. My job as a screenwriter is to take notes as they run the course of obstacles to their destiny. I'm an observer in their lives. But, you have to build complete characters to be able to wind them up and let them go.

Understanding your character's attributes, such as his age, height, weight, color of hair (or lack there of), or if he walks confidently or with a limp from a war wound, for example, should be conveyed to the reader. The script is a visual medium. You must build a picture of the character in the mind of the reader. You will provide some of this when the character is first introduced, but you will provide more insights into their character as the story progresses.

Sometimes the character is so strong that they drive the story themselves. If we look to some famous characters in history like Muhammad Ali for example or the fictional character of Forrest Gump, the sheer magnitude of their character drives the story. Two things inspired the story, *Mister Christmas*, a story in our book, *Family Movies Hollywood Didn't Make But Should*. First, while observing several young handicapped workers that cleaned the building I worked at, I knew I wanted to show how they looked at life differently from me, and I sensed that it would make a great heartfelt story. I just didn't know what story to put these characters into. Second, I read an article about a man in Chicago that started a Christmas tree decorating service. Suddenly, it became clear. I wanted my character to be a handicapped young man, whose family was dysfunctional (they were torn apart from the guilt associated with his illness), but was the one who started a tree decoration service in his father's hardware store. The decorating service catapults the story and finally brings the family together. So you see, initially it was the character that intrigued me and all I needed was an original story line to put him into.

For me, I love characters that are not quite equipped for what lay ahead of them. This is a double-edged sword. First, just about everyone loves an underdog because they can relate to that character more than the character who is perfectly ready to battle any foe. Look at the latest Batman sequels, like *Dark Knight.* Even Batman is not sure if he's ready to make the sacrifices required of him to defeat evil or even if he is the answer to Gotham City's needs. However, the mistake that's made too often in B movies is thrusting a character into a situation where they all of a sudden are experts with weapons or outsmarting the enemy who is a professional at what they do – kill people. If the character in Act 0 had served in the Marines in a previous war but had developed an aversion to killing people, then we have something to base their skill on and something to work with. Your characters should have both skills and flaws, just like humans.

PROTAGONISTS AND ANTAGONISTS

LET'S BEGIN BY AGREEING that if every character in a film got along with every other character in the film, it would be absolutely boring. Without an antagonist, we would be watching an episode of *Mr. Rogers' Neighborhood*. Simply put, if there is no antagonist to throw rocks at our protagonist, we might as well stay home and watch the paint on the wall dry. It would be just as exciting. Conflict is at the heart of drama or storytelling. In fact, some level of conflict, whether internal or external, should exist in every scene. Conflict is the result of a protagonist trying to get something such as money, love, revenge, or redemption, and an antagonist trying to stop him or at least making it difficult for him.

Think of a film's characters in football terms. Let's say you have the Bears at one end of the field and the Packers at the other end. Maybe you're a Packers fan, so to you, they're the protagonist of the film; the main character or the good guy, let's say. The Bears are the antagonist, who are going to do everything they can to stop you from moving down the field toward the goal. However, the antagonist has a goal of their own as well. They want to get to the other end for a touchdown. The point? Just don't throw an antagonist at your character to create conflict. Give your antagonist goals just as viable as your main character's. And from another perspective, that of the Bear fans, perhaps they, even though they are the antagonist, have a legitimate claim for creating problems for the protagonist.

Not only should you look for and try to write great characters as your protagonist, but do as much for the antagonist as well. Some of the characters that come to mind that we loved to hate or considered equals to our protagonist are: An unmatched Anthony Hopkins as Hannibal Lector, a riveting Heith Ledger as the Joker, Joaquin Phoenix as Commodus in *The Gladiator,* Alan Rickman as Hans Gruber in *Die Hard,* and the list goes on and on. Make them worthy of our protagonist.

CHARACTER ARCS

What is a character arc? The character arc is when a character changes over the course of the story. When a character, whether main or supporting, takes a journey through one of your stories, they can either learn from the experiences, or they can be the same person that started on the journey at the end of the story. A story should present our hero with conflict at every turn, and try to stop him or her from realizing happiness or whatever else they are trying to achieve. Likewise, the supporting characters should also be changed by the events in the story. Many times, we notice that a main character has not changed over the course of the story; they're still the same person, but as you look deeper, you may find that the supporting character has changed. They are the ones with the arcs. They have changed because of what the main character has done. Although the main character walks away at the end never having learned anything, everyone else has been changed by his actions.

In fact, you'll find these arcs coinciding with plot points in your story. Wouldn't a shift in what the character believes force them on a different path or a different decision? Wouldn't this result in a turning point in the story?

Some writers even map the arcs of all of the characters in their paradigm. My stories are more organic. I don't orchestrate arcs on paradigms, but use my gut feeling instead. I'm not saying it's not useful. I just don't do it.

GRAY CHARACTERS

Today's characters are more gray than ever. If you've ever watched any vintage movies from the early days of Hollywood, you'll quickly discover that Hollywood colored their characters very black and white. The bad guy was very bad, and the good guy was very good. They were clearly defined. Gray characters confused the audience. Maybe we were a naïve nation then or not yet corrupted. Nevertheless, audiences associated with this. Since then, audiences have become much more sophisticated. Good and evil have become blurred and so have our characters. Maybe we've become a more cynical nation because now when we see the perfect character that is straight, polite, does the right thing all the time, polishes his shoes, we have to ask ourselves, "What's he hiding in the closet?"

Take the Dustin Hoffman character in *Hero*. He's the perfect example of a gray character. He's got a little hero in him and yet he's a thief at the same time. Hollywood, as well as audiences, like these characters who aren't predictable, who may all of a sudden take a turn that you didn't expect. Now, don't think that I'm saying that your character should do something out of character, because they shouldn't. What I'm saying is that this type of character has a different value system and it's up to you to understand what that is. A more complicated character makes him more appealing. Think of some of the most interesting characters that you've watched in films and you'll realize that they are very complex. Think gray.

Dysfunctional characters have also crept into our mainstream films. Although these aren't really what I consider gray characters, they still have attributes that we see in many of our films today. Have you noticed how many of the characters in today's films are either socially dysfunctional or from dysfunctional homes? Many of the hit teen movies, such as *American Pie* or *Napoleon Dynamite,* have main characters that are socially or sexually dysfunctional. So when you are considering your characters, look for complex personalities.

CONCEIVING CHARACTERS

The more you know about the characters you create, the more realistic they will become and operate. As I mentioned, new characters for your story can be pieced together from people you know or knew, or can be a combination of those persons, picking attributes that make them operate uniquely. It helps to be able to visualize the character that you are writing about, naturally, so you can bring them to life. For a couple of my screenplays, I felt it was important to go one-step further than visualizing. I actually needed to draw them out. If you're not an artist, perhaps you know one who can help you to visualize your character by putting them on paper. For *Manimals,* my short film (feature length screenplay, though), we had to work with a special makeup person, so I needed to know what they looked like. I started with five characters, (see below) and they were pretty crude drawings. I then honed it down to three characters (MaryAnn, the pig-girl, and Howey, the horse-boy, got dropped). Then I sat down with the makeup artist to come up with the final renderings for the three characters.

However, the actual actors' makeup was quite different. See below:

Another screenplay, *The Return of the Great Zombie Killers*, which I collaborated on with my son, Nick, needed an artist rendering of our characters as well. We eventually decided that the storyline would make a great concept for a game. So we brainstormed what our characters would look like, what they would wear, their age, and so on. Nick, being a gamer, designed the costumes, battle gear, and weapons, and I focused on the characters faces and profiles. We also collaborated on the history of the family that killed zombies. Below is a short history of the family and the result of our collaboration.

"RETURN OF THE GREAT ZOMBIE KILLERS"

For one and a half centuries, the McDonald family has been killing the undead. It began during the Civil War when the McDonald ancestry was called upon by the federal government to stop an army of the undead created by the government itself. Since then, in every war, the McDonald family has been called to duty to stop or destroy the undead on the battlefields all around the world. In each war, the McDonalds pay a high price. Each time, one McDonald does not return, a victim of a vicious zombie attack.

Jake (Mac) McDonald: Mac is fifty-eight years old and has been killing zombies since he was seventeen. He began his career in Vietnam with his brother Tom (Lisa and Chip's father). Tom was killed by the leader of the zombies (Caine).

Jake McDonald Jr.: Jake is twenty-one, was an all-star athlete in high school, and knows weapons, Karate, and Kung Fu. He is independent and stubborn like his old man. He will meet his first zombie in the mountains.

Lisa McDonald: Lisa is twenty, independent, and outspoken. Her knowledge and skills of weaponry and the Martial Arts is exceeded by nobody, except her Uncle Mac. She is aware that a zombie killed her father and wants payback.

Charles (Chip) McDonald: Chip is nineteen and not a fighter. He's extremely intelligent and has a head for technology like his father did. He's unaware of zombies and his own talents.

Colonel Sam Mallard: Col. Mallard runs the E.L.I. Project, which is a covert top secret project that reanimates the dead for use on the battlefield. The colonel also has a morbid curiosity about life and death itself.

Doctor Carl Lichtenberg: "Doc" as he's called, was brought onto the project a decade earlier to develop a new serum that would allow reanimation of corpses with a synthetically engineered formula. The new formula does not rely on the use of Eli Caine's blood to create new zombies.

Doug Bruester: Although Bruester is Doc's assistant, he secretly keeps the colonel informed as to the professor's progress on the serum development. Unbeknownst to the professor, not only will the serum free the government from Caine, but the colonel has been creating his own stash of serum that reverts to the original "contagious" effects of Caine's blood prior to the Vietnam War. The serum developed from Caine's blood to reanimate the dead also caused them to be contagious as well. The government found that a virus was the cause and removed it. Bruester is a sneaky and greedy little worm

Elisha Caine: Elisha fought in the Civil War as a youth and was killed on the battlefield. However, when he continued to walk the Earth, the government used him in an experiment to create an army of the undead. He's the first recorded undead. Since then, he has served the government in every war when they needed the unbeatable armies conquered. He is the king of the undead and wields power over the dead. Myth has it that he is un-killable.

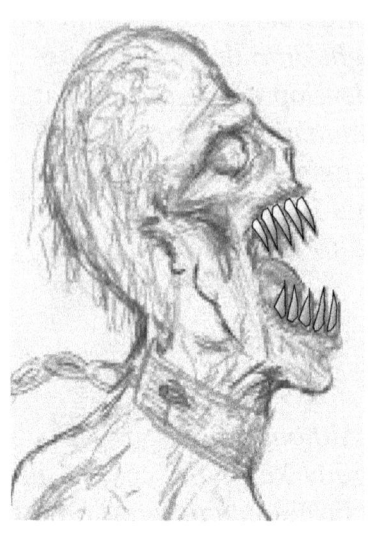

The Zombies: After the discovery that Elisha Caine could not die, the government used a serum developed from Caine's blood to reanimate its own army of the undead. Whenever the government was in a pinch in a battle or war, they turned to this secret army to turn a defeat into victory. It was also decided, in the government's best wisdom, that the best place to get zombies was the battlefield itself. So they claimed the casualties of the wars for themselves to maintain their own secret army. It was the job of the McDonald family to go into the war zones after the government had let loose their secret army, to kill the rampaging undead and to bring the situation under control. They were the government's own cleanup crew. The government also took it upon themselves to "improve" the zombies. They added sharpened steel teeth and claws to the undead to make them more effective on the battlefield. This was true, but it also made them a lot more dangerous for the McDonalds when doing cleanup.

The Freak: Col. Mallard's morbid curiosity with the undead resulted in a secret lab where different combinations of body parts and creatures were experimented on. The result of on experiment was a creature with four arms and various body parts that stood over eight foot tall.

Not all screenplays need this sort of detail on characters. However, in sci-fi, action adventure and possible game related screenplays, it never hurts to have the research done, just in case Hollywood comes knocking... or the gaming industry.

SCENES AND DIALOGUE

As I PREVIOUSLY MENTIONED, screenplays are works of art for a visual medium. How do readers or directors get visual images from your screenplay? Every word that you put into the screenplay must translate into an image. If what you're typing into your script cannot be translated into an image, then you are wasting the person's time. If the image is not a location or you are not describing the location elements, or you are not describing how the actor looks or moves, or you are not presenting dialogue for the actors, then it doesn't add to the final product, which is the film. Some of the famous screenwriters, like Tarantino, add personal comments in their screenplays. You're probably not famous at this point so I wouldn't try it. Stick to the rule that if it doesn't translate to a visual image, leave it out.

The scene description section of the screenplay immediately follows the scene heading. The scene heading not only sets the location and time of day for the scene to unfold, but it also informs the director of what locations he needs and how many. I've had several independent film producers request a screenplay that has ONE location. They are on such a tight budget that all they can come up with is their uncle's cabin and that's it. Okay. Don't do this. Not many of us can pull this one off. There's a term in the industry for this. It's called "talking heads." It's when we have one location and people are talking back and forth and there's no scene changes or action. There are instances, however, where this has been done successfully. A great example of this can be seen in the movie *Twelve Men*. In this film about twelve jurors, it was done successfully, but for most of us, it's certain death.

The Scene Description allows us to visually describe the environment, whether it's a majestic interior of a mansion or a run-down slum. It also allows us to describe the tone and demeanor of the characters in the scene by having them racing in the room frightened, or mad, or happy, or carrying a sawed off shotgun. You set the tone of the scene for the supporting dialogue.

Let's talk about dialogue. Dialogue reveals character. This is how they interact with each other, in addition to their facial gestures, body movements or other actions described in the scene description or parenthetical. As I mentioned earlier, people have favorite words or ways of saying something.

Also, when characters have "on the nose dialogue," this means they are stating the obvious. For instance in *Jerry McGuire*, Renee Zellweger tells her love interest that he "*...had me at hello.*" How would it have sounded if she had blandly said that she had fallen in love with him at first sight? It wouldn't have been memorable. Having her say that she fell in love with him at first sight would have been considered "on the nose dialogue." In one of my screenplays, the main character meets the girl of his dreams and falls for her the first time they meet. During his conversation with her, he can hardly get a word out of his mouth that makes sense. When she leaves, his brother asks him what he said to her. That exact minute, I stopped writing. I knew that I wanted something different to come out of his mouth. The radio was on for some mood music and a song came on about angels. The line, "*What do you say to an angel?*" popped into my head. He could have easily said, "*I just babbled... I didn't know what to say.*" The inspired line worked much better!

In, *Mister Christmas*, the main character is handicapped and has a speech impediment. I knew that I had two options. One is that I could have noted that he had a speech impediment at the beginning of the screenplay and write his dialogue as normal dialogue, or I could write his dialogue just as he spoke it, impediment and all. I chose the latter because it was more effective and put you more in touch with the character.

Dialogue for screenplays is not written in English proper unless the person talking is perhaps a professor or well-educated gentleman.

Most of us talk in broken language and rarely have a chance to finish a complete sentence when conversing with others. Dialogue for film is like that, fragments and broken language. Avoid needless dialogue, like discussions about the weather or busy talk. If it's unrelated to the story or doesn't move it forward, ditch it! I can't tell you how many screenplays that I've read where the writer will have the characters carry on a conversation to try and convince me they are real. They are NOT real and nobody wants to listen to chitchat from characters unless it's understood that the character is trying to get something from another character. Avoid using needless dialogue.

Each character should rush into a scene with a purpose or goal, and the dialogue is used to get what they are after, or not after. Remember what I said about a beginning, a middle, and an end. The scene serves a purpose — to move the story each and every time, and the dialogue is used to accomplish this. Keep the dialogue to the point and do NOT use it for exposition. What I mean is, do not have the character explaining what is going on to the audience. They can figure that out on their own. Also, keep the conversation down to short bursts of dialogue between the characters. Don't have the characters making speeches, unless, of course it's a politician and it's needed.

THE INSANITY OF IT ALL

ON THE SURFACE, it looks like we sanely approach the process of creating something from nothing, a story from air, characters that never existed or never will exist, and words that no man or woman ever said. It looks as if we deliberately and methodically write words on paper from start to finish, all which results in a screenplay. Well, not quite. I'm not sure how other screenwriters' brains work, but mine is chaotic and unpredictable as to what it will spit out. They initially look more like the ramblings of a madman than they do of a writer. They seem disorganized and disconnected, but yet they are more like pieces of a puzzle that needs assembling. This is how my thought process works when I'm brainstorming or creating story structure. Below are my actual notes for the screenplay entitled, *In Your Dreams*, which I introduced to you as a synopsis on page 17.

This screenplay originated from a short story that I wrote many years earlier during some of my first fiction writing attempts. I had given that early version the title "Charlie's Worlds". It was about a comatose man who was capable of bringing other people into his dreams. Although the short story never panned out too much, it did provide inspiration for this screenplay. So, dig out your short stories. As you'll see in my notes, I started out with the original premise, but after putting Jim Carrey in as my lead I started to think more about the characters and new ideas began to come to me. Then the story started to unfold.

I actually did two sets of notes. The original notes provided me with the major sequences that would drive the story. These notes that outlined the story will give you insight into the workings of a mind as it tries to conjure up the story elements that will eventually form the screenplay. Then, I provide you with my complete notes after having gone through the original ones a second time. I think it helps to write down all of your ideas for scenes or sequences a couple of times. However, you don't have to do this if you feel comfortable with the notes you created the first time through.

I have numbered the notes sequentially for reference purposes only. I have also numbered the scenes in the screenplay. Don't do this! It's only for my own reference. As I discuss the random scenes that came to me during my brainstorming sessions, I will refer to which scene in the screenplay that it finally developed into. For me, I think about the story and what scenes will help me to develop the story. It doesn't matter if the scene is not sequential, as I can fit it into the structure afterward. Later in my notes, you will see an outline forming from the ideas, and then you will see them listed somewhat sequentially.

The reader can compare the raw idea with the final scene of the screenplay to understand how these ideas translate into scenes. I will reference the notes as Note 1, etc., and the screenplay scenes as Scene 1, etc. Below, I have mapped a couple of example notes to the corresponding scenes to give you an idea.

Opening Scene: What looks like a real cop chase scene - a car squeals around the corner."

> (5) Opening Scene: What looks like a real cop chase scene - a car squeals around the corner.

```
1) EXT. CITY STREETS - DAY

A police car is in hot pursuit of an old sedan.  The
CRIMINAL hangs out of the speeding car's driver's side
window and fires a large caliber gun back at the police car
blowing the exterior mirror into pieces.
```

HOW TO WRITE A SCREENPLAY IN 3-DAYS

"Suddenly: we cut to the driver a small boy (5) in a cop uniform - (Walter)"

```
1) Suddenly: we cut to the driver
   a small boy (5) in a cop
   uniform — (Walter)
```

```
2) INT. POLICE CAR - DAY

From the back seat, we watch as HARRY, 30s, the policeman
riding shotgun, hangs his weapon out the window and fires
several rounds with no success.

A small hand (of a child) holds a very large caliber gun out
the window and firing. A direct hit takes the fleeing car's
back window out. Harry is impressed.
                        HARRY
                Good shooting Officer Morris.

CLOSEUP: On MORRIS, 6 years old, driving the police car,
dressed in full policeman gear and uniform, his hat brim
pulled down to the top of his eyes. He peers out determined
as he cuts a corner.
                        MORRIS
                Thanks Harry. It's nothing.
```

In Note 1 on the next page, you can see the old title of the short story that I started with and in Note 3, I give a brief logline of the story: "Jim Carrey plays a down on his luck dog catcher in a small town with no life." Note 6 gives more insight into the character (named Walter at this point) suggesting that he's a "daydreamer" who imagines himself as a hero and a tough guy. Note 8 expands this concept in that his daydreams begin to merge with the real world and this creates problems. These first notes gave me the essence of the story.

① "IN MY DREAMS"
~~Worlds of Charlie~~

② — Jim Carrie ~~plays~~ a ~~down on~~ his luck ~~investigator~~ CATCHER on a small town with no life. (WALTER)

③ — Tone of Central Characters?

④ — ~~Charlie Brankton — at Inlaw — have fun~~
walter

⑤ — ~~Frank~~ Googlebe? — a failure at his life — stuck in a rut — doesn't really [think] that he is alive — 2 years study criminology at local college. Father was a real cop. —

⑥ — Daydreamer — imagining himself as a hero + tough guy — does impressions then is zapped back to reality.

⑦ — His daydreams get sharper + sharper and a man (Charlie) begins showing up in his daydream — causing him to get totally messed up.).

⑧ — His daydream begin to merge with the real world and create problems.

Notes 9 to 13 were about ideas that kept trying to pull me back to the previous short story theme. I didn't use them. I wanted to move ahead to something new. Notes 14 and 15 provided me with key themes or sequences important to our character. Note 14 lets us know that he is in love with a waitress who is sexually harassed by the town sheriff. Although he imagines himself doing something about it, he can't bring himself to do anything in the "real" world. Note 15 tells us that he still lives with his parents and that his mother still does his hair.

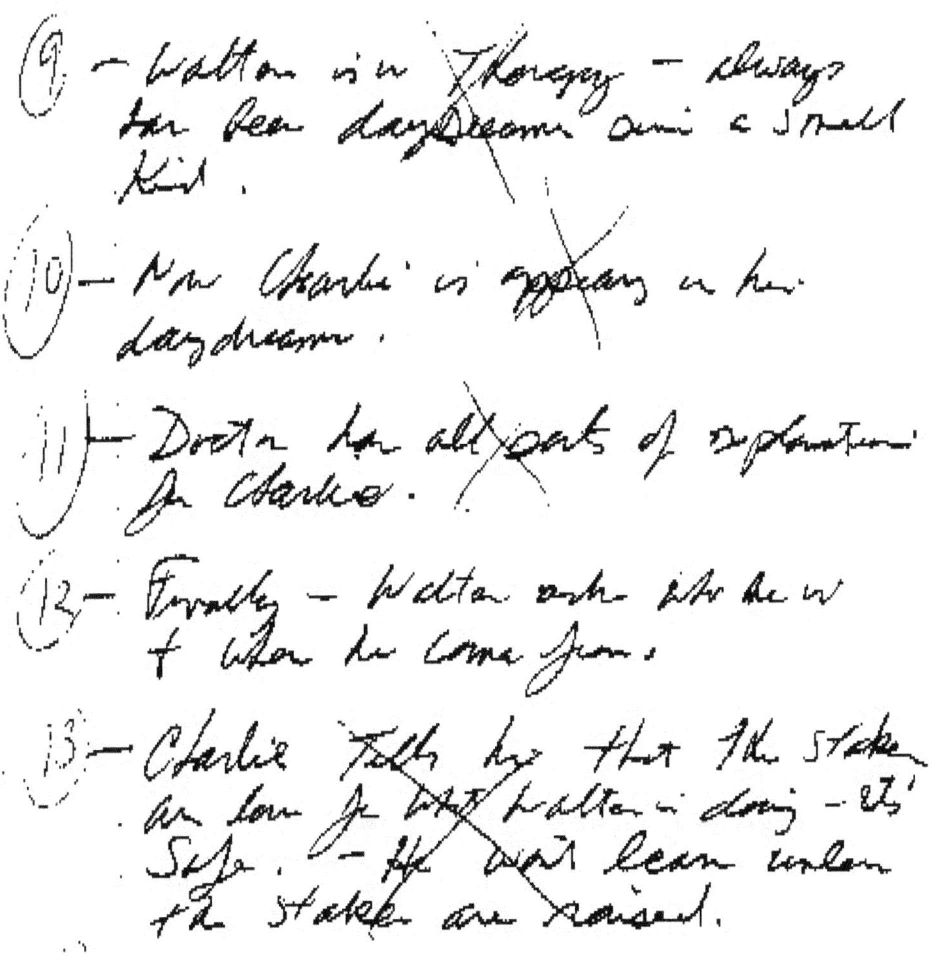

[Handwritten notes:]

9 — Walton is in therapy — always has been daydreaming since a small kid.

10 — Now Charlie is appearing in his daydreams.

11 — Doctor has all sorts of explanations for Charlie.

12 — Finally — Walton asks who he is & where he comes from.

13 — Charlie tells him that the stakes are low for what Walton is doing — it's safe. — He won't learn unless the stakes are raised.

In Notes 17 and 18, I was trying to figure out how the sheriff is connected to the other characters. I realized that the sheriff was from the same high school and had done something that put our hero in his shell (where he still is at this point). As soon as I asked the question, an idea came to me to make Morris a male cheerleader and that the future sheriff had orchestrated a practical joke on our hero. These ideas turn into sequences early in the story and tell us why our character is the way he is. Note 23 was an idea for a scene. In Note 24, the sheriff is running for reelection and became a theme or sequence that was very important to the story. Many of the other notes on that page weren't used. They, again, were trying to drag me back to themes in the short story I had written earlier.

16) His father is a retired cop and thinks he's a sissy.

17) The sheriff did something to him or pighooted in front of the whole school. What?

18) Put ladies cream in his underwear in locker room before the school meeting (what coaches) before the game. — He was a cheerleader. It started with, oh boy, he finally gave in & showed he's hum down his pants and massaged himself — everyone thought he was playing with himself. So much for self respect and a career as an ___.

19) He never found out that the sheriff did it.

20) At end — he sneaks in police department to does his shorts right before a press conference?

21) Sheriff is the town bully. He was the star quarterback.

22) He throws Walter bones, like lost dogs, etc.

(23) — Traps him in a joke in restaurant.

(24) Sheriff has an election coming up. People in town actually like him because he always helps people — but they don't think he has the spunk to be sheriff.

(25) Up on the hill lives Charlie — a man who has lived a full & rich life and has been to every corner of the world — now 90 years old — his dying. A caretaker takes care of him but he's now comatose.

(26) The walls are adorned with collections of artifacts from all over the world. A strange eerie cloud hangs over it. — Something suspicious is going on.

(27) He has been a benefactor to many — a philanthropist — a student of the occult — the mystic. He has volumes of books on the occult — the

(28) mystical — magic — history, etc.

(29) He's everything that Walter is not.

In Notes 30 to 32 I was brainstorming some of the practical jokes that Ben plays on Morris while in high school. One of them is the itching powder scene where Morris is seen digging into his shorts and scratching himself in front of the whole school. Other ideas that came out during Notes 33, and 35 to 37 weren't used.

(30) — opening scene of jokes putting itch powder in Walter's shorts in locker room. Walter dressing for Pep Meeting. — [illegible] — Pep Meeting.

(31) — Walter (a cheerleader) [illegible] — does cheerleader routine. The [illegible] laugh [illegible].

(32) — At beginning itching. Walter digs deep & [illegible] audition [illegible] laughter — [illegible]

(33) — At Restaurant — Walter now, older sits at the bar drinking his coffee.

(34) — Maybe Walter is the dog catcher. He has a way with animals — but not human ones.

(35) — Sheriff is always making dog jokes. Heard you were out with a real dog the other night.

(36) — ~~Heard you [illegible]~~ What's his comeback? [illegible] — [illegible].

(37) — has daydream that animals can talk as they say some really stupid shit.

In Notes 44 and 45, my first idea about pets humping came up. I tried to figure out what animals would dream about. Humping things would probably be pretty close. I first wanted our waitress to have dreams about college, but then it struck me that her NOT having dreams would be more dramatic and symbolic of her life. This appears in Notes 46 and 47.

Notes 52 to 204 of my first notes are repetitions of the notes that I later did. I wanted to show you some of the first original notes so you could see where a majority of the sequences came from.

The following notes are from my second round of brainstorming:

Notes 1 through 3 on the following page actually end up in Scenes 200 and 201 at the end of the screenplay. Note 4 inspired me for words at the beginning, dedicated to those who dream. However, Notes 5, 6, and 7 find themselves as Scenes 1 and 2 in the screenplay, as shown in the example. I wanted to open with a couple of dramatic and comical scenes that lets the audience see how our main character does not differentiate between his imagination and the real world.

JWT

① - Where we at?

② - Sevin you don't have dreams. I thought you ask to share mine. Look. She turns to look at a sunset on the water. They stand on a tropical beach resort. Etc. Feature.

③ - No. He turns her. You do. He kisses her.

④ - Words on screen don't dream like: "Dream in what different than from carnival... dream on..."
opening — NO

⑤ - Opening Scene: What looks like a real cop chase scene — a car squeals around the corner.

⑥ - The Bad guys hang out + fire back.

⑦ - Suddenly: we cut to the driver — a small boy (5) in a cop uniform — (batter)

The Marathon Method

200) INT. HOPEVILLE CAFÉ - MORNING

The café door opens. CLOSEUP: On the Sheriff badge and follow it as the guy wearing it moves to the counter and sits. We move up to reveal a smiling Morris. Jenny moves in close to his face, so close he can smell her breath.

> JENNY
> Good morning...Sheriff.

> MORRIS
> You can call me Morris or Moe.

> JENNY
> Are you sure? How would that look? The Sheriff flirting with a waitress? You might get a reputation.

> MORRIS
> You have a point there.

Just then, Ben enters, and yeah, guess what? He's wearing the dogcatcher uniform that Morris used to wear. Ben pats Morris on the shoulder as he passes.

> BEN
> Morning, Moe.

> MORRIS
> (Without taking eyes off Jenny)
> Morning Ben.
> (To Jenny)
> Maybe I can save my reputation.

> JENNY
> You have an idea?

> MORRIS
> Yeah, but I can't share it here.

> JENNY
> Ohhhhh, I see. Maybe we should step into my office.

Jenny tries to poke Morris in the eyes. He blocks it.

> MORRIS
> That would work.

Jenny turns and heads towards the storage room. She opens the door. Morris follows and steps into the room. She closes it. It's pitch dark. We can't see either one.

                    JENNY
          Maybe we should turn on the
          light.

                    MORRIS
          I have a better idea.

A dream cloud begins to form above their heads. It lights
the closet and their faces. Jenny looks up at it. It's a
beautiful beach with white sand and sky blue water.

                    JENNY
          Now maybe I'm crazy, but I think
          there's a dream above us.

                    MORRIS
          It's mine.

                    JENNY
          That's your dream?

Morris takes her hand and lifts it towards the dream.
Whoosh, they're sucked into the dream.

201) INT. BEACH DREAM - DAY

There they are standing on that beautiful beach. Morris
takes her hand.

                    MORRIS
          It's my dream of our honeymoon.

                    JENNY
          Honeymoon?

                    MORRIS
          Only one problem.

                    JENNY
          Yes...I will.

Jenny wraps her arms around his neck. They passionately
kiss. She pulls back and looks at him.

                    JENNY
          I only have one question.

                    MORRIS
          What's that?

                    JENNY
          How do we get back? Knuck
          Knuck.

                    MORRIS
          Who cares?

They passionately kiss again.

HOW TO WRITE A SCREENPLAY IN 3-DAYS

Notes 8 and 9 were not used in the screenplay. The idea is to throw out scene ideas and get into the creative mode. Don't worry if you come up with scenes that never get used. I did find the name of the town, Hopeville, while brainstorming about corn and corn parades. Note 10 generated ideas about the sheriff's name (Ben). While I was thinking about the office in Note 11, I got inspiration for scene 155, where our character sees his heritage being removed from the walls of the courthouse.

[Handwritten notes:]

"WALTER HILL"

(8) — Corn? They have a Corn Festival — Corn Parade — People wear Corn hats —

(9) — "King & Queen of the Corn Parade"

— HopeVille Indiana
  What River?
  or Ohio?
  or Nebraska or Iowa?

(10) When Walter stops by to talk with the Sheriff — okay give him a name — "BEN McKay"

(11) He sees that the office is being redecorated. 4 square clean space on the wall are lighter because of the sun. Walter sees the frames laying against the wall or the corner. He thumbs through them — They are all pictures of his relatives all have last names — "HILL".

(12) Ben enters and sees him going through the pictures. Walter people why they're down.

155) INT. CITY HALL - LATE AFTERNOON

Morris enters the lobby, which is currently being remodeled, and checks the room listing on the wall for city offices. An old man, RUPUS, 70s, dressed in white coveralls and speckled with paint, is removing a series of portraits from the wall and placing them into a box. The last one that Rupus takes down is of Morris' father, Walter, as Sheriff.

Morris walks to the box and looks down. He lifts his Father's portrait out of the box. Rupus sees him at the box and approaches.

> RUPUS
> Can I help you, son?

> MORRIS
> This is my Father.

Rupus moves around to get a better look at him.

> RUPUS
> So you're Morris? You probably don't remember me.

Rupus offers his hand likes it's an honor. Morris looks up at him and studies his wrinkled face.

> MORRIS
> I don't think so.

> RUPUS
> Rupus Smith. Folks call me Smitty. I knew your Father, Walter, when he were Sheriff. I knew your Grandfather too, Moe. I was a little bit of a troublemaker back then.

> MORRIS
> I see.

Morris puts the portrait back and lifts another. It's his Grandfather "Moe Hill", also a previous Sheriff. Another portrait is of his Great Grandfather "Morris Hill".

> RUPUS
> It's a real honor, Mr. Hill. And I mean that with all my heart. Your father was a good man. He put me up many a cold night when I had no place to go.

Morris gently puts the portrait back and wipes the dust from his hands.

> RUPUS
> I quit drinking and carrying on years ago. Even got back with my family. My wife passed a few years back, but I've got some great boys.

Rupus takes out his wallet and shows a picture of him and his two SONS.

The Marathon Method

                    MORRIS
          They look nice. I'm glad
          things worked out for you.

Rupus puts his wallet away. He notices that Morris is still
focused on the portraits.

                    RUPUS
          The Sheriff's idea. Said he's
          gonna change things around here.
          I just cleanup 'round here and
          take orders.

                    MORRIS
          So these aren't going back up?

                    RUPUS
          Said to put them into storage. We're
          starting a new era, is what he
          said.

Morris turns and walks away.

                    MORRIS (O.S.)
          We'll see about that.

A big grin comes over Rupus' face. He quickly follows
Morris.

INT. CITY CLERK'S OFFICE - LATE AFTERNOON

Morris waits patiently as the Clerk, DIANA, 30s, finishes
some filing work. She then turns her attention to Morris.

                    DIANA
          How may I help you, sir?

Rupus sneaks up to see what's going on. Diana looks at him,
wondering what he's doing. Rupus looks around as if he's
looking for something.

                    MORRIS
          I'd like to officially run
          for office.

                    DIANA
          I see. What office, sir?

                    MORRIS
          Sheriff.

Several of the other OFFICE WORKERS all perk up and look.
Rupus smiles a big smile. Diana is a little shook by it.
She obviously hasn't had a request like this for a while.

65

She searches though her paperwork and finally finds the forms. She takes out a pen.

>   DIANA
>   Your name?

>   MORRIS
>   Morris Hill. No, make that
>   Morris Moe Hill.

She stares at him, her mouth parted.

>   MORRIS
>   Something wrong?

She snaps away from her stupor and begins writing.

>   DIANA
>   No.

Diana looks back over her shoulder at the other Girls. They all smile. She smiles and turns back to finish the form.

TRANSITION TO:

Diana finishes the form and turns it around for his signature. Morris signs.

>   MORRIS
>   Is that it?

>   DIANA
>   Yeah. We'll just attach the
>   signatures when you bring them
>   in. But we'll need them by close
>   of business Monday since the
>   election is Tuesday. You're
>   cutting it short by-

>   MORRIS
>   What signatures?

>   DIANA
>   The two hundred you need to
>   get on the ballot. I thought
>   you knew.

>   MORRIS
>   I need two hundred signatures?

>   DIANA
>   Yes. Why?

                    MORRIS
          Because, I don't have them.

                    DIANA
          Oh. I'm sorry. Maybe you can-

                    MORRIS
          I'm going out of town. Besides
          I couldn't get that many signatures
          by Monday.

Diana puts the form under the counter.

                    DIANA
          Maybe next election?

                    MORRIS
          Yeah. Thanks anyway.

Morris turns and almost bumps into Rupus. He tries to smile.

                    RUPUS
          Tell your pops that I said
          hello.

Morris offers his hand to Rupus. They shake.

                    MORRIS
          I will. Take care Rup- Smitty.

Morris exits. Rupus scratches his unshaven face then looks at Diana. He approaches the counter.

Note 12 wasn't used in the screenplay. On the next page, I didn't use Note 13, and only used some words from the idea "end of an era" in Scene 155. Note 15 started out as the idea that our character wanted to tell the girl he loves about his weird dreams. The idea was used in Scene 116 of the screenplay but with different wording.

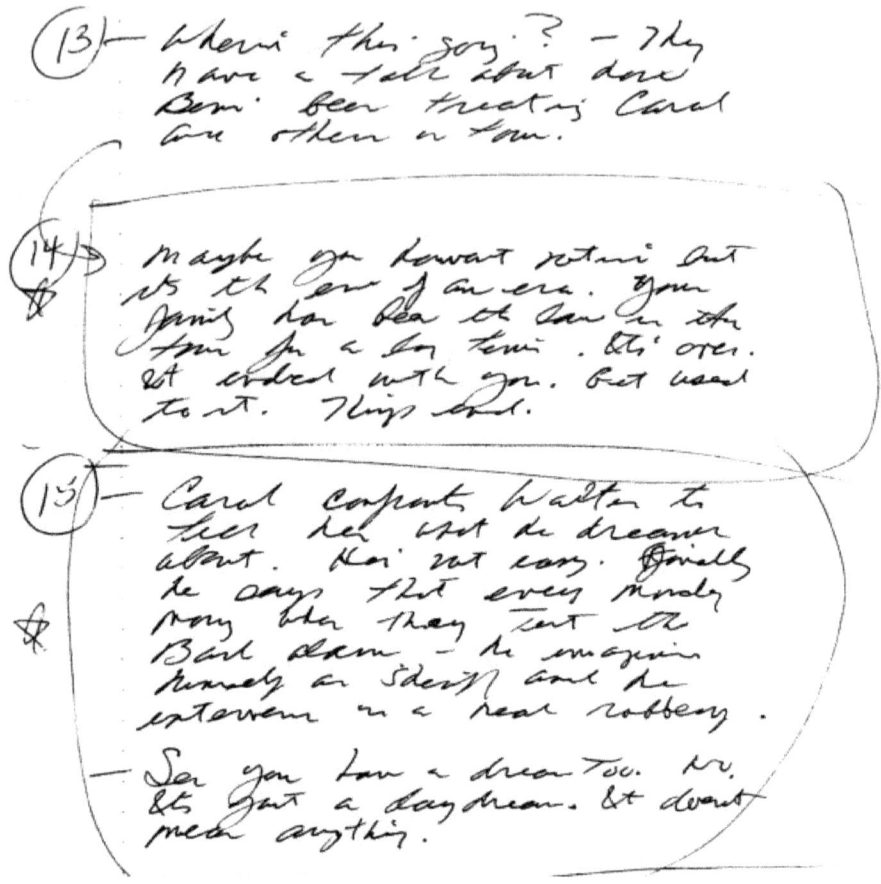

116) EXT. MORRIS BALCONY - NIGHT

As Jenny and Morris sip their tea, Morris is busy studying the dreams that hover above the sleeping citizens' homes. He takes out a black notebook and takes notes then puts it away.

                    JENNY
          Something's happening to you
          Morris.

                    MORRIS
          It is?

                    JENNY
          I mean a good something.

                    MORRIS
          Oh. Thanks.

Morris puts his cup down and turns to her.

MORRIS
Do you believe in dreams?

Jenny searches for an answer, then.

JENNY
I don't think I have dreams. I mean, I don't remember them. I don't know why. I suppose we just lower our expectations and finally get to the point where there are none anymore. If you don't expect, you won't be let down.

MORRIS
Wow. I guess that's safe. But isn't it lonely?

JENNY
Sometimes. But you can always count on men like Ben, who has more hands than an octopus to keep things lively.

MORRIS
Ever since I was a boy, I had these expectations of myself that were really so out there.. that they couldn't even happen ..in the real world, anyway. I wanted to be like my Dad so bad that I created this world in my head where I could. It was real to me.

JENNY
What happened?

Morris turns and looks off in the distance.

MORRIS
Nothing. Nothing at all.

Jenny looks down.

MORRIS
But, in my mind, everything could happen..and everything did..until.

JENNY
Until what?

MORRIS
I'm not sure. But now it's gone.

JENNY
I'm sorry.

MORRIS
Oh, no. It's okay. Because now I see that there's a lot of dreams out there besides mine. Hopeville is still a town of hopes and dreams. They're just not being realized, that's all.

He shifts and leans against the railing.

MORRIS
Am I crazy or insane?

JENNY
No. I think it's wonderful.

Morris slides towards her.

MORRIS
You do?

JENNY
I think that it's great that you would spend the time to talk with people about their dreams and-

Morris moves closer.

MORRIS
Oh no. I can see them as clear as day. That's what I was trying to tell you the other day. I really see them.

Now he's starting to scare her.

JENNY
Oh. You can really see them?

Morris stands and points.

MORRIS
(Excited)
Yeah, old Mr. Lacasta the music teacher always dreams of Marilyn Monroe.

                    JENNY
               (Unbelieving)
          He does?

                    MORRIS Continuing
          ..and my Mother dreams of these
          Barry Mantilow strippers..
          and the pets in the kennel dream
          of home and chewies and -

Jenny puts her cup of tea down. She's becoming frightened.

                    MORRIS
          and- what's wrong?

Jenny pulls her robe tight.

                    JENNY
          I really should be going.
          It's late and I have to open
          at five. Goodnight, Morris.

                    MORRIS
          You're afraid.

                    JENNY
          Afraid? Afraid of what?

                    MORRIS
          Afraid to hope...to dream.

                    JENNY
          What's the point? I'm a waitress
          with bills. I hope for tips.

                    MORRIS
          That's sad.

                    JENNY
          I'm sad? You just moved out your
          parent's house and chase dogs and
          cats for a living. Goodnight.

She exits. Morris is deflated. He leans forward on the balcony and looks out. Max plops down beside his leg.

EXT. MORRIS' APARTMENT - NIGHT

Jenny slams the door to Morris' apartment and leans back against it, regretting her remarks. Pulling her robe together, she steps away into the night.

INT. MORRIS' BEDROOM - NIGHT

Morris enters. The dream cloud is still next to his bed of Butch the Bulldog humping the hydrant. Morris sneaks close and whips the covers off of the bed. He looks down at Max.

                        MORRIS
            That dog has taken humping to
            a new level.

He turns and leaves.

Note 16 of the next page provided me the inspiration for Scene 155. Just above the note, I finally wrote the character's name, Morris. I had been calling him Walter (after Walter Mitty) but ended up giving that name to his father. In Note 17, I realized that, although as a kid he idolized his father who was a policeman, somewhere he had reexamined his view of him and this had changed the direction of his life. This happens in Scene 17 of the screenplay.

17) INT. LOCKER ROOM - DAY

Ben and the other football players laugh and do a high five but immediately stop and begin dressing for practice upon noticing Morris' Father, Walter, Chief of Police, standing with his arms crossed in the doorway. Walter adjusts his gun-belt and approaches Ben. Ben starts to open his locker but Walter slams it shut.

                WALTER
    That was a funny stunt you
    boys pulled. Why don't you
    tell me who set it up. I'd
    like to talk to him.

Ben ignores him and tries to open his locker. Again, Walter slams it shut.

                WALTER
    Maybe it was you.

Morris rounds the corner of the locker room just as his Father, Walter, grabs Ben and violently throws him up against his locker. Morris is seeing a side of his Father he's never seen before.

Back to Walter:

Walter gets in Ben's face. Ben struggles to get free.

                BEN
    Come on, man. Let me
    go. You're hurting me.

                WALTER
    I'm the law around here. Know
    what that means?

                BEN
    No. What?

                WALTER
    Means I can do what I want and
    It would be my word against yours.
    Who do you think they'll believe?

                BEN
      (Struggles)
    What's your problem?

                WALTER
    You. You're my problem. If
    you know what's good for you,
    you'll keep away from my son.

Walter releases him, turns and sees Morris watching. He walks away.

Back to Morris:

Morris looks down disturbed by his Father's actions. The pristine image of the father that he'd held so highly has just been permanently tarnished.

Note 18 was the development of a support character, Willard the janitor, who dreams of getting his high school diploma. It was the idea that developed into several scenes with Willard, starting at Scene 41. Willard turned out to be great comic relief as the straight man who thought that aliens were behind everything that was going on. In Note 19 and 20, I began playing with the idea of Morris' mother dreaming of things from men in leopard G-strings to Barry Manilow. That note idea was used for scenes 141, 142, 145, and 149. Note 20 wasn't used. I was able to work in something similar in another Scene (58). Note 21 gave me an idea for a "Butchy" short order cook at the café (Scene 57), a great dream for Morris to be trapped in!

41) EXT. HOPEVILLE ANIMAL SHELTER-LATE AFTERNOON

Morris has the back doors open and is unloading the cages. As he turns towards the building, he notices another strange dream cloud above the building. This one is bigger and brighter that the one before and involves Alice. Alice is dressed in a very skimpy outfit and is dancing on a stage to a room full of cheering men.

As Morris stares at the dream cloud, he starts getting into the music and starts swaying, then he's really getting into the action...thrusting his pelvis. As he swings around, he's surprised to find himself facing the Janitor, WILLARD, 65 and black, who's staring at him.

Morris makes one last move and stops. Morris looks back up at the dream cloud. Willard looks up to see what he's looking at then gives Morris a strange look.

                      WILLARD
            You feeling alright, Morris?

Morris turns and finishes unloading the cages and slams the door. The dream vanishes. He turns to notice it's gone. Willard looks up again.

                      WILLARD
            You ain't having one of them
            close encounters like I saw
            on TV. They say ten percent
            of the people have one.

Morris thinks about it.

                      MORRIS
            No. I'm not seeing little
            green men.
                (To himself)
            Wish I were.

Willard picks up a couple of the cages.

                      WILLARD
            They's ain't green. They's
            gray. Gray with big black eyes.

Morris picks up a couple of the cages.

                      MORRIS
            Ohhhkay..I stand corrected.

They enter with the cages.

141) INT. MUSIC STORE - DAY

Morris studies a Music CD in his hand titled "*Barry Mantilow's Greatest Hits*"

142) INT. MEN'S STORE - DAY

Morris holds up a pair of men's leopard briefs.

145) INT. HILL'S GARAGE - DAY

Morris enters with a small package under his arm. His Father is under the car changing the oil. His legs protrude out from under the car.

                    MORRIS
              Where's Mom?

                    FATHER (O.S.)
              Shopping.
                  (Realizes it's Morris)
              Oh, is that you Morris?

Suddenly he slides out on the coaster, his hands and face oily. He struggles to get to his feet. Morris helps to pull him up. Walter wipes his hands and then leans over the engine.

                    FATHER
              So how are things going, Mr. Bachelor?

Morris leans over to see what he's doing.

                    MORRIS
              Dad, did you ever daydream?

                    FATHER
            Are you kidding? I was the king.

                    MORRIS
            You were? What kind did you have?

Walter straightens up.

                    FATHER
          Oh boy, I was Flash Gordon and
          Buck Rogers zooming through the
          universe. Saving gorgeous damsels
          in distress, of course.

                    MORRIS
          Of course.

Walter begins to stroll the garage, his imagination taking
over. Morris follows, intrigued.

                    FATHER
          I was John Wayne with my six guns
          blazing.

Walter pretends to draw his guns on Morris.

                    FATHER
          Blam, Blam, Blam!

Morris pretends to be shot and staggers against the car.

                    MORRIS
          You dirty coward, I thought
          we were partners..ooohhhh

                    FATHER
              (Blows smoke from barrel)
          Now you're partners with the grave.

Morris stands having gotten over his own death.

                    MORRIS
          And what else?

Walter begins a smooth dance.

                    FATHER
          I was Fred Astair dancing with
          the lovely ladies all night. They
          couldn't get enough of my fancy
          dancing.

Morris steps up.

                    MORRIS
          May I have this dance Mr. Astair?

Walter takes the lead.

                    FATHER
          Be my pleasure Miss Rogers.

The Marathon Method

As they dance around the garage, Walter twirls Morris away.
Morris curtseys and Walter bows. Walter then rejoins the
real world and grabs several quarts of oil from the shelf.

                    MORRIS
          What about being a policeman?
          Was that one of your dreams?

Walter opens a quart and pours it in the engine.

                    FATHER
          That was the one that got me.
          That's why I did it for thirty
          years.

                    MORRIS
          So I got it from you?

                    FATHER
          I guess so.

                    MORRIS
          Do you still daydream?

                    FATHER
          Right now, I'm getting my
          car ready for the NASCAR 500.

                    MORRIS
          I love you, dad.

Walter stops, wipes his hands and hugs Morris.

                    FATHER
          I love you too.

Morris hands him the present.

                    MORRIS
          I got you something.

Walter takes it and looks at it.

                    FATHER
          It's not my birthday. What is
          it?

                    MORRIS
          It's really for you and Mom.

                    FATHER
          Oh, thanks.

Morris turns to leave.

                    MORRIS
            I'll see you later.

                    FATHER
            Morris?

Morris turns back around.

                    MORRIS
            Yeah?

                    FATHER
            I'm happy. Maybe I wasn't an
            astronaut or a big star like
            Fred Astair, but I have you and
            your Mother. That makes me happy.
            Only you know what your dream is.
            Go be happy. Do what you have to
            do.

                    MORRIS
            Thanks, Dad.

Morris exits the garage. Walter goes back to work.

149) INT. HILL HOUSE-KITCHEN

Walter is sitting at the kitchen table. The Barry Mantilow
CD sits on the table in front of him. He holds up the skimpy
leopard underwear and examines them. His wife, Ann enters
the kitchen from a trip to the store. She places two bags
of groceries on the counter and puts her purse down.
Turning to go for more groceries, she steps from the
kitchen.

                    ANN (O.S.)
            Dear, could you help me
            with the rest of the-

Okay, it just hit her that her husband is holding up a pair
of leopard underwear. She slowly backs into the room, her
eyes now locked on the underwear he's holding. Walter looks
at her odd.

                    WALTER
            Now isn't that strange? Morris
            came by and gave these to me.

Walter then picks up the CD and shows it to her.

                    WALTER
                (Puzzled)
            And a Barry somebody CD.

As he looks at his wife, there's this strange animal lust
look coming over her face. She throws off her coat, grabs
the CD and Walter by his arm. She pulls him straight up from
the chair.

                    ANN
            Screw the groceries!

The Marathon Method

58) CLOSEUP: of Morris' closed eyelids. The Bell ends and Morris opens his eyes. He looks around. Nothing had happened. Ben and the other patrons are setting their watches by the clock.

Morris clinches his eyes closed and tries even harder. He opens them... Still nothing. He looks at the clock again. It shows 8:02. Something's wrong. He's becoming panicked.

Suddenly, he sees a small daydream cloud floating above Deloris, the cook. It's close enough to touch. Inside the dream cloud, Deloris (remember that she's a "butchy" woman) is dressed in S&M gear (black leather and skimpy). Morris can't believe his eyes. As he leans forward, the PATRON on the left side asks for the salt.

     PATRON
  Morris could you-

Morris is sucked up into the dream. The Patron looks around for Morris as Jenny steps up to refill his cup.

     JENNY
  Where'd he go?

The Patron shrugs his shoulders and reaches for the salt.

57) INT. HOPEVILLE CAFÉ - MORNING

Morris enters. The café is filled with its usual crowd. Morris makes his way past Ben and to his usual chair. Jenny

Note 22 was an idea that the pictures in the courthouse needed to be put back up (which had been taken down by Ben) as a symbolic gesture that the Hill legacy had been restored. This happens in Scene 199. I didn't take my own advice in Note 23 to have the janitor do it. They end up back on the wall, but we don't know who did it. Note 24 is an elaborate idea for a scene where Morris rescues the day like he's Dirty Harry, but in the end embarrasses himself in front of Jenny. This idea finds itself in the makings of Scenes 24 through 26.

(22) — at end of scene — Momeni hangs the pendant that is he bought her, puts next to her dad's.

(23) Maybe have the Janitor do it. — (Same guy who helps get her BED)

(24) — When he daydreams of stopping the Robbery, he stops + hands the roll he's eating to Jenny. He takes Ben's gun, doesn't go, I'll take care of this. Here Jenny, hold this. I'll be right back. He stops the Robbery + returns. He hands the gun back. Jenny hands him the roll. It's filthy. She sees the rag on his hand. Oh, I'm sorry. She licks the rag off his hand. She starts getting a little crazy, licking all over his hand. He starts getting into it. Then the laughter brings him back. The Customer has a dog with him and it's licking the wrist of Momeni hand that's hanging down

more

199) INT. CITY HALL - AFTERNOON

Morris enters the main doors and sees that the pictures of his past relatives who held office have been put back up. As Morris steps towards the office, Jenny steps up, hands him the signatures, and kisses him on the cheek. Before he can take another step, Ben steps up wearing an arm sling. He offers his hand. Morris shakes it.

> BEN
> It might sound weird, but I wanted to wish you luck.

> MORRIS
> Thanks. And thanks for hanging the portraits back up.

> BEN
> They're heroes..like you. They belong there.

Ben steps back to allow Morris to continue.

24) INT. HOPEVILLE CAFÉ - MORNING

Morris enters. The café is already busy with the morning customers. A single stool at the counter is empty (Morris' stool). Sitting at the first counter seat is Ben Harris, his archenemy, now in his 30s also, wearing the police chief's uniform. He's chatting with JENNY, late 20s and attractive with short dark hair, who's holding a full coffee pot. Morris makes it a point not to make eye contact with Ben as he passes. Jenny spots Morris and smiles.

Morris makes his way through the busy café to his seat. Jenny tears herself away from Ben to grab Morris' morning Danish and a clean cup.

Morris compares his watch with the café clock as Jenny places his Danish in front of him and pours his coffee. It shows 7:50.

> MORRIS
> Morning, Jenny. How are things?

> JENNY
> It's Monday. What can I say?

The cook, DELORIS, 50 and a large woman who could easily be mistaken for a trucker, works the grill. She puts another order up.

> DELORIS
> (To Jenny)
> Order's up!

                          BEN
                But they have guns.

Morris hands Jenny his half-eaten roll, and still chewing a
mouthful of roll, unfastens Ben's holster and takes his gun.

                          MORRIS
                       (To Jenny)
                Hold this. I'll be right back.

Morris steps calmly from the café, the large gun dangling at
his side.

25) EXT. TOWN STREET - MORNING

Morris calmly steps out onto the street while watching the
two Bank Robbers climbing into their getaway car. They see
Morris with the gun and fire a couple of random shots. The
glass of the café shatters. Morris calmly looks back at the
shattered glass and shakes his head. Stepping forward
towards the now moving car, he aims the huge gun.

                          MORRIS
                Halt!

The car speeds wildly towards Morris.

At the Café: A crowd of patrons gathers at the café windows
to watch.

Back to Morris:

Morris calmly takes aim at the car that's quickly
approaching him and fires. The windshield is blown out.
The car veers away just missing Morris and careens out of
control. It slams into a dumpster. The driver slams against
the steering wheel and is knocked out. The HORN is stuck
on. The passenger door flies open and a bloodied Bank
Robber staggers out with a shotgun. Morris turns and slowly
walks towards the crashed vehicle. The Bank Robber fires
and misses. Morris aims and fires. The Bank robber is hit.
He falls over.

26) INT. HOPEVILLE CAFÉ - MORNING

Morris enters dragging the two Bank Robbers. He deposits
them at Ben's feet. Ben, still shook by fear, looks down at
them. Morris puts the gun back into Ben's holster and
buttons it.

                          BEN
                Might want to lock up these
                fellas when you get time.

He grabs Ben by his collar and pulls him up to his face.

> MORRIS
> And if you ever pinch or touch Jenny gain, I'll break your fingers.

Morris releases him. Ben thinks about it, then.

> BEN
> Yes, sir, Mr. Hill.

Morris steps to Jenny.

> MORRIS
> You have something for me?

Jenny lunges into his arms and passionately kisses him. Everyone in the Café CHEERS. She steps back and smiles.

> MORRIS
> I meant the Danish, honey.

He holds out his hand. She lays the sticky Danish back into his open palm. He takes the Danish with his other hand and looks at the icy mess on his palm. Jenny sees it.

> JENNY
> Oh, I'm so sorry.

Jenny takes his hand and licks the icing. She licks again and begins licking it aggressively to the point where she's lapping it like a dog. Morris is starting to experience something wonderful. He lets it out.

> MORRIS
> Oooohhh Yeah!

A burst of LAUGHTER takes us to.

Morris is seated at the counter with his arms at his side engrossed in his daydream. A PATRON'S Dog is lapping at the icing on Morris' hand that's hanging to his side. Another PATRON (one of Ben's friends) quickly finishes tying Morris' shoelaces together and scurries away.

Morris looks up at the clock. It shows 8:00. Slowly he looks around. Everyone behind the counter has stopped in their tracks and is staring at Morris. Ben is leaning forward at the counter staring at Morris. Slowly they go about their business. Morris stands and starts to walk away. He falls over flat onto his face. Everyone LAUGHS.

Morris pulls his face from the floor and looks down. His shoes are tied together. Ben nearly gags on his coffee, then holds it out for a refill. Jenny refreshes it.

      JENNY
   That wasn't funny.

Ben tries not to smile, but can't help it.

      BEN
   Yeah. You're right. It wasn't
   funny... It was hilarious!

Everyone laughs again as Morris quickly fixes his laces. He stands and turns to face Ben. Everyone becomes quiet as Ben swivels around in his seat. Morris looks at the badge that says "Sheriff."

      BEN
    (Now serious)
   Yeah, Morris? What can I do
   for you?

Morris looks over at Jenny. She looks down, embarrassed for Morris.

      BEN
   That's what I thought.

Ben spins around as Morris contemplates some kind of gesture that would prove he's a man. His fists tighten then relax and open. He can't find it. He turns and walks out.

Ben and the other patrons set their watch for 8:00. Jenny leans against the counter during a lull in orders. She sips a cup of coffee. Ben looks up after adjusting his watch.

      BEN
   If it weren't for Mr. Hodges
   testing that old Bank Alarm
   every Monday mornin', none
   of us would have the right
   time.

Ben stands and stretches. He takes out a five and holds it out to Jenny. She starts to take it, but he doesn't let go.

      BEN
   You know, if I get reelected
   it'll mean a raise.

She tries to pull the money away. He finally lets go.

                    JENNY
                (Not impressed)
            Yeah, that's great.

Ben moves around the end of the counter towards her as she
goes to the register and gets his change. She holds it out.
He folds her hand around it.

                    BEN
            A man shouldn't be alone.
            A woman either.

Jenny waits for him to release her hand then puts the change
in her tip jar.

                    JENNY
                (Cold)
            Thanks Sheriff.

Ben exits. Jenny watches him leave and the door close.
Maybe he was right. She didn't know but it made her think.

                    DELORIS (O.S.)
            He may not be the man of
            your dreams but you could do
            worse.

Jenny turns to pickup another order while giving Deloris a
dirty look.

                    DELORIS
            Just trying to help.

                    JENNY
            Don't.

Jenny shoots her a half smile as she steps away with the
order.

Notes 25, 26, and 27 didn't develop into scenes in the screenplay. Some of it was dialogue and the last note, 27, was an idea to have her have the greatest dream of all. I didn't feel it was needed, so I never used it.

(25) — She closes her eyes. nothing happens. I'm sorry I can't do it.

(26) — Sure you can. just try harder.
— I don't want to.
— Oh come on its easy.
— No. I said no. I have to go. She runs off.

(27) [28] When she finally has a dream its the biggest & most colorful in the town.

Note 28 is a pivotal idea about the use of dreams in the story. When the shaman performs the ritual on Morris and he begins to look outside his own dreams, he begins a different path that will change his life.

Notes 29 and 30 weren't used. However, in Note 31, I realized that it would be a pivotal point when Morris FINALLY stood up to Ben, who had been his adversary from high school and who had the job that had been in his family for generations. Although the note discusses a scene where Morris stands up to him, it happens in Scene 90 in a more subtle way, and different from what I expected. Characters WILL surprise you in their actions and in when they pick the times to do the things they need to do.

Note 32 brings up the reference to the fact that Morris' family had a legacy that had ended with Morris.

HOW TO WRITE A SCREENPLAY IN 3-DAYS

scene 63 starts

(28) — When Morris starts helping the people dreams come true — the attitude begins to change —

(29) — When they discover that it's Morris who is behind it, and Ben accuses Morris of doing it as a campaign to become sheriff, it suggests to the townsfolk that he's running. People keep stopping him & saying that they support him. — Didn't this way

(30) — Bof goes back to her father. They visit Morris & tell him about that. Her dad asks him about it and says that he'll support Morris. Morris denies he's running for sheriff. His father becomes upset?

(31) — It's when Ben makes another pass at Jenny that Morris has had enough. He tells Ben to stop it. Everyone is hushed. — Doesn't appear exhibit this yet — why not or 90

(32) — This is when Ben says that Morris' joking reign is over — You saw to that Morris — he says — well maybe I made yourself

90) INT. HOPEVILLE CAFÉ - MORNING

Morris drags his body into the café. He looks like crap. Jenny takes note as he finds his seat and melts into it. Ben is in his usual seat, but Morris is so worn out he doesn't even notice him today or Jenny approach with his usual Danish and coffee.

                    JENNY (O.S.)
        Rough night?

Morris jumps then collects himself enough to get his hands around the coffee and find his mouth. After a sip, he looks up at Jenny.

                    MORRIS
        If you consider being chased
        by a horny old geezer with no teeth
        aaaall niiiiight bad, yeah it was-

It dawns on Morris of what just came out of his mouth. He wasn't in a dream. He was in reality and that may have been a little TOO MUCH.

As he turns to face the jeering crowd in the café, he notices that nobody's paying attention. It's just Jenny who's still standing in front of him.

                    JENNY
        I see. That sounds a little
        strange, Morris.

                    MORRIS
          (Over confident)
        And I was dressed like Marylyn
        Monroe. Yeah.

THAT DID IT! Every dull conversation in the place comes to a screeching halt on that note. Forget about hearing a pin drop, you could hear a dust mite flossing. Morris notices this and turns to face his fear. Yep, everyone has their eyes on Morris, including Ben.

                    MORRIS
        Costume party.

And with that, as suddenly as it had stopped, it starts again...the murmur, the chatter. But Jenny is not satisfied. She's concerned.

                    JENNY
        Are you alright?

Morris takes a big gulp of coffee to wash his stupidity away.

                    MORRIS
        Yeah. Sure.

                    JENNY
        Good. Then maybe you'd like
        to follow me.

Jenny puts the coffeepot down and walks back towards the stock room. Morris follows. Jenny swings open the stockroom door to reveal Max, who is lying on the floor. A small dream cloud floats over him, showing him in the arms of Morris. Morris smiles.

                              MORRIS
                    Oh, Max.

Max perks up. The dream disappears as he rushes to Morris'
arms. Morris stands.

                              JENNY
                    I found him outside my door this
                    morning on the way to work. What
                    happened to you last night? For
                    real.

                              MORRIS
                    If I told you, you wouldn't
                    believe me.

                              JENNY
                    Trust me. You hear some whoppers
                    as a waitress.

Morris looks around for witnesses within ear range.

                              MORRIS
                    I can see dreams.

It takes a minute for her to digest it.

                              JENNY
                    You mean you have visions?

                              MORRIS
                    No. I mean DREAMS. You know when
                    you sleep or daydream?

                              JENNY
                    You can read people's minds? I
                    don't understand.

                              BEN (O.S.)
                    Then read mine. Let me help
                    you. I'd like to pay my tab
                    so I can leave.

They both turn to find Ben leaning against the doorway with
his arms crossed.

                              MORRIS
                    I have to go. I'll be late
                    for work.

Morris approaches the doorway. Ben doesn't make any effort
to move out of the way.

                              MORRIS
                         (Looking down)
                    Excuse me.

Ben leans forward towards him.

                              BEN
                         (Hushed voice)
                    You need help Morris. Stop by
                    my office and I'll make some
                    phone calls to reserve you a
                    nice little padded room.

                    Morris finally looks up at Ben. Reaching up, he puts his
                    hand on Ben's arm.

                                        MORRIS
                              I said excuse me. That means
                              move out of my way.

                    Ben looks down at Morris' hand, then steps aside. Ben turns
                    to watch him leave not sure what to think of Morris' sudden
                    possession of guts. Jenny steps up beside him.

                                        BEN
                              Did you see the way he talked to
                              me?

                                        JENNY
                              Yep. It's about time.

                    She walks away. Ben shakes his head and follows.

Notes 33 and 34 were not used. Note 35 was the idea to introduce a subplot of two convicts on the run. We had setup early on in the story that Morris had a ritual daydream of saving the bank from a robbery every Monday morning when the bank alarm was tested.

The introduction of two convicts on the run and on a rendezvous with Morris' destiny was too hard to resist. The cons are introduced in Scene 169, late in the story.

(33) a mistake. He can't believe what he's just said.

- What's done is done, Morris. I'm the Sheriff and I plan to keep the job.
- I guess we'll see about that.
- What's that mean.
- Everyone waits — Jenny nods here on
- I'll be running against you, Ben. Ben's startled.

---

(34) at school gym the votes are being tallied as Ben & Morris wait.

- Morris wins. Everyone leaves.

---

(35) — Subplot of two escaped cons on the run. —

- They need cash & decide to hold up the bank of the little rich town.

169) EXT. COUNTY JAIL-NOT FAR AWAY - DAY

Two inmates, LARRY (the leader) and ALBERT (the dummy), both in their late thirties and wearing jumpsuits, are on a work detail, unloading a truck at the back of the jail. As the Guard, BILL, 40s, turns his attention to a car that speeds by, Larry and Albert overpower him, knocking him out. Larry, the leader, takes his gun. They make their break over a six-foot wire fence. As the other Guard, KEVIN, 30s, runs over to help Bill up, he looks up to see that the cons are gone.

BILL
Damn it. They got my gun!

Note 36 was a logistical thought about the location of the sheriff's office. This sets up the courthouse as a pivotal location where not only does the antagonist, the sheriff, reside, but it is also where the history of Morris' ancestors who were previous sheriffs begins. Notes 37 through 40 support Scene 155. It's also where Morris will go to try and get on the ballot for sheriff. Note 41 was not used.

HOW TO WRITE A SCREENPLAY IN 3-DAYS

Note 42 was not used. Notes 43-45 provide ideas for Scenes 104 through 109. The idea was that Morris was seeing that others had dreams like him (he could now see their dreams and not his own, thanks to the shaman) and was taking actions to help their dreams come true. He stops and picks up the GED package for the janitor and helps Mr. Lacasta, realize his dreams of Marilyn Monroe. By the way, I named Mr. Lacasta after my seventh Grade music teacher. Remember when I told you that when building characters; take a look around at those you know? When you do this, it also helps you to visualize the character.

104) EXT. HOPEVILLE STREET-LATE AFTERNOON

Morris' truck moves down the street. In front of the HopeVille Beauty Salon, Mr. Lacasta is escorting his wife BETTY, 70s, into the salon. Morris' truck stops and backs up.

105) INT. MORRIS' TRUCK-LATE AFTERNOON

Morris watches them enter the beauty salon. Moments later, Mr. Lacasta exits and drives away. Morris looks at Max.

> MORRIS
> Are you thinking what I'm thinking?

Max barks.

106) INT. BEAUTY SALON - AFTERNOON

Morris and the BEAUTICIAN, 20s, stand behind Betty having an animated discussion about a great hairdo for Betty. The Beautician nods in agreement. As the Beautician begins, Morris spots a dress shop across the street through the salon window.

107) INT. DRESS SHOP - AFTERNOON

Morris lays a Marilyn Monroe look-a-like dress on the counter.

108) INT. SALON - AFTERNOON

Morris and the Beautician impatiently wait at the bathroom door. Finally, the door swings open and Betty steps out. She looks like a Marilyn Monroe look-a-like (except older) with her blond hair, red lips, and white dress.

109) INT. MORRIS TRUCK-LATE AFTERNOON

Morris watches as Mr. Lacasta, like a boy in love, carries his wife in his arms from the salon as he smooches on her. He puts her in the car. The car speeds away. Morris puts his hand up for a high five from Max. Max doesn't get it. With his free hand, Morris gives him some help with the high five. Morris throws it in gear and drives away.

Note 46 started me thinking about the two cons we brought in as a subplot. It leads to additional notes (47-50) that begin to formulate scenes in the town for later on when Ben and Morris confront the crooks. The ideas in the notes were used to develop Scenes 169, 192, 196, and 199. Note 50 wasn't used. As you see, the scenes in the screenplay may not play out exactly as the notes suggest, but they made me realize some of the scenes that I needed.

169) EXT. COUNTY JAIL-NOT FAR AWAY - DAY

Two inmates, LARRY (the leader) and ALBERT (the dummy), both in their late thirties and wearing jumpsuits, are on a work detail, unloading a truck at the back of the jail. As the Guard, BILL, 40s, turns his attention to a car that speeds by, Larry and Albert overpower him, knocking him out. Larry, the leader, takes his gun. They make their break over a six-foot wire fence. As the other Guard, KEVIN, 30s, runs over to help Bill up, he looks up to see that the cons are gone.

> BILL
> Damn it. They got my gun!

192) EXT. MAIN STREET - DAY

Larry steps up to the door of the truck as Ben runs towards them with his gun raised. Larry takes aim and fires. Ben is struck and tumbles to the ground. The truck starts pulling away as Ben struggles to get to his feet. As the truck passes, Ben leaps forward and hangs onto the door of the truck bed door. He's dragged as the truck keeps moving.

196) INT. FARMER'S TRUCK - DAY

Albert flinches with every whack.

> ALBERT
> Ouch! Hey stop that!

The truck careens and crashes into a telephone booth. Morris and Ben are thrown free from the truck.

TO BEN: As Ben comes to and looks up, Larry is standing over him with his gun aimed at him.

> LARRY
> You stupid cop. You just
> couldn't stay out of it.
> Now it's gonna cost you.

Larry cocks the gun and aims it. Suddenly, his gun hand is hit with a windshield wiper. The gun fires and drops, but misses Ben. Ben ducks to the ground as Morris steps forward with the wiper. Larry rubs his hand as he turns to see his aggressor. Just then, Albert staggers up to them. He pulls his knife from his back pocket.

> LARRY
> Kill these Mayberry hicks.

The Marathon Method

Albert looks at the knife then tosses it towards Larry. It lands at his feet.

>   ALBERT
>   You do it. I'm tired of you
>   telling me what to do.

Larry sneers at Albert, then dives for the knife. Morris dives at the same time. They collide and fight on the ground, struggling over the knife. Larry jabs the knife over and over towards Morris' mid section as they fight. Finally, Morris grabs him, pulls him up to his feet and punches him. Larry staggers back.

The café CROWD "Oooohhs" with the punch. Morris pulls him back and aims his fist.

>   MORRIS
>   We ain't hicks and this ain't
>   Mayberry. It's Hopeville.

WHAM, he punches him out. Larry collapses onto the ground. The crowd CHEERS and runs to gather around them. Albert quickly raises his hands and collapses to his knees in surrender. As the crowd surrounds them, Morris steps to Ben and helps him up. Jenny pushes through the crowd to embrace Morris. Jenny sees that Ben is bleeding.

>   JENNY
>   Someone call an ambulance!

Jenny feels something strange on her hand that's around Morris' waist. She lifts her hand and looks at the blood.

>   MORRIS
>   (Oozy)
>   I guess he got me.

199) INT. CITY HALL - AFTERNOON

Morris enters the main doors and sees that the pictures of his past relatives who held office have been put back up. As Morris steps towards the office, Jenny steps up, hands him the signatures, and kisses him on the cheek. Before he can take another step, Ben steps up wearing an arm sling. He offers his hand. Morris shakes it.

>   BEN
>   It might sound weird, but I
>   wanted to wish you luck.

                    MORRIS
          Thanks. And thanks for hanging
          the portraits back up.

                     BEN
          They're heroes..like you. They
          belong there.

   Ben steps back to allow Morris to continue.

Note 51 wasn't used. Note 52 brings up the two cons, and throws out some names for them. I knew that since this was a comedy, I wanted one to be the straight man and one the idiot. This info is relevant in Scene 169. Note 53 was a reminder that since Ben was the town sheriff, he would probably notice Morris acting strange when it came to the dreams and his actions. This happens in Scene 110. Note 54 introduces Jenny's dog, Butch. Her dog amplifies her frustration with her life by his constant dreams of humping a fire hydrant, which Morris gets to experience first hand since he lives above her apartment. This materializes in and influences Scenes 114, 116, 147, 152, 153, and 160. It becomes a device to bring Morris and Jenny together. Note 55 was just a reminder to think about other dreams that Morris could get sucked in to. Note 56 was another reminder that it was important that Morris talk with Jenny about dreams. This is important because Jenny doesn't believe in dreams (lost hope). This happens in Scene 116. It's important as noted in Note 57 that Ben is running for sheriff and although no one else is running, he's still putting up posters for his reelection (Scene 120).

I didn't use Note 58. Something similar does happen in Scene 191, though. Note 59 is a reminder to have Morris deface one of the posters for Ben's reelection to show that he is changing, rebelling. He does this in a grocery store and I used it as a pivotal point in the story. He overhears two ladies discussing the sheriff's reelection and how they feel somewhat disappointed that no one is running against him. So, although Note 59 was really insignificant to begin with, it provided a pivotal point in the story in Scene 148.

51) Added scene when Morris is handing out Toys & clothing (as he needs a List) to annual 1/4 of the cases are now empty.

52) Jerry & Larry — Two Cons — Unshaven — Couple of Small Time Crooks
    Happens a few scenes before the Robbery occurs

53) Add scene where Ben sees Morris at Beauty Parlor — doesn't get what he's doing.

54) — Even Jenny's dog is frustrated — Buy Hydrant toy

55) — What other schemes does Morris get involved in? — Show them

56) — Later — Morris & Jenny talk about schemes

57) Ben puts up Poster for Re-election Sees Morris doing stuff & uses a list.

58) — Ben tells Jenny that he knows what Morris is up to

59) Morris makes Sign for Ben's Poster for Re-election

110) INT. SHERIFF'S CAR- LATE AFTERNOON

The Sheriff, Ben, has been watching. He doesn't know what to make of it.

114) INT. MORRIS' APARTMENT-BEDROOM - NIGHT

Morris is asleep, when he rolls over to find himself inches from Jenny's dog, Butch's dream. Butch is humping a fire hydrant and making god-awful slobbering noise.

Realizing the importance of getting away from THIS dream, Morris immediately lunges backwards and lands on the floor with a loud THUD. Trying to maintain his distance from the dream cloud, he crawls across the floor and pulls his robe from the chair. Dragging it, he makes his way out of the room.

115) EXT. MORRIS BALCONY - NIGHT

Morris sips on a cup of tea. There's a slight KNOCKING at his door. He enters from the balcony and answers it. It's Jenny in her robe. She looks half-asleep.

                    JENNY
          Are you okay? I heard this loud
          noise and-

                    MORRIS
          Everything is fine. I'm sorry
          I woke you.

                    JENNY
          What are you drinking?

                    MORRIS
          Tea. Want some?

                    JENNY
          Sure.

She enters.

116) EXT. MORRIS BALCONY - NIGHT

As Jenny and Morris sip their tea, Morris is busy studying the dreams that hover above the sleeping citizens' homes. He takes out a black notebook and takes notes then puts it away.

                    JENNY
          Something's happening to you
          Morris.

                    MORRIS
          It is?

                    JENNY
          I mean a good something.

                    MORRIS
          Oh. Thanks.

Morris puts his cup down and turns to her.

The Marathon Method

147) PET SUPPLY STORE - DAY

Morris loads up a cart with half a dozen large bags of dog and cat food. As he's pushing the cart towards the counter, he passes the pet toy aisle. Slowly he backs up. A foot-high yellow toy hydrant comes into view.

152) INT. MORRIS' TRUCK - AFTERNOON

Morris climbs in and sees the fire hydrant. He smiles and starts the truck.

153) EXT. JENNY'S APARTMENT - AFTERNOON

Morris places the hydrant in front of the door. The note attached reads "To Butch from Moe"

160) EXT. JENNY'S APARTMENT - EVENING

Jenny steps up and looks down at the fire hydrant. She reaches down and picks it up.

She reads the note as she opens the door. Butch rushes to greet her.

      JENNY
   Hey, boy. Someone left you
   a present.

She closes the door.

120) INT. MORRIS' TRUCK - MORNING

As Morris drives out of town, he notices that Ben is putting up a re-election poster on a telephone pole.

191) INT. HOPEVILLE CAFÉ - MORNING

Morris enters and doesn't notice that everyone is watching him and smiling. Jenny smiles as Morris sits down at the counter. Jenny quickly attends to him.

      JENNY
   Welcome back..Moe. How was your
   trip?

Morris looks up and smiles.

      MORRIS
   The van broke down.

      JENNY
    (Still smiling)
   I heard.

      MORRIS
   Jenny, there's something that-

Suddenly Ben stands and steps to the center of the café. He adjusts his gun belt (tough guy).

                    BEN
            Okay, everybody listen up.

Everybody stops talking and looks. Morris turns in his chair.

                  BEN Continues
            I know what you've all been
            up to this weekend. I'm very
            disappointed in all of you.

Ben steps over to Morris.

                    BEN
            And you don't have a chance of
            beating me for Sheriff. You'll
            find that out.

Puzzled, Morris looks around at everyone then Jenny. She smiles. He turns to Ben.

                  MORRIS
            I don't know what you're talking
            about. I'm not running against
            you.

                    BEN
            Oh, no?

Ben walks out the front door and to a nearby pole. He takes down a poster and walks back in. He steps to Morris and hands it to him.

CLOSEUP: Of Morris holding a poster with "Elect Morris Moe Hill as Hopeville Sheriff." The picture has Morris with the little curly "Q" in his hair.

                    BEN
            Then explain that?

                  MORRIS
            Oh God, not that picture. Tell
            me you didn't use that one?

Jenny smiles.

                  JENNY
            Sorry. It's the only one your Mother
            had and –

Alarmed, a PATRON stands and points at the clock:

                  PATRON
            Hey it's eight O'clock! What
            happened to the bank alarm?

Everyone starts talking and agreeing that something is wrong. As they turn to look at the bank, the stolen farmer's truck slowly pulls up and parks in front of the bank. Ben steps up to the window.

                    BEN
            What the-?

Just then, Larry rushes out of the bank and rushes for the awaiting truck. Immediately Ben draws his gun and heads out the door.

148) EXT. PET SHOP - DAY

As Morris exits the pet shop, he gets stuck behind two OLD WOMEN, 80s, who are moving very slow and jabbering. They're both reading the re-election poster of Ben's.

                OLD WOMAN # 1
      Why does he put those up?

                OLD WOMAN # 2
      Yeah, it isn't like there's
      anybody running against him.

                OLD WOMAN # 1
      Right man for the job. Hah.

As they move on, Morris finds himself staring at the poster. The poster boasts "The Right man for the job." The smile disappears. Morris takes out his pen and draws buggers hanging from his nose and blacks out several of his teeth. A CUSTOMER enters and Morris quickly departs the scene.

149) INT. HILL HOUSE-KITCHEN

Walter is sitting at the kitchen table. The Barry Mantilow CD sits on the table in front of him. He holds up the skimpy leopard underwear and examines them. His wife, Ann enters the kitchen from a trip to the store. She places two bags of groceries on the counter and puts her purse down. Turning to go for more groceries, she steps from the kitchen.

                ANN (O.S.)
      Dear, could you help me
      with the rest of the-

Okay, it just hit her that her husband is holding up a pair of leopard underwear. She slowly backs into the room, her eyes now locked on the underwear he's holding. Walter looks at her odd.

                WALTER
      Now isn't that strange? Morris
      came by and gave these to me.

Walter then picks up the CD and shows it to her.

                WALTER
              (Puzzled)
      And a Barry somebody CD.

As he looks at his wife, there's this strange animal lust look coming over her face. She throws off her coat, grabs the CD and Walter by his arm. She pulls him straight up from the chair.

                ANN
      Screw the groceries!

150) INT. ANIMAL SHELTER - AFTERNOON

Morris unloads the pet food and is storing it away when Alice approaches him.

Note 60 was about having Morris talk with Jenny about his dreams. This happens in Scene 116. Although Morris has a problem with dreams, it really is a metaphor for one having hopes and dreams of a better future and life. When he talks about his dreams, Jenny misunderstands and doesn't really get what's going on with him. Note 61 was an idea that when people's dreams or wants come true, they change and become more pleasant. I wanted to show that by Morris helping the town citizens to realize their dreams, they become better citizens. This is shown in Scene 154. Note 62 wasn't used. Note 63 is a repeat of an earlier note as well as Note 64. Note 65 is related to Alice who dreams of dancing and a reminder to have a scene where Morris stops at a dance club. This happens in Scene 131.

60) - Morris explains to Jenny how he'd always had daydreams but now things changed?

61) - The attitude began to change?
 - Stare.
 - a lady says good morning to Sheriff?
 - People in Café are pleasant
 - Bar notices & comments to Jenny that somehow Morris is behind it.

62) - Morris' Father has heart attack. - They have talk.

63) - Morris goes to City Hall to register - meets old man whose life was changed by Morris Jekle - see picture.

64) - Escape scene & crooks start

65) - Stops at Strip Club when he sees sign for Part time Stripper. - Talks about alien and she has move - Buys Stripper outfit or talks with Stripper about getting one. - She has extra that is too small (she just got a boob job)

154) INT. HOPEVILLE-CAFÉ' - AFTERNOON

Jenny serves a table. At the table are seated Mr. Lacasta and his now blond wife, Betty. They're jovial and romantic. There's a couple of suitcases next to the table.

                  JENNY
        Going on a trip, Mr. Lacasta?

                MR. LACASTA
        A weekend getaway. (He winks)

                  JENNY
        Okaaaaaay.

She turns to bump into Mrs. Avery.

                MRS. AVERY
        Oh, my. Excuse me, dear.

Jenny starts to step around her.

                MRS. AVERY
        Dear, could you do me a
        favor?

Jenny turns. Mrs. Avery is holding out a stack of fliers for her Web site.

                MRS. AVERY
        Could I leave some of these here?
        They're fliers for my new antique
        web site.

Jenny takes them.

                  JENNY
        Sure. I guess.

Mrs. Avery casually puts her hand on Jenny's forearm.

                MRS. AVERY
        Ain't technology great!
        Thank you, dear.

She waddles away, cordially greeting other patrons as she leaves. Jenny looks around and suddenly realizes that everyone is smiling and laughing and being ever so nice to each other. Something is off. As she makes her way back to the counter, she feels her head to see if she has a fever. The cook, Deloris, approaches and stands next to her, spatula in her hand.

                DELORIS
        It ain't you, honey. I see it
        too. Very strange.

Deloris goes back to work, as Jenny tries to make sense of it. She opens a beer for Ben and places it in front of him. Willard, the janitor, is seated a couple of seats down and is reading a book and taking notes.

In another seat, eating lunch is Mr. Henderson and his Wife. Mr. Henderson is dressed in painting clothes and they are in a very enjoyable discussion about how they are going to remodel the kitchen.

> JENNY
> (To Ben)
> What's going on?

Ben, naturally, is oblivious to the people.

> BEN
> (While eating)
> Maybe it's a virus. Who knows?

> JENNY
> They're not sick. They're alive.

131) EXT. AL'S FANCY LADIES STRIP CLUB - LATE AFTERNOON

Morris stares at a small sign in the window "Part Time Help Needed- Free Costumes"

> MORRIS
> I wish I could take you in with me boy.

Max lays his head down and whimpers.

> MORRIS
> You're not going to miss much, just voluptuous big breasted woman in very tiny revealing-

Morris quickly opens the door.

> MORRIS
> Be right back.

Max jumps up and barks.

Note 66 is a repeat of an earlier note that reminds me to have Morris see all of the town's dreams. See Scene 86. Note 67 doesn't really show up as dialogue in any scene. Notes 68 and 69 weren't used. Note 70 is a repeat. Note 71 wasn't used. Note 72 developed into Scene 202. I wanted a scene where the town shows up to celebrate Alice's new job as a dancer. Note 73 is about Morris asking her to marry him. He does this in Scene 200. It also has a note about the Indian shaman doing the second ritual. The first ritual allowed him to see other people's dreams. The second allows him to share his dreams with others. This explains his ability at the end to pull another person into a dream (the beach scene).

86) INT. MORRIS' APARTMENT - NIGHT

Morris has fallen asleep on the couch with Max. A car door SLAM wakes him from his sleep. The local news is on the Television. He clicks it off, groggily stumbles to the balcony, and looks out over the parking lot. It's Ben bringing Jenny home from the date.

Max trots up and sits next to Morris. He cocks his head, trying to figure out what Morris is doing. Morris lifts him so he can see. Max growls.

                    MORRIS
          Yeah, I don't like him either.

Jenny quickly climbs out of the car. Ben exits and tries to cut her off. Grabbing her arm, he tries to pull her to him. Max growls again as Morris watches intensely. Jenny looks up at Morris then hastily makes her way towards the apartment. Ben is obviously frustrated with how the date went and slams the door when he climbs back in. He speeds away.

Morris turns with Max to go inside, then stops, something out of the ordinary having caught the edge of his vision. With Max still in his arms, he slowly turns back around to face the night landscape of the small town.

His mouth drops at the sight of hundreds and hundreds of dreams floating above the houses in the town. Creeping slowly towards the balcony railing, he gapes in wonder.

                    MORRIS
          Look boy. Look at all of the
          dreams. What's wrong with me?
          Why am I seeing all of this?

Max whimpers.

                    MORRIS
          Yeah, maybe I'm crazy, huh?

Morris turns with Max.

                    MORRIS
          Maybe we should get a closer
          look.

202) INT. AL'S FANCY LADIES STRIP-CLUB - NIGHT

The club is packed with Hopeville Townspeople. Alice, dressed in her skimpy cowboy outfit is gyrating and dancing to a steamy song. Everyone from the film is applauding and cheering, including Morris, Jenny, Ben, and Morris' parents.

200) INT. HOPEVILLE CAFÉ - MORNING

The café door opens. CLOSEUP: On the Sheriff badge and follow it as the guy wearing it moves to the counter and sits. We move up to reveal a smiling Morris. Jenny moves in close to his face, so close he can smell her breath.

      JENNY
  Good morning...Sheriff.

      MORRIS
  You can call me Morris or Moe.

      JENNY
  Are you sure? How would that
  look? The Sheriff flirting
  with a waitress? You might
  get a reputation.

      MORRIS
  You have a point there.

Just then, Ben enters, and yeah, guess what? He's wearing the dogcatcher uniform that Morris used to wear. Ben pats Morris on the shoulder as he passes.

      BEN
  Morning, Moe.

      MORRIS
   (Without taking eyes off Jenny)
  Morning Ben.
   (To Jenny)
  Maybe I can save my reputation.

      JENNY
  You have an idea?

      MORRIS
  Yeah, but I can't share it
  here.

      JENNY
  Ohhhhh, I see. Maybe we should
  step into my office.

Jenny tries to poke Morris in the eyes. He blocks it.

      MORRIS
  That would work.

Jenny turns and heads towards the storage room. She opens the door. Morris follows and steps into the room. She closes it. It's pitch dark. We can't see either one.

      JENNY
  Maybe we should turn on the
  light.

      MORRIS
  I have a better idea.

A dream cloud begins to form above their heads. It lights the closet and their faces. Jenny looks up at it. It's a beautiful beach with white sand and sky blue water.

      JENNY
  Now maybe I'm crazy, but I think
  there's a dream above us.

      MORRIS
  It's mine.

      JENNY
  That's your dream?

```
201) INT. BEACH DREAM - DAY
```

There they are standing on that beautiful beach. Morris takes her hand.

                    MORRIS
          It's my dream of our honeymoon.

                    JENNY
          Honeymoon?

                    MORRIS
          Only one problem.

                    JENNY
          Yes...I will.

Jenny wraps her arms around his neck. They passionately kiss. She pulls back and looks at him.

                    JENNY
          I only have one question.

                    MORRIS
          What's that?

                    JENNY
          How do we get back? Knuck
          Knuck.

                    MORRIS
          Who cares?

They passionately kiss again.

Note 74 was an idea to show Ben in Morris' old job at the end. Scene 200 actually handled this differently from the note. Note 75 refers to the sharing dream idea that happens in Scene 200. Note 77 reminds me to add a scene of Willard graduating. This is Scene 203. Notes 77 and 78 are repeat notes. Note 79 was an idea to highlight the fact that in the end, Hopeville really was a place of hope and this was exemplified by repainting the sign. However, I did use the sign theme in Scene 29 in a different way.

[Handwritten notes 74-79, partially legible:]

- 74) *Ben is in Cafe - looking for work - Morris says to her a job on animal shelter - gives his dog umm - lucky powder in it - Run out & down street screaming.*
- 75) *Then he shares dream End*
- 76) *Don't forget Willard's graduation scene - his wife & grown children in there*
- 77) *Also his dad & Morris scene where he burys dad something. Under car & Barry Manilow tape.*
- 78) *Later - He stays B & they in bedroom - he hears Barry Manilow*
- 79) *As Morris walks for Police car to Cafe - he looks up and someone is putting a fresh coat of paint on the Hopeville sign. He smiles as the guy waves.*

203) INT. HIGH SCHOOL GYM - GRADUATION SCENE

Willard dressed in his high school gown and hat receives his GED diploma from a State Education representative as the whole town applauds.

29) INT. MORRIS' TRUCK - DAY

Morris climbs into the truck and starts it. He stares at an old weathered sign that says "Welcome to Hopeville, Town of Hopes and Dreams." He shakes his head and drives away.

Note 80 was an idea for Morris to give Jenny's dog a plastic fire hydrant in hopes of ending Butch's recurring dream. This also brings Morris closer to Jenny. This is in Scene 147. Although Note 81 wasn't actually used in dialogue, it drives the Morris character and is the heart of the story, where people give up on their dreams.

Note 82 was just a restatement of previous notes. Note 83 dealt with animals that dream and what they would dream about. It lead me to the idea that if lost animals could dream of home, Morris could use this to get them back to where they belonged. He does this in Scene 63 for the first time with Max.

Note 84 and 85 weren't used. I toyed with the idea of having the shaman return once more to remove the charm from Morris and then have Morris state what he had learned. It was better to let Morris' actions tell us that. Note 86 was the original idea for the ending where Morris gets the girl and becomes sheriff. I did do something similar in Scenes 200 and 201.

ENDING

(84) — at end, the Indian removes the charm from Walter. Walter says he understands why dreams exist. Those who have not achieved dreams of achieving, those who do not dream, are either happy with their lives or are afraid to dream... afraid of being let down.

(85) — Chief says (Holds up finger) — one more — Some dreams are just for you & meant to be shared with others. He says "oh". The chief does his chant & throws some dust on Walter. So I'm back to normal. Chief nods. Then says something in Indian talk. "What'd he say?" He said "Share your dream" oh.

(86) — Later: Walter is sitting at counter (AS New Sheriff) daydreaming about Carol. It dawns on him what the chief said. "Carol" she says yes. Come here. She walks over. They disappear. The glasses & trays drop a gun. Cheyenne looks around for Carol. She's gone.

Hard Dream.

63) INT. MAX'S DREAM - DAY

Morris runs along side of Max as he races towards the house, BARKING (I'm home!). Morris stops at the end of the sidewalk by the mailbox as Max races up to the door and scratches at it.

Morris looks at the name on the mailbox. It reads like Greek. He studies it as the front door opens. Max races up to greet them.

The owners ELMER, 70s, and ELEANOR, 70s, step out. Max jumps up, trying to give them a kiss. They both scratch and pet him. Morris smiles.

                    MORRIS
        Hi. I guess he's yours, huh?

                    ELMER
            (Most words are Garble)
     Garble, Garble, Garble, Max good boy.

Morris looks at him strange. Then he understands. It's Max's dream and Dogs have a limited vocabulary. Morris nods in agreement.

Morris looks at the address of the house and it too is Greek. Dogs don't know numbers either. Scanning the surrounding community for landmarks, he spots several large white irrigation windmills. The SLAMMING of a cage takes us back to:

Note 87 incorporates the idea that since Morris could see dreams, it would be funny to see what Ben was thinking when he was around Jenny. This manifests into Scenes 83, 84, and 85. Note 88 was a thought about what animals must be thinking. It turned out that animals only thought about humping everything. This was used in Scene 60. Note 89 was an idea that came to me while thinking about how animals perceive the world. I thought that since they don't have an understanding of mechanics and language, their world would be very strange. This was used in Scene 63. Some ideas for the following scenes appear in Notes 90 and 92 (I'm not sure what happened to Note 91. I think the dog ate it.)

[Handwritten notes in margin:]

87) Morris sees Ben daydream about disrobing Jenny — he clears his throat extremely loud to knock him out of the daydream.

88) Morris seen on dog's daydream of home — goes on to telling Alice that all animals think of is sex.

89) — He disappears into dream-dog (MAX) has weird dream. See people — Home. Weird smell. — Car is more weird — (Dog's concept of car) — Weird smells

90) However when he gets there at house — he's happy — dog's happy, but neighbor says they died a little while back one after the other. Guess they couldn't live without each other. Hey that's Max. I heard they gave him away. I wish I could tell him but my wife's death and I've got plenty to do. Sorry.

92) He brings Max back home. Tries to explain to him that they gone. He takes dog.

83) INT. MORRIS APARTMENT-BEDROOM - EVENING

As Ben, unimpressed by the apartment, surveys it, Jenny enters with several pair of Morris' underwear not realizing that Ben's in the room.

                    JENNY
         Your Mother must have put these
         in with your toiletries-

Jenny is caught off guard by Ben's appearance then she recalls the date.

                    JENNY
         Oh ..our date.

Ben silently looks at the underwear she's holding, then approaches her. He holds out the flowers.

                    BEN
          I got you flowers.

She starts to take them, but realizes she's holding the
underwear. Morris quickly grabs the underwear so she can
take the flowers. She examines the flowers then smells
them.
                    JENNY
          They're beautiful.

As Morris helplessly looks on, he sees Ben eyes roaming
Jenny's body. A dream cloud begins forming over Ben.

84) INT. DREAM CLOUD

Ben, dressed in a robe, has Jenny on the couch of his
apartment. The lights are low and a Sinatra song is playing.
Ben caresses her shoulder and then kisses it romantically.
Jenny throws her head back.
                    JENNY
                  (Sexy)
          Take me, you big stud.

Ben pulls her dress strap down to reveal-

Morris CLEARS his throat extremely LOUD. The dream vanishes
as Jenny and Ben both look at him. Morris grabs his throat
and does a couple of pretend throat clears.
                    JENNY
          I think there's a couple of
          old vases under your sink. You
          mind?
                    MORRIS
          NO.

Jenny enters the kitchen and digs under the sink. Ben steps
to the doorway and eyes Jenny's body bent over. The dream
cloud reappears.

85) INT. DREAM CLOUD

Now Ben is in bed, undressed, his hairy chest exposed above
the covers. Jenny sexily steps into the frame and undoes
her sexy nightgown straps and it falls revealing-

Morris CLEARS his throat LOUDLY again. The dream cloud
vanishes. Ben looks at him strangely again.

Jenny fills a vase with water and puts the flowers into it,
then exits the kitchen.
                    JENNY
          Okay, I'm ready.

Ben leads her towards the door and opens it. Morris follows
and closes the door after them. A moment later, there's a
knock at the door. He opens it to reveal Jenny holding a
house key.
                    JENNY
          Almost forgot...your key.
                    MORRIS
          Thanks for everything.
                    JENNY
          Thank you. I enjoyed meeting
          your family. It was fun.

She turns and leaves. Morris hangs on the door watching her
leave; regretful that he doesn't have the guts to stop her,
then slowly closes the door.

```
60) INT. ANIMAL SHELTER - MORNING

Morris opens the door to the back room, where the cages are
located.  He stops cold in his tracks.  Every animal in the
place is having a dream.  The room is filled with dreams of
the pets humping other animals.  He spots one of a dog
humping a squirrel.  Morris feels his breakfast coming up.

                    MORRIS
             Uhhh.oh..ah…eeeeh

He jumps back outside the door, slams it, and throws his
body against it.
```

In Note 93, I have Max meet Jenny and the two hit it off. I also have Ben seeing Morris and Jenny walking together. This will drive an additional scene later when Max dreams of Jenny for Morris. This drives Scene 70. In Note 94, I decided to make Jenny the landlord of the apartment building she lives in. Even though she's a waitress, she's obviously got some smarts. This drives Scene 72. In Note 95, I have Jenny helping Morris move. This gives me the opportunity to have her meet his parents and witness the Three Stooges ritual that they perform. Note 96 is a repeat of a previous note (I do this a lot). I didn't use Note 97. I wanted to show Jenny trying to bolster Morris to stand up to Ben, but I decided not to use it.

HOW TO WRITE A SCREENPLAY IN 3-DAYS

(93) — He meets Jenny with MAX. She immediately likes dog. They walk Home or Bar watch?

(94) — She shows apartment — He wants to spend landlord. She says she owns it. He writes her check.

(95) — She helps him move. Ben shows up + has dirty thoughts. Mom has to keep clean. Mr. throat to break th up.

(96) — Later: He watches over the city, she comes up. Says he couldn't keep hands to himself. They talk about dreams + people etc.

(97) — She asks "Why do you take that for Ben + oth others? I guess I grew up thnk I had it coming.
— Nobody has it coming. Especially you.
— I know that now.
— Good.

70) INT. HOPEVILLE SHERIFF'S OFFICE - EVENING

Ben pulls a blind down to get a better view of Morris and Jenny in front of the restaurant. He watches them walk away together with Max, then lets the blind flip back up.

121

72) INT. VACANT APARTMENT - EVENING

The door is unlocked. Jenny leads Morris and Max into the sparsely furnished apartment. Max sprints away joyously for his own tour of the apartment.

                    JENNY
          Looks like Max likes it.

                    MORRIS
          So the landlord doesn't mind
          pets?

                    JENNY
          I guess I'd better not, or I'll
          have to get rid of my dog, Butch.

                    MORRIS
          You're the landlord?

                    JENNY
          What's the matter? A girl
          can't own property?

                    MORRIS
          Oh no. I didn't mean that.

                    JENNY
          It's okay. It was a steal. I
          live downstairs and rent this
          one out. It helps pay the bills.

She turns.

78) INT. MORRIS' BEDROOM - EVENING

As Morris packs his belongings into a box, Jenny lifts a picture from his dresser. It's one of his Father and him when he was a boy. His Father's dressed in Police Blues and Morris is dressed in his toy cop gear. She then lifts the Associate Degree from the wall and examines it.

                    JENNY
          I remember when your Dad was
          the police chief.

She walks over and hands the pictures to Morris. Morris takes them and studies them for a moment.

                    JENNY
          We use to see him on our
          bikes. He always waved to us.
          My Dad said he was the best
          Sheriff we'd ever had.

Morris packs the pictures and diploma.

>   JENNY
>   In that picture, you look like
>   you're standing with your hero. You
>   wanted to be like him didn't you?

>   MORRIS
>   I suppose.

>   JENNY
>   Can I ask what happened?

Morris moves to the wall and removes a Dirty Harry poster.

>   MORRIS
>   Yeah, but I'm not sure I have
>   an answer.

Jenny is puzzled by his remark and starts to inquire when Morris' Mother enters the room carrying a bag of his toiletries. His Dad follows but stops at the doorway and watches. She lays it on the bed.

>   MOTHER
>   I brought your toiletries.

>   MORRIS
>   Thanks, Mom.

She sniffs and waits. Morris puts the poster into a box and approaches his Mother. Gently putting his hands on her shoulders, he kisses her on the cheek.

>   MORRIS
>   It's just across town, Mom.

>   MOTHER
>   Could we...you know?

Morris steps back and rubs his hands together like he's going to do a magic feat.

>   MORRIS
>   Okay.

Jenny is curiously watching, not quite sure where all of this is leading.

>   MOTHER
>   Your Father too?

Morris sighs.

                    MORRIS
            I guess.

His Father beams a smile and quickly joins them. He messes
up his hair so it's stretched in every direction as Morris'
Mother comes to life and quickly grabs the pillow stuffing
it under her blouse, creating a fake stomach.

Jenny oddly studies them.

Morris checks himself in the dresser mirror. Using a comb
from the dresser, he combs his hair down in the front so he
resembles Moe Howard as his Mother and Father move together
side-by-side. As Morris moves to the bedroom door for his
entrance, he sees that Jenny has a confused look on her
face.

                    MORRIS
                (To Jenny)
            You might want to cover your
            eyes. This could be scary.

                    JENNY
            I'm fine. Pretend I'm not here.

Here we go with their 3-Stooges routine...Morris steps up
and pushes his Mother and Father aside.

                    MORRIS
            Spread out.

His Mother, doing her imitation of Curley, wipes her hands
across her face and shoves her stomach out towards Morris.

                    MOTHER
            Mmmmmmmm.

His Father turns to him to do his Larry impression.

                    FATHER
            Hey, what gives?

Morris bops him in the forehead with the palm of his hand
then slaps him on the back of the head.

                    MORRIS
            How about that?

His Father rubs his head.

                    FATHER
            Okay...okay.

The Marathon Method

His Mother does the Curley routine with the wavering hand that moves past Morris' face. Morris watches the hand go up and down.

>   MOTHER
>   Knuck knuck knuck.

Morris holds out his two fingers to his Mother.

>   MORRIS
>   See dat?

>   MOTHER
>   (In Curley voice)
>   Yeah. So what?

Morris tries to jab her in the eyes. She blocks it with her hand.

>   MOTHER
>   Knuck knuck knuck.

Jenny bursts out laughing at their antics. The three stop and look at her. Morris' Mother wraps her arms around him and hugs him tight. Jenny stops when she sees that it has turned emotional. His Father looks down and tries to smooth down his hair.

Note 98 is just a reminder to think about the midpoint and where it should be. I estimated it to be at page 52. Since the screenplay turned out to be 106 pages, that's a good guess. The midpoint is when Morris realizes that everybody in town has their own dream just as he does and get's pulled into one of them. Note 99 was a repeat note. I didn't use Notes 101, 102, and 103. I wanted Ben to be more proactive with what Morris was doing with dreams and the town and to show how Ben didn't want people dreaming or wanting a better life. I decided to make Ben a little less bright. I wanted him to think that Morris was losing his mind, but it turns out that Ben is the one who is oblivious.

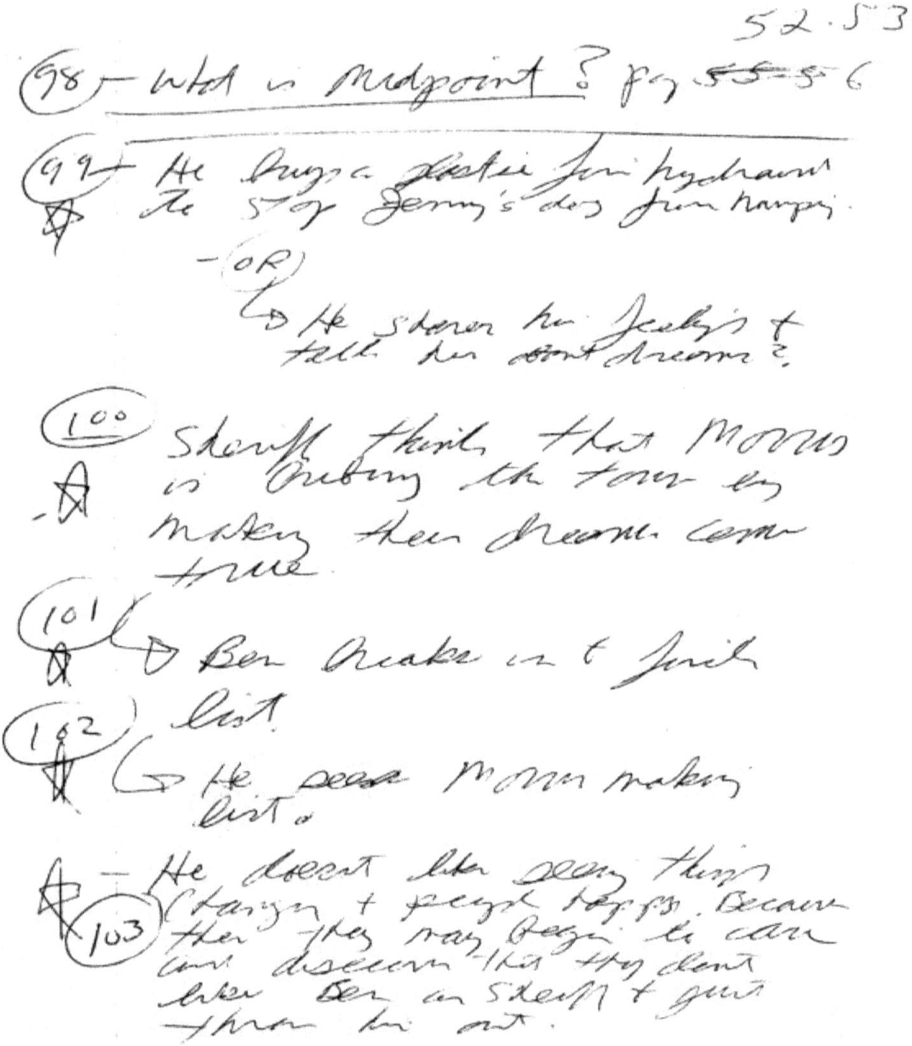

[Handwritten notes:]

- 98 — What is Midpoint? pg 55-56   52·53
- 99 — He buys a [?] for hydrant to stop Jenny's dog from [Harry?].
  — (OR)
  → He shares w/ Jerky's & tells her don't dream?
- 100 Sheriff thinks that Morris is [?] the town by making their dreams come true.
- 101 → Ben sneaks in to find list.
- 102 → He sees Morris making list.
- 103 — He doesn't like seeing things changing & people [?]. Because then they may begin to care and discover that they don't like Ben or Sheriff & quit — throw him out.

Note 104 is more an outline than a note. At this point, I was trying to reevaluate where I was in the story development and was reviewing the scenes to make sure I knew which had been done. The checkmarks indicate that I had completed the scenes. They're not sequential but just a quick bullet list of scenes. You'll notice page numbers in the left hand column as well. This is a page count for the scene. I estimate how many pages it will take me to complete the scene. This depends on the complexity of the scene and the amount of dialogue that I might need. You'll get a better feel for estimating page counts with experience.

(104) pg 85 †   35/15   ORDER

pg 1 ✓ Hydrant for Butch (104.1)
2 † ✓ Indian Remover charm – dream mins to starid (104.2)
1 † ✓ Morris shares dream with Jenny (104.3)
2-3 — ✓ City Hall Scene – Removing portraits (104.4)
— bets applied to job for sheriff
2 † ✓ Ben speech about "end of an era" (104.5) for Hill
→ ✓ Ben talks about Morris' father & how it changed his life (at City Hall) (104.6)
1-2 — Janitor (Willard graduates) (104.7) (104.8) ①
1-2 ✓ Gives her class G story to Marilyn
1 † ✓ Stops at House – Hears Marilyn come from Bedroom – "Stroke it Baby" – Mother says (104.9)
1 † ✓ Morris & old man Re-hang portraits in City Hall (104.10)
3-4 ✓ Ben gets shot & Morris stops Real Robbery (104.11)
1 — Morris accepts nomination as sheriff – at gym (104.12)
1 — Cafe Scene – Puts powder on Ben's ashes – (104.13)
1 — Ben announces that Morris has been trying to buy people votes (104.14)
1 ✓ Bank Robber escapes from prison & steals car (104.15)
1 ✓ Morris draws on Poster – (104.15) (104.16) old
1 — Carolyn stow owner – says hi – website etc
1 † Someone paints Sign for Hopeville (104.17)
2-3 — Jenny overdue Patient – says Sorry (104.18) is gery on – Ben says Virus – She says life!
3 ✓ Talks with Dad about Daydreaming (104.19) ②

Notes 105 through 109 are about developing the subplot with the conmen who escaped. I wanted one to refer to Hopeville as "Mayberry" and to use other hick-town type references. I also wanted them robbing a farmer, to show they were out in a rural area, and arguing about weapons. I wanted our cons to be tough, but I also knew that this was a comedy. Scenes 196 and 178 used some of these notes or ideas for scene development.

196) INT. FARMER'S TRUCK - DAY

Albert flinches with every whack.

                    ALBERT
          Ouch! Hey stop that!

The truck careens and crashes into a telephone booth. Morris and Ben are thrown free from the truck.

TO BEN: As Ben comes to and looks up, Larry is standing over him with his gun aimed at him.

                    LARRY
          You stupid cop. You just
          couldn't stay out of it.
          Now it's gonna cost you.

Larry cocks the gun and aims it. Suddenly, his gun hand is hit with a windshield wiper. The gun fires and drops, but misses Ben. Ben ducks to the ground as Morris steps forward with the wiper. Larry rubs his hand as he turns to see his aggressor. Just then, Albert staggers up to them. He pulls his knife from his back pocket.

                    LARRY
          Kill these Mayberry hicks.

Albert looks at the knife then tosses it towards Larry. It lands at his feet.

                    ALBERT
          You do it. I'm tired of you
          telling me what to do.

Larry sneers at Albert, then dives for the knife. Morris dives at the same time. They collide and fight on the ground, struggling over the knife. Larry jabs the knife over and over towards Morris' mid section as they fight. Finally, Morris grabs him, pulls him up to his feet and punches him. Larry staggers back.

The café CROWD "Oooohhs" with the punch. Morris pulls him back and aims his fist.

                    MORRIS
          We ain't hicks and this ain't
          Mayberry. It's Hopeville.

WHAM, he punches him out. Larry collapses onto the ground. The crowd CHEERS and runs to gather around them. Albert quickly raises his hands and collapses to his knees in surrender. As the crowd surrounds them, Morris steps to Ben and helps him up. Jenny pushes through the crowd to embrace Morris. Jenny sees that Ben is bleeding.

                    JENNY
          Someone call an ambulance!

Jenny feels something strange on her hand that's around Morris' waist. She lifts her hand and looks at the blood.

                    MORRIS
                 (Oozy)
          I guess he got me.

Morris collapses.

178) INT. FARMHOUSE KITCHEN - LATE SUNDAY NIGHT

Larry finishes tying and gagging the FARMER into his kitchen chair while Albert holds the gun. Larry goes through the Farmer's wallet and takes out a few bills, then tosses it over his shoulder. Then he turns and grabs the car keys from a hook on the wall and exits.

HOW TO WRITE A SCREENPLAY IN 3-DAYS

Note 110 suggests a series of scenes. Note 111 has a similar idea. Note 111 goes into more detail than Scene 110 about the type of scenes needed. This may have been mentioned before, but serves as a reminder and an interesting idea comes up for comedic relief. Morris learns to enter the dreams of the lost animals in order to return them to their rightful owners. In one scene, Alice has to poke a lost pet awake to get Morris free from its dream.

Although I have the janitor studying his GED books, he takes an interest in Morris' odd behavior with the animals. This is laid out in Scenes 94-101. Note 113 talks about a black book. Although I originally wanted the black book to be stolen by Ben because he is curious as to what Morris is up to, I never pursued it. Nevertheless, I kept the book, and it shows up in Scene 116.

94) INT. KENNEL - MORNING

The door slowly creeps open. They poke their heads around the edge of the door again.

                    ALICE
                  (Whispers)
        Call me when you want out. I'll
        poke him with a stick to wake
        him up.

Morris rolls his eyes to her and gives her a strange look for the absurdity of her comment.

95) Morris and Alice crawl on all fours across the darkened kennel. Morris puts his hand over his eyes as he passes one cage.

                    ALICE
                  (Whispers)
        Is it bad?

                    MORRIS
        You don't want to know.

Morris stops.

                    MORRIS
                  (Whispers)
        Good. Here's one.

Morris puts the cell phone into his pocket and quietly moves closer to the cage. Whoosh. He's gone. Alice's eyes slowly rotate around looking for Morris. She feels the floor where he was kneeling.

                    ALICE
                  (Whispers)
        Wow.

Alice creeps backwards towards the exit.

96) INT. HOPEVILLE-ANIMAL SHELTER-OFFICE - MORNING

As Alice backs out of the door on all fours, she bumps into Willard, the janitor, who's waiting with his mop and mop bucket. She looks at his work shoes and bucket then quickly springs to her feet. He starts to move past her with his bucket into the kennel.

                    ALICE
        Uh, where are you going, Willard?

                    WILLARD
        To mop the kennel. Why?

                    ALICE
        Uh..you can't.

                    WILLARD
        Why?

                    ALICE
        I don't know.

                    WILLARD
        Okay.

He turns and pushes the mop bucket away as she scurries to her desk and checks her phone for dial tone. She hangs it up and sits, tapping her fingers on the desk.

Willard collects the trash as he keeps an eye on her because of her strange behavior. She gives him an "I'm normal" smile as she acts as if she's doing paperwork.

There's a knock on the front door glass. Willard unlocks the door and talks to someone briefly. He closes it and approaches Alice.

                    WILLARD
        There's a lady at the door.
        Said she lost a cat. I told her
        we weren't open. She wants to talk
        with you.

Alice stands, looks at the phone then steps away. Every few steps, she turns and looks back at the phone. Willard looks at the phone, then at Alice. He takes off his hat and scratches his head.

97) EXT. HOPEVILLE-ANIMAL SHELTER - MORNING

Alice steps out and closes the door behind her.

                    ALICE
        Can I help you?

A robust woman, MRS. WHITE, 50s, starts in.

                    MRS. WHITE
        I hope so, dear. Missy, my
        precious and darling cat was
        outside last night..

98) INT. HOPEVILLE-ANIMAL SHELTER-OFFICE - MORNING

The phone rings. Willard picks it up, holds it up, and listens.

                    MORRIS (V.O.)
        You got get me out of here. Hurry.
        I've got a pit bull on my ass.

                    WILLARD
        Hello. Is this Morris?

                    MORRIS (V.O.)
        Who's this?

                    WILLARD
            Willard, sir.

                    MORRIS (V.O.)
            Oh. Is Alice there-Ouch!

Willard pulls the phone away and looks at it weird then puts it back.

                    WILLARD
            You at home, sir?

                    MORRIS (V.O.)
            No. I'm stuck in this crappin'
            dream! Get Alice please. I need
            to get out. Ouch!..you little shit!

                    WILLARD
            Just a minute.

Willard lays the phone down and walks to the front door.

99) EXT. HOPEVILLE-ANIMAL SHELTER - MORNING

Willard sticks his head out the front door. Alice is busy writing down information from the woman.

                    MRS. WHITE
            And if you can't reach me on
            that cell phone number-

                    ALICE
            No that's fine ma'am.

                    WILLARD
            Excuse me.

They both look at Willard.

                    WILLARD
            It's Mr. Hill. He's having a
            nightmare or something weird.

Alice moves towards the door.

                    ALICE
            Okay Mrs. White, we'll see
            what we can do.

Alice and Willard quickly disappear. Mrs. White stares at the door for a minute then walks away as we go to:

100) INT. HOPEVILLE-ANIMAL SHELTER-OFFICE - MORNING

Alice rushes to the phone and almost knocks it off the desk answering it. Willard follows, curious as to what the Hell is going on. Alice turns away from him.

                    MORRIS (V.O.)
            Get me the hell out of here!

                    ALICE
          Have you got it?

                    MORRIS (V.O.)
          Yeah. yeah. I got it. Ouch!

Alice throws the phone down and runs around the room looking
for something she can poke the dog with to wake it. She
grabs several things but they won't do. She tosses them over
her shoulder as Willard watches her puzzled. Finally, she
spots the mop bucket and grabs the mop from it. Dropping to
all fours, she crawls through the kennel door. Willard
follows.

INT. KENNEL - MORNING

Alice crawls along the floor pulling the mop behind her. The
door slowly creeps open. Willard peeks around the corner to
see what she's doing. There she is, in front of the cage,
poking a sleeping dog with the mop handle. He scratches his
head. With a whoosh, Morris falls out of nowhere and rolls
across the floor. Willard's eyes widen then he disappears.

101) INT. HOPEVILLE-ANIMAL SHELTER-OFFICE - MORNING

Alice and Morris work on descriptions of the homes of the
dogs. Morris is busy writing out the descriptions on a long
list.

                    ALICE
          You think that's enough to
          go on?

                    MORRIS
          It'd be nice if animals could
          read and write in English. Then
          I could just write down the addresses.
          Everything in their dreams is in
          some sort of weird language.

Alice lifts the list and examines it.

                    ALICE
          Some of these don't make sense.
          They're just a list of toys and
          stuff.

                    MORRIS
          Not all of them had dreams of
          home. Happiness for some of
          them is just a chewy or stuffed
          animal away.

Then they suddenly realize that Willard has stopped mopping
and is staring at them. They both look up, realizing how
weird it must sound. Willard guards his mop as if they
might want it back. He quickly looks away and whistles.

```
116) EXT. MORRIS BALCONY - NIGHT

As Jenny and Morris sip their tea, Morris is busy studying
the dreams that hover above the sleeping citizens' homes. He
takes out a black notebook and takes notes then puts it
away.
                    JENNY
          Something's happening to you
          Morris.

                    MORRIS
          It is?

                    JENNY
          I mean a good something.

                    MORRIS
          Oh. Thanks.

Morris puts his cup down and turns to her.
```

Note 114 is about Morris helping his balding neighbor with his hair problem. This is the same man who had previously told him, "Bite me, dog boy." This is in Scene 136. Note 115 is a repeat note about getting the leopard underwear, a Barry Manilow CD, as well as discussing the dreams with his father. This is in Scene 145. Note 116 is about seeing the results of Morris' work to help people with their dreams which was mentioned in a previous note.

Note 117 wasn't used. Note 118 shows how Morris is changing people's lives in the town. The old lady whose antique shop wasn't doing well and was continually in a bad mood, is shown doing much better. Instead of having Morris bump into her and finding this out, I had her reveal some of this to Jenny in the restaurant. This added to the results. I had the other townsfolk at the same time in the restaurant, which resulted in a more powerful outcome. This ends up in Scene 154. Note 119 refers to setting up the robbery and is a repeat note. (Again. Sorry.) Note 120 is another pivotal point. It simply states that things have changed in the town. Since the café is a focal or meeting place for the town, it's a great place to show that the work Morris is doing is paying off. It is an important note, although previously mentioned. I didn't use notes 121 through 124. It deals with the black book again and this time, we have Jenny finding out what Morris has been up to by finding the book. I found it more powerful to have Jenny influenced by the events going on instead of simply reading the black book.

HOW TO WRITE A SCREENPLAY IN 3-DAYS

(117) Ben has Bernadean watch Moni & follow him. — He takes stop at g mailing errand. Her puzzled why.

(118) Meets lady on street who now has website —

(119) Decides to stop in Cafe

— After scene — Cut to Crooks escaping. — Set up for Robbery.

? (120) Scene in Cafe when they have Changed.

(121) At Animal Shelter Alice has a depressing day — Needs to have Mom go in — Mom leaves Plan Book out

(122) Jerry is feeling sorry aunt fell & goes to Animal Shelter — Just as Mom is going in — Talks with Alice about Mom & how she feels bad — She sees Plan book Mom is reading it when Alice approach — she hides it in her jacket or pocket (Jean)

(123) Alice drops her to see him after phony call

(124) Later that Night — Jerry gets the Jury book — she reads it & is startled that Mom is actually doing it. Ben comes by

```
136) INT. JOHN'S HAIR CLINIC - DAY

A man, JOHN, 30s, with a bad toupee shows Morris hair
options with several brochures.
```

Note 125 didn't happen in the story. Ben never got the book. Note 126 is a repeat of a previous note. Note 127 pursues the idea that the janitor in the courthouse (Rufus) is told why Morris can't run for sheriff, but because the Hill family had helped turn his life around, he gets involved and goes to visit Morris' father. This materializes in Scene 155 and 158. Note 129 talks about fliers and the campaign that goes on behind Morris' back to elect him sheriff while he's gone. This materializes in a different way in Scene 197. Note 130 wasn't used.

(124 cont) and create dennis on P done rings its Morris - He tries to apologize. Ben sees the book + lifts it - then he starts and talking Morris asks if that's Ben - He Hangs up - or says he is decides to Run for Sheriff.

(125) Now Ben has book -

(126) - Morris goes to courthouse or City Hall to register for election. Sees portraits - learns stories for Bum.

(127) Clerk says to Bum - its only two days till election - there's no way that he can get the votes in time.

(128) - Bum goes to Morris' father - tells him.

(129) - Somehow Her mother + father get together with Jenny to quickly get them out + do a door to door campaign all night.

- Where's Morris?

Election is on Monday

(130) The recount until ... after - its Saturday morning

158) EXT. HILL'S HOUSE - LATE AFTERNOON

Rupus steps to the door and rings the doorbell. He waits and waits. Then he moves his head closer to the door. He can hear faint "Barry Mantilow" music.

                    ANN (O.S.)
                 (Faint)
         Shake that booty baby!

He draws his head back.

                    RUPUS
         Booty?

He turns and starts to leave, then realizing the importance of his mission, he turns back around and pushes the doorbell with determination. Then the door swings open. Walter is wearing a robe. Some of his leopard underwear is showing. Rupus stares at it. Walter quickly covers it then recognizes him.

                    WALTER
         Smitty!? What are you doing
         here?

                    RUPUS
         Could I could in? I need
         to talk to you about your son.

                    WALTER
         Come in.

The door closes.

197) INT. HOSPITAL ROOM - AFTERNOON

POV: Of Morris as he comes to. His Father, Mother, Jenny, and Alice come into focus. His Father leans towards him.

                    FATHER
         Morris? Morris, are you okay?

                    MORRIS
         (Sluggish)
         I'm fine. I just had this strange
         dream where I jumped on this truck
         and someone stabbed me and-

                    FATHER
         It wasn't a dream, Morris. They
         were only flesh wounds but you
         needed stitches.

                    MORRIS
         Oh, and the Sheriff part?

```
                        FATHER
            That was Jenny's idea.

Jenny leans in.

                        JENNY
            Everybody got together and-

Jenny digs into her bag and pulls out a stack of papers.

                     JENNY Continues
            We get over three hundred signatures.
            More than enough to put you on
            the ballot for Sheriff.  You're
            gonna be the next Sheriff of
            Hopeville, Morris.

She puts them back into her bag.

                        JENNY
                     (To Walter)
            I have to get these in today
            to get him on the ballot.

Morris tries to sit up. His Mother stops him.

                        MOTHER
            You have to stay -

                        MORRIS
            No, Mother. I want to do it.
```

Note 131 presents a problem for Morris. He'll need to have two hundred signatures to get on the ballot for Monday. This is used in Scene 155. Note 131 was a logistics issue. I needed Morris unavailable on the road while Jenny worked her magic and the community came together. I also wanted Morris to reflect on things and to realize not only what he wanted, but also to face the fact that he was in love. I wanted the same for Jenny, as well. This note served this purpose and helped to create Scene 150. Note 133 orchestrated the cons into position for a meeting with Morris and Ben (Scene 187). More setup with the cons in Note 134 that results in Scene 181. Note 135 drives the Ben character in Scene 191. Note 136 was only a reminder of the robbery (Scene 191) that needed to happen. Note 137 was a reminder of the election on Tuesday (no scene). And Note 138 reminds me when Morris gets back in town, although it doesn't play out as in the note. He goes to the café in Scene 191.

(131) The county clerk says that he'll need 200 signatures to get on the ballot — (The Burns' history) — I see, Never mind.

(132) Morris has to go out of town to a city to deliver several cats — (Someone a buck wants them) — he'll have to drive 8 hours to get there. Spend the night & drive back Sunday.

— Election Tuesday

(133) Monday morning the crowd drunk at Red Barn before it opens.

(134) The Escape on Saturday on work detail — Sunday they steal truck for church party lot.

(135) Monday morning — le Café — Burns confident that they haven't reach enough people to carry the election.

(136) Robbery

(137) Election (Tuesday)

(138) Sunday afternoon he gets back — alone or is out there — can't find anyone at Café or at his house

150) INT. ANIMAL SHELTER - AFTERNOON

Morris unloads the pet food and is storing it away when Alice approaches him.

                    ALICE
          I've got good news and I've got
          bad news.

Morris stacks the food.

                    MORRIS
          Good news first.

                    ALICE
          I got homes for three of the
          dogs on a farm from the website.

Still working.

                    MORRIS
          That's great..and the bad news?

                    ALICE
          It's a ten-hour drive from here.

Morris stands and stretches.

                    MORRIS
          That's fine.

Alice is perplexed.

                    ALICE
          You complain when it's a half
          hour drive. What gives?

Morris removes his gloves.

                    MORRIS
          I'm gonna run for Sheriff.

Alice is in shock.

                    ALICE
          What?

                    MORRIS
          I'm gonna run for-

                    ALICE
          I heard that part. Why?

                    MORRIS
          If you can go after your dream,
          why can't I?

She slides over and puts her arm around his shoulder.

                    ALICE
          Do you know how long we've
          been waiting for you to say
          that?

                    MORRIS
          About as long as I've been
          wanting to say it.

                    ALICE
          And since we're sharing good
          news, I took off an hour this
          morning and went over for an
          audition.

She beams a smile.

                    MORRIS
          Well?

                    ALICE
          I blew them away!

Morris embraces her and twirls with her.

                    MORRIS
          I knew you could do it.

She kisses him on the cheek.

                    ALICE
          Thanks.

                    MORRIS
          I've got to go. I have to
          stop by City Hall before
          I leave town. There is money
          in the budget for a motel room?

Alice squeezes her two fingers together.

                    ALICE
          A little bit.

                    MORRIS
          Great, roach motel, here I come.

187) INT. FARMER'S STOLEN TRUCK - MORNING

Larry checks his gun and looks out the windshield at the small bank in town.

181) EXT. FARMHOUSE-LATE SUNDAY NIGHT

Larry climbs into the Farmer's old truck and starts it. Albert runs out of the house and jumps into the truck just as it takes off.

>   ALBERT (O.S.)
>   Where we going now, Larry?

>   LARRY (O.S.)
>   To find some cash. One of these
>   hick towns has got to have a
>   bank.

Notes 139 and 140 weren't used. Note 140 was replaced with the hospital scene (Scene 197). Note 141 was about getting his name on the ballot. This was Scene 197 again. Note 142 was a reminder that I wanted the town to rally behind Morris at the end. This happens in Scene 198.

198) EXT. CITY HALL BUILDING - AFTERNOON

Morris is helped up the steps to the front steps, his midsection covered with bandages, as the town is crowded on both sides of the steps watching. When he gets to the top at the entrance, he turns and looks back at the crowd. They cheer.

Note 143 wasn't used but would have been funny. Here it is in screenplay format (If I had written it):

Ben steps back to allow Morris to continue. The butchy cook, Deloris, steps through the crowd.

                    DELORIS
        If it makes you feel any better,
        I m voting for you on Tuesday. I
        love a man in uniform. Maybe we
        can get together so you can show
        me your appreciation.

Jenny raises an eyebrow and smiles as Morris fumbles for an answer.

                    MORRIS
        Let me get back with you on
        that, Deloris.

The crowd bursts out laughing.

Note 144 thru 149 are repeats of earlier notes

(144) After Elect — They go to the bradwin of Wellford.

(145) The Party at Club & San Alici dance

(146) Cafe Scene — he asks her to Marry her — IN DREAM

(147) Itchy Powder Scene?

(148) Last Dream — Share

On way back from Trip
(149) He seen' the unleain —
They tell him that he must share his dreams!

Note 150 shows up in Scene 163 and shows Jenny realizing that she's in love with Morris. Notes 151 through 156 weren't used.

163) INT. JENNY'S APARTMENT - NIGHT

Jenny lays in bed, motionless, staring at the ceiling. A love for Morris is growing to the point of bursting out. She rolls over and looks down at Butch. He's cuddling the toy hydrant like a lover. Throwing back the covers, she springs to her feet, grabs her robe and rushes out.

164) INT. ALICE'S APARTMENT - LATE NIGHT

Alice covers her head to hide from whoever is POUNDING on her door. From underneath the covers, she bellows.

>ALICE
>Go away. I don't do pets at home.

>JENNY (O.S.)
>It's about Morris.

That registers with her. Slowly, she comes around and slumps up to a stand, her eyes still closed.

>ALICE
>Coming..

165) EXT. ALICE APARTMENT - LATE NIGHT

The door swings open to reveal the half-asleep Alice.

>ALICE
>This better be good.

>JENNY
>I think I love him.

>ALICE
>That'll do. Come in.

Note 157 wasn't used. Note 158 was a repeat of an earlier note, but it let me know that I wanted the motel where he was staying to be desolate. This appears in Scene 162. Note 159 wasn't used. We don't show how the signatures were obtained. Note 160 is a repeat of an earlier note. I didn't use Note 161 or 162.

162) EXT. CHEAP MOTEL - NIGHT

As the Sun sets, Morris climbs wearily from the truck. Max follows as he walks towards the desolate motel in the disappearing sunlight.

Note 163 reminds me to remove the scenes where the town comes together for Morris. I've added a scene on the following page that got removed (among others) because of this suggestion. I didn't use Notes 164 and 165 and had thought about an alternative ending where Morris wakes up and he's only six years old. The whole movie had only been a dream (Note 166).

Here's the scene)If I had used it of Jenny getting together with the tpwnsfolk to help Morris:

INT. HOPEVILLE CAFÉ - SATURDAY MORNING

CLOSEUP: on Ben as he sips his morning coffee. There is NO noise whatsoever other than the slurping noise coming from Ben. Ben lowers the cup, his eyes rotate around the room. Something isn't right and he knows it. It's too damn quiet in the café.

We PAN the patrons of the café. It's unusually crowded for a Saturday. They sit quietly, as if waiting. All eyes are on Ben. We pan past Alice and some of her longhaired FRIENDS. Willard is there, as well as Morris' parents, Walter and Ann (wearing hats and sunglasses) hiding in the corner.

Ben stands and scans the faces of the patrons of the café. He takes out his wallet and walks to the register. Jenny takes his money and hands back his change. He takes it and leans toward her;

> BEN
> I know when I'm not wanted.
> I'll be watching you.

> JENNY
> Good. You do that.

Ben slides on his sunglasses and steps toward the door. He scans them one last time and then slowly pushes open the door. He stops then steps out, letting the door slowly close.

Everyone watches him climb into his car and drive away. Then everyone CHEERS. Jenny races to the door and flips the OPEN sign around. Hurrying to the counter, she reaches under and pulls out a large backpack. Everyone begins crowding around the counter. Jenny pulls out stacks of empty signature pages. Alice joins her side as they begin handing them out. Hands fly out to grab some;

> JENNY
> Now remember, we have until
> Monday to get at least two
> hundred signatures to put
> Morris on the ballot. Make
> sure you get ALL of the
> information or it won't
> count.

Hands fly out to get some as Alice and Jenny get buried in people.

153

These notes are about the town citizens' dreams. Some are repeat notes. Note 167 drives Scene 122, Note 168 wasn't used. Note 169 is a repeat note. Note 171 (the fireman dream) drives Scene 126. Both Notes 172 and 173 are repeats about the antique dealer and his bald neighbor, who's dog poops on the Hill's lawn.

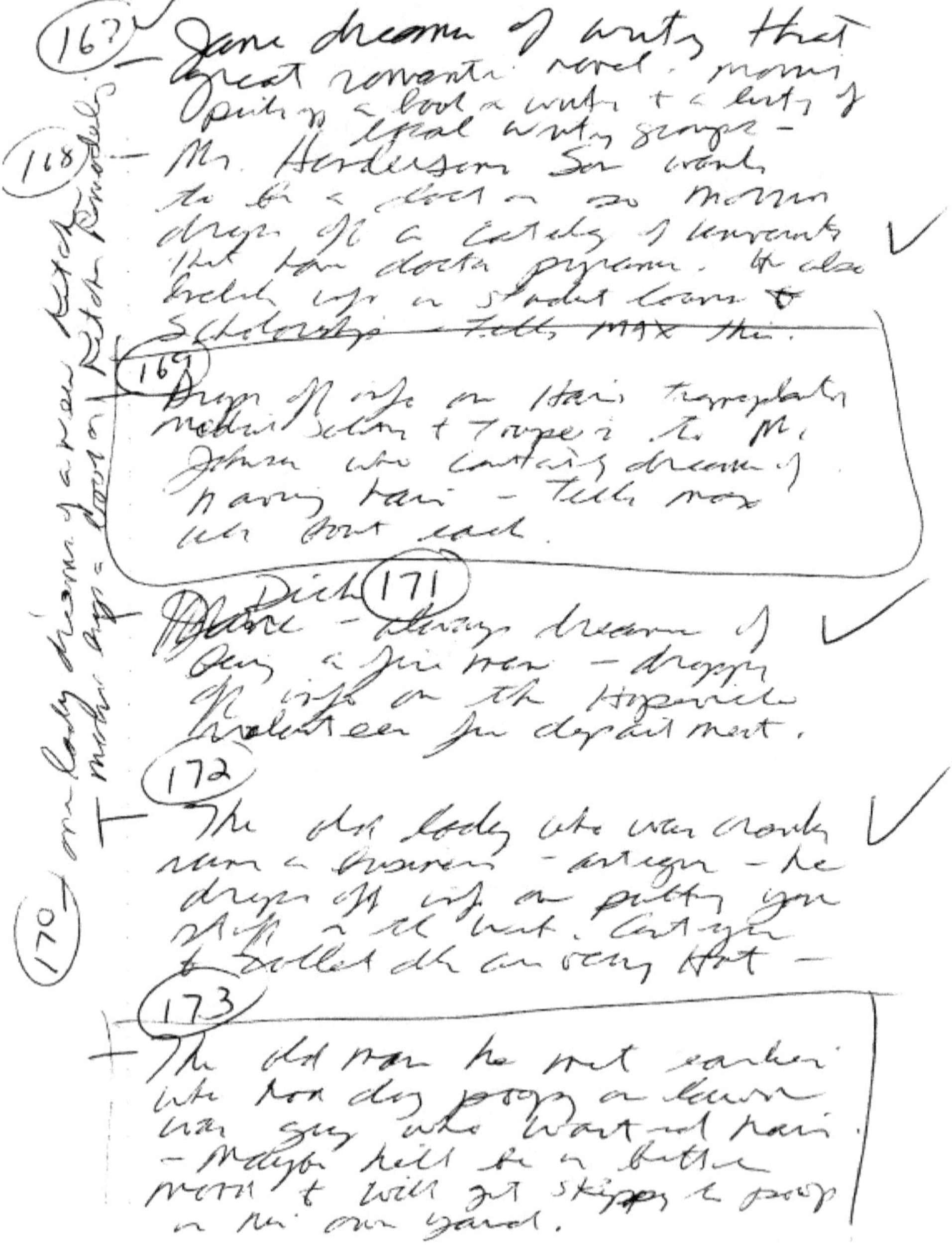

(167) — Jane dreams of writing that great romantic novel. Morrison putting up a book on writing + a listing of local writing groups —

(168) — Mr. Henderson's son wants to be a doctor so Morrison drops off a catalog of universities that have doctor programs. He also includes info on student loans & ~~scholarships — Tells Max this.~~

(169) Drops off info on Hair transplants medical salon + toupee to Mr. Johnson who constantly dreams of having hair — Tells Max later about each.

(171) Dick ~~Dave~~ — always dreams of being a fireman — dropping off info on the Hopeville volunteer fire department.

(172) The old lady who was clearly running a business — antique — he drops off info on putting your stuff on the net. Can't you [illegible] collect ... very Hot —

(173) The old man he met earlier whose dog poops on lawn was guy who wanted hair. — Maybe he'll be in better mood + will get Skipper to poop on his own yard.

(170) one lady dreams of a new kitchen — Morrison drops off brochure on Kitchen Remodels

122) INT. MORRIS' TRUCK - AFTERNOON

As Morris drives towards town with the strays, he passes a bookstore. He turns around the truck and parks in the bookstore parking lot. Pulling out his black book of dreams he scans it with his finger, stopping on one.

>   MORRIS
>   (To Max)
>   Mr. Henderson's wife is dreaming
>   of a new kitchen. Think they might
>   have some remodeling books?

Max barks.

>   MORRIS
>   While I'm in there I'll see if
>   they have anything for Ms Jansen
>   who's dreaming of writing the
>   great romantic novel.

Max barks again.

126) INT. MORRIS' TRUCK - LATE AFTERNOON

Morris crosses out more names. He taps the pen on Dick Randal's name. He ponders Dick's dream.

>   MORRIS
>   (To Max)
>   Dick's always dreams of being
>   a fireman. Instead, he works in
>   a shoe store. Big difference.

Max barks. Morris looks up at the fire station through the window.

>   MORRIS
>   You think being a volunteer
>   fireman would make him happy?

Max barks twice.

>   MORRIS
>   Me too.

Morris climbs out.

Most of the following notes (174, 175, 176, 178, 179, and 180) weren't used. Note 177 simply says that a man shows up with his wife who looks like Marilyn Monroe. This did happen for Mr. Lacasta in Scene 154. I didn't have people whistling though.

Note 181 drives Scene 91. Morris uses his ability to interact with dreams to find Max's home but finds that they have been deceased for some time. Alice (the girl referenced in Note 181) thinks that Morris could use his newfound talent to help find the homes of the other pets. They realize that the pet needs to wake up before Morris can get back out. The note also provided some dialogue used in Scene 93 when Morris gets stuck in a dream with Marilyn Monroe and an "old geezer."

[Handwritten notes:]

pg 64

(181) Goes back to Dog Pound. Girl there asks what happened. It (he) came yesterday, says he knew Max's owner. As they look over past dreams. He's sort of calm me now, good. She says, Too bad you couldn't work some of that magic on the others — it's getting awfully crowded in there.

✓ — Okay — I'll try.

— But I'll need your help. I spent the night dreaming about Marilyn Monroe and being chased by a horny old geezer with no teeth.

✓ — Wow. I don't even want to hear that. I'm a visual person — ew.

(182) Just give me 5 minutes then make some noise to get me out.

(183) She falls asleep. He calls on cell phone. Remember me. I'm stuck in this crappin dream. GET ME OUT.

In Note 183, while Morris is stuck in a pet's dream, I needed Alice to be unavailable so the janitor, Willard, could get involved. I didn't have her fall asleep (lame reason) but rather had her distracted by a customer instead. This is in Scene 98.

```
93) INT. HOPEVILLE-ANIMAL SHELTER-OFFICE - MORNING

Morris motions her away from the door.

                    MORRIS
          We've got a problem.

                    ALICE
          What is it?

                    MORRIS
          I'm gonna need your help. I
          spent the other night dressed as
          Marilyn Monroe being chased by
          an old geezer with no teeth.

                    ALICE
          Wow. I didn't even want to hear
          that.  I'm a visual person. Ouch.

                    MORRIS
          What I mean is that I can only
          get out if they wake up. You'll
          have to make noise to wake them.

                    ALICE
          Won't it wake up all of them?

                    MORRIS
          Yeah, you're right.

Alice hands him her cell phone. He studies it.

                    ALICE
          ET phone home.
```

In Note 184, we continue the pet dream theme with Morris going into dreams and Alice witnessing. See Scenes 101 and 102. I didn't use Note 185. Notes 186 and 187 deal with the dreams pets have and what they want. It drives Scene 101. Okay, Note 188 sounds strange but it's when Morris realizes that one dog dreams of humping a squirrel. That is in Scene 62. I didn't use Notes 189 and 190.

184) At water — Series of scenes where he goes in. She's convinced that he can do it. She sees his designs.

185) He makes runs around the county + people are happy, etc.

He has a full day

186) Several of the pets just miss things like special toys — are chewies.

187) The day is very productive 1/4 of the animals are placed.

188) There is one that only dreams of humpy in square. He buys a toy square + change on the throne it in. "Sorry fella"—

189) He comes home feels great.

190) That night Jerry comes by with some wine — Sort of a housewarming gift

95) Morris and Alice crawl on all fours across the darkened kennel. Morris puts his hand over his eyes as he passes one cage.

                        ALICE
                     (Whispers)
              Is it bad?

                      MORRIS
            You don't want to know.

Morris stops.

                      MORRIS
                     (Whispers)
            Good.   Here's one.

Morris puts the cell phone into his pocket and quietly moves closer to the cage. Whoosh. He's gone. Alice's eyes slowly rotate around looking for Morris. She feels the floor where he was kneeling.

                      ALICE
                     (Whispers)
            Wow.

Alice creeps backwards towards the exit.

62) INT. ANIMAL SHELTER - DAY

LATER: Morris goes over his pickup list.

                      MORRIS
            I'm telling you all animals
            think about is humping
            something.

Over Alice's shoulder, he sees that Max (the Cockapoo) is having a daydream and it's not about humping. He steps around her without taking the ticket. She follows. Morris approaches the cage and is in awe. Above Max's cage is a fairytale scene of a beautiful farm cottage and an apple orchard. Alice doesn't see what he's in awe of. The phone RINGS. She turns to get it just as Morris reaches towards the dream. He's gone. As she's talking on the phone, she notices that Morris is gone.

In Note 191, Jenny realizes that Morris is changing. She says that something is happening to Morris in a good way and they enjoy talking about dreams (Note 192). This happens in Scene 116. Notes 193 and 194 were repeats of previous notes.

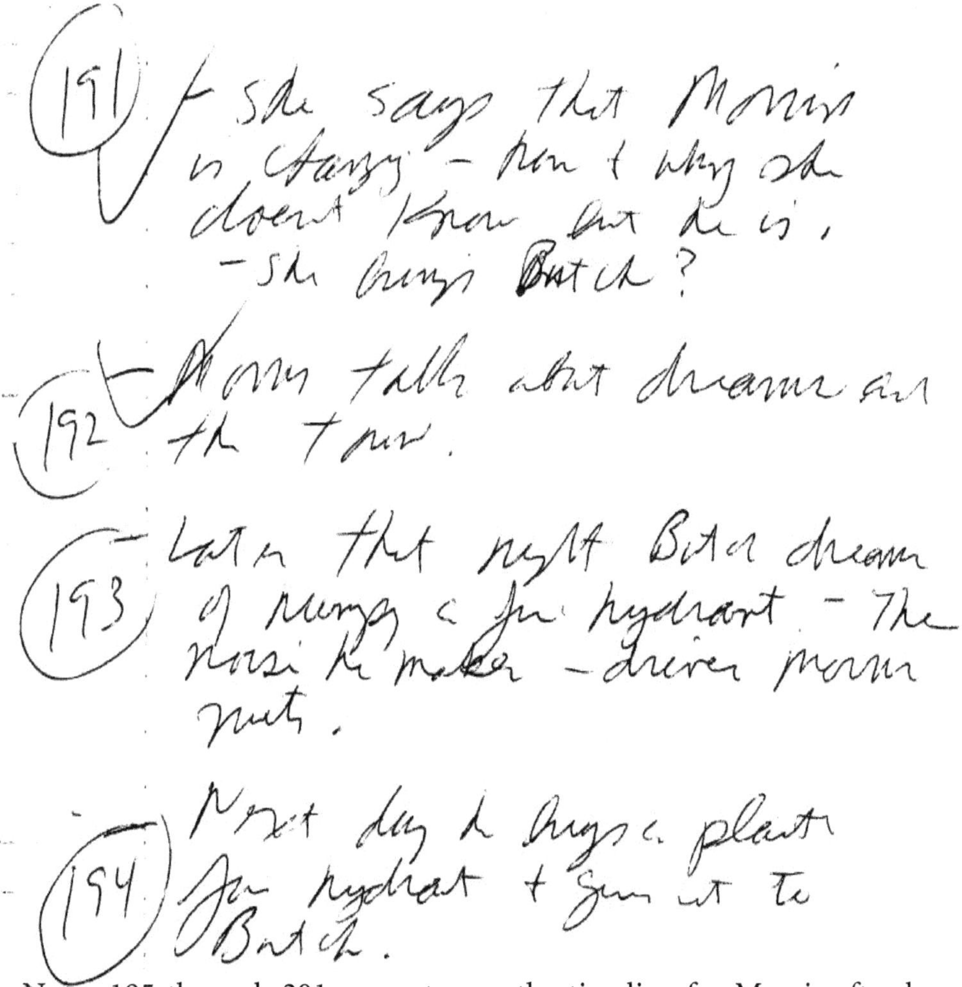
191 She says that Morris is changing – how & why she doesn't know but he is. – She brings Butch?

192 Morris talks about dreams and the Tour.

193 Later that night Butch dreams of humping a fire hydrant – The noise he makes – drives Morris nuts.

194 Next day he brings a plastic fire hydrant & gives it to Butch.

Notes 195 through 201 are notes on the timeline for Morris after he starts having car problems. They drive Scenes 171, 172, 164, 165, 182-185, and 188. Notes 202 and 203 weren't used. In Note 196, Scene 164 and 165, Jenny tells Alice that she loves Morris. This is a pivotal scene. When Morris tries to call home with car problems, he can't reach Alice. She's busy with the petition. In Note 198, (Scenes 182-185) I have Morris getting a second dose of Indian magic and then the shaman mysteriously disappears.

~~195~~

More outline

FRIday - leaves at 5:00 PM - gets there at 3:00 in Morning SAT - ⓐ Afternoon - delivers dogs - gets back at 6:00 - stays Saturday night - Sunday - Ted Fried

195 - Morris has car problem
196 - Jerry goes to Alicia's - says he loves her — Jerry at given
197 - Morris has car Still Towed - tries to call Alicia - no answer, each party to answer

198 - Morris comes home - on way he picks up Indian again - they appear & disappear mysteriously — were they only a dream?

199 - Gets home Sunday evening or ~~Monday Morning~~ Monday night - Bar gets Robbed December.

200 - When Morris drives into town, he drives past a poster on a pole that proclaims "Morris Moe Heil,

201 - Sets p crooker & they're plan on debts bank before they — He stays at Jerry's apartment over shop put home

202 - He gets into town at 7:45 - stops at Cafe - Jerry is going to surprise him - Parents are there - South goes on -

203 - Phone call that he's driving back home that night or in early in morning.

171) EXT. MOTEL - DAY

Morris has the hood of the truck open. Max is sitting nearby, watching. Morris bends down and looks under the truck. There's a pool of antifreeze under the truck. Morris stands, puts his hands up on the hood, and stares at the motor.

172) INT. HOPEVILLE ANIMAL SHELTER - DAY

The phone rings and rings and rings until.

                    MORRIS (V.O.)
      Alice. You must not be into
      work yet. I'm stuck at the
      motel. The truck is broke
      down. I think it's the
      water pump. The Motel manager
      said the nearest garage is
      an hour or so from here. He's
      not sure when they open. I'll
      call when I know more. Bye.

163) INT. JENNY'S APARTMENT - NIGHT

Jenny lays in bed, motionless, staring at the ceiling. A love for Morris is growing to the point of bursting out. She rolls over and looks down at Butch. He's cuddling the toy hydrant like a lover. Throwing back the covers, she springs to her feet, grabs her robe and rushes out.

164) INT. ALICE'S APARTMENT - LATE NIGHT

Alice covers her head to hide from whoever is POUNDING on her door. From underneath the covers, she bellows.

                    ALICE
     Go away. I don't do pets at home.

                    JENNY (O.S.)
     It's about Morris.

That registers with her. Slowly, she comes around and slumps up to a stand, her eyes still closed.

                    ALICE
     Coming..

181) EXT. FARMHOUSE-LATE SUNDAY NIGHT

Larry climbs into the Farmer's old truck and starts it. Albert runs out of the house and jumps into the truck just as it takes off.

                ALBERT (O.S.)
      Where we going now, Larry?

                LARRY (O.S.)
      To find some cash. One of these
      hick towns has got to have a
      bank.

182) EXT. HIGHWAY - NIGHT

As Morris drives, the two Indians, John John and his Grandfather appear out of nowhere. John John has his thumb out. Morris pulls over and stops. As before, they somehow appear next to the truck. John John opens the passenger door and sticks his head in.

                JOHN JOHN
      Hello again. We're going home.

                MORRIS
      Climb in. I can take you as
      as far as the Hopeville exit.

John John holds the door open as his Grandfather, Jack climbs in. John John follows.

183) INT. MORRIS TRUCK - NIGHT

Morris drives as John John and his Grandfather are having a quite conversation.

                MORRIS
      How was your sister's wedding?

                JOHN JOHN
      We stayed at her house
      a while. Grandfather had too
      much spirits at the wedding party.
      He was not well for a while. He
      is better now.

                MORRIS
      That's good.

Jack leans towards John John and whispers.

188) EXT. HOPEVILLE STREET - MORNING

Morris parks the van and walks down the sidewalk towards the café. He passes a storefront without noticing the new poster that is now replacing Ben's reelection poster.

HOW TO WRITE A SCREENPLAY IN 3-DAYS

Note 204 is a repeat note. Note 205 relates to the fight scene at the end (Scene 196) where Morris gets stabbed. The notes that follow are fairly sequential with scenes 197, 198, and 199 and shows the town, and even Ben, supporting Morris.

204) Bank is Robbed — Ben is shot by pistol — other has knife

205) Morris comes to rescue — gets stabbed

206) Wakes up in Hospital — Parents are there — + Alvin + Jenny.

207) Morris says he don't mean that he was saying for Sheriff — they fought.

208) The stab is only a flesh wound — no organs — stitches up — Doctor is willing to let him leave —

209) Half the Town is waiting — they have signs — Morris for Sheriff. They wheel him out — he is surprised — He asks about signatures — Doris says Jenny + Alvin got everyone together + they spent weekend getting signatures. She says they have over 1200 signatures. They go to City Hall to officially get him on ballot

211) Sheriff is outside — his arm in sling.

165

Note 212 is a note on my FAVORITE scene (Scene 166). Morris realizes that he loves Jenny, but because of the shaman magic, he can only see other people's dreams and CAN'T dream himself. So, Max, his new friend and companion, stops under a tree on the hill and lies on the ground. Max has the dream of Jenny for Morris because Morris can't dream and misses her. The dream of Jenny coming from Max lights up the night sky like a movie as Morris sits down to enjoy it. One day, when I asked one of Spielberg's readers what they were looking for, she said "magic." Okay, how's that, Steven?

---

(212) That night — Morris walks under the stars & moon — with MAX. He stops & looks up at the moon.

"I wish I could at least dream of her." He barks. Max lays down and a small dream cloud appears — of showing Jenny petting MAX. "Thanks, MAX."

166) EXT. MOTEL - LATE NIGHT

Morris and Max walk out on a deserted landscape with a few straggling trees. The stars and moon are bright and near. Morris stops and looks up at the full, large moon.

                    MORRIS
          You know what sucks, Max? I
          can't even dream of her.

Morris takes a few steps but notices that Max isn't following. Max has decided to take a break and is lying on the ground. Morris walks back to join him and sits. A small dream cloud appears over Max. It's Jenny and she's bending down and petting Max.

                    MORRIS
          Thanks, Max.

Morris props his elbow on his knee and rests his chin on his fist. The dream plays like a personal movie, magically glowing, lighting the night sky and Morris' smiling face.

167) INT. JENNY'S APARTMENT - NIGHT

Jenny lies on her side, watching Butch cuddle the hydrant. She rolls over on her back and stares at the ceiling.

168) EXT. MOTEL - LATE NIGHT

Morris lies on his side watching the dream of Jenny play over Max.

Notes 213 and 214 (Scene 191) comprise the scenes where Morris finally returns and Ben confronts him about his running for sheriff. I used a lot of the dialogue that spewed from that note in Scene 191.

- Band – Barker open door – Hair pushed in by Rotten.

(213) Cafe – Morris enters – everyone is looking at her & smiling. Ben stands & says he knows what's been going on over the weekend. Walks over to Morris. "You don't have a chance in hell, me." Morris "Oh" "The vault is on timer – It doesn't go open until 8:00 –

(214) He doesn't set off alarm test at 8:01 – People at bank are concerned.

No Runnin'.
oh you try.
Ben freaks out & rips down a poster. He comes over & hands it to Morris. "Then what's this?" It's a clear Morris for sheriff
"He has a curly Q"
"Morris – oh god, you didn't use that picture Jerry – Sorry, it's the only your mom had."

Sell gift as gag in act

The tone, whether it's a drama or comedy, comes from the dialogue and the situations that you create as well. For instance, even though I knew that in Scene 2 I wanted to introduce Morris as a six-year-old truly engrossed in a daydream, I also wanted to create some comedic moments. The comedic tone did not come out until later as I sat down to write the scene.

The forty-one pages of notes are merely a sounding board for me to toss out my ideas on the story line, the scenes, etc. Although some writers would call the forty-one pages of notes an outline, I consider them a practice run and only refer to them when I get stuck. As I mentioned, many of the practice lines of dialogue and scene ideas never got used because once I got into the story, better scene ideas and dialogue came to me. A lot of times, my notes are the mere essence of a scene and I know that I will need to write in more detail later. Upon completion of this chapter, you should be prepared to enter the three day marathon.

PREPARING FOR THE MARATHON

YOU HAVE FLUSHED OUT your story and feel comfortable that you know the whole narrative. Are you ready to start? Personally, I know I'm ready to start when I have about thirty to forty pages of notes on scenes and dialogue to back me up. Although, I normally don't have to rely much on the notes once I start, it gives me a warm fuzzy just in case I get stuck in the mud in the second act. Act II is where most writers get stuck. I've had it happen to me on several occasions and I have several half-written scripts to prove it. This happens when you don't have a complete story line either in your head or on paper and run out of steam. The notes provide some assurance that if you lose your way, or get stuck, you can refer to them and go, "Ahah, now I remember…"

It is critical that you carve out 3 days of uninterrupted writing time from your schedule. This is absolutely necessary. Would you expect a runner to run a marathon with his telephone strapped to his hip and have to stop every mile to answer his phone? No. Prepare for the marathon because interruptions like the telephone and your friends stopping by will do nothing but take time away from your writing. The best way to do this is to let everyone know that you are embarking upon a screenwriting adventure. You will enter the 3-day weekend with one goal. That is to walk away Sunday night with a draft screenplay in your hands. It can be done, I've done it dozens of times and you can do it, too. There is no feeling in the world like the completion of your first screenplay. It is quite an accomplishment, and it will bring you to your feet in excitement when you type the words: The End.

But listen carefully, you must have the 3 days, and you must let everyone know that you cannot be disturbed unless it's an emergency! If you only have a two-day weekend, burn a day of vacation or use comp time for the Friday to get your 3 days. Set a target date for the marathon and stick to it. Although the writing part of the marathon only takes 3 days, you should spend a minimum of two weeks researching characters, story theme, locations or any subject matter that you are not familiar with and two weeks drafting the story outline and supporting notes. So give yourself a month to flush everything out before you hit the 3-day marathon date.

A quick note on research: Let's say that you are writing a western. I wrote one called, *Sheriffs Incorporated*. What did I know about the old west? Not much. So I researched it, everything from trains to the Chisam Trail, as well as any other elements that came into play during the writing. However, you are NOT obligated to use all of the research in the screenplay. Don't beat the reader in the head with all that you've found out. Do the research until you are comfortable with the topic you are researching. When the time comes for the details you need, you'll know what to do. You'll be surprised how much you'll actually need to use to be convincing. Do the research but only use what you really need to.

If you write in your office at home, in a spare bedroom, a dorm, or in your basement, make sure you have a door between you and the outside world. Because that's where you are going to post your DO NOT DISTURB: SCREENWRITER WORKING sign. Yes, you will post a sign. I'll tell you why. The first time you are interrupted, take the person to the door and politely point at the sign. They'll get it! This will prevent future interruptions. Believe me, this works. I was married with two small children at the time and it didn't take long before they understood the sign hanging on the door had significance. If you are married or living with someone, sit them down and explain what you are going to do. Make sure that you don't have a wedding or birthday party to attend on the scheduled weekend and can devote yourself to the marathon. Are you ready?

THE MARATHON

TAKE A BREATH and let's run through a checklist to see if you're ready for the marathon. I also wanted to mention that when you have completed the screenplay, move ahead and read about how to protect your screenplay by registering with the Writers Guild of America (WGA), polishing and editing your screenplay, marketing your screenplay, and additional reading and resources to continue as a screenwriter.

CAUTION: Before attempting to do the marathon screenwriting session, make sure your health is not a factor and that you are healthy enough to put in twelve-hour days for three days!

To accomplish your goal of writing between 105 to 110 pages of screenplay, you must be prepared to spend approximately twelve hours a day for 3 days to complete the full screenplay. Not being a real typist (I hunt and peck more or less) I can type about three pages an hour. If you are a skilled typist, all the power to you and you are ahead of the game. Based on three pages per hour, the goal is to write 36 pages a day. On day one, you will complete Act I and begin Act II. On day two, you will have completed more than half of Act II and be approximately on page 76. On day three you will finish Act II and Act III.

I usually get a fresh early start, about 7:30 AM, and work until 7:00 or 8:00 in the evening. Be sure to get a good night's rest Thursday night, because the first day will be the roughest. Once you have accomplished the writing for the first day, the second and third day will go easier. Okay, let's go over what you need to do to prepare for your 3-day Screenplay Marathon:

- Be sure to have enough paper on hand (at least a hundred pages). I find that as I complete sections of the script, I like to print them out. It's kind of a reassuring factor to print out sections and when you can physically see the pages, it provides additional motivation.

- Have the story notes nearby for reassurance and reference.

- Be sure to hang up your DO NOT DISTURB sign on the door. It'll save you a lot of aggravation.

A VISUAL REHEARSAL

One thing I do before the big day is lie on the bed (not because I'm tired) to relax and concentrate on the complete story flow. I will start at the beginning with screen credits and all. Fade from black and roll the credits. What's the opening scene? Start there and play the whole story in your mind as if you are a viewer in the audience at the theater. Play the whole story, picturing the locations and the characters, hearing the dialogue, the scoring, and the WHOLE thing. I will do this a couple of times before I get to the writing. It will help you to reinforce the story line, find dialogue and scenes you missed and will prepare you for the marathon.

Since you will be sitting at the keyboard for extended periods, plan to take an occasional break, walk around the room (don't leave unless you need a quick snack or drink) and stretch. Do this every couple of hours.

For me, music helps to set the mood for some scenes. I know that if I'm writing action, horror, or sci-fi, I like to listen to rock. For romantic comedies or serious scenes, I may switch to lighter more moody music. It's up to the writer. Pick music that encourages your creativity. What you will find is that the more you try to create, or write, the more that will come to you. You will find that ideas will begin to rain down on you as you open yourself to the creative forces.

PEP TALKS

Think of this segment as your own personal coaching section. It will coach you through the 3-Day writing marathon. I want you to read these pep talks on days one, two, and three. The first pep talk prepares you for day one before beginning the screenplay. The second pep talk, to be read on day two, assumes that you have completed your goals for day one and prepares you for the writing and challenges of day two. The third and final pep talk assumes that you made it through day two and prepares you for the final writing day of the marathon. So each day, read the pep talk for that day and good luck!

DAY ONE PEP TALK

Hopefully, you have read the rest of the book and have gotten some helpful ideas on writing your screenplay. You have also come up with a great idea and have given it lots of thought and have even written down your notes on the scenes, the characters (with names), and even some dialogue bits and pieces. Great!

You're sitting at the PC and have a comfortable chair. You are rested from a good night's sleep and have a cup of coffee or tea (if you're like me) that you're sipping on. You have already typed the title and your name and have "FADE IN:" at the top of the page. Great! You have set your left margin at 1½ inches, and the right margin, as well as your top and bottom margins, to 1 inch. Terrific! Let's get started.

Your goal for today is to get through Act I and hopefully a few (or more) pages into Act II. You are going to introduce your characters today to the audience and are going to open your story with several scenes that will set the tone for the rest of the movie. Not only will you introduce the characters, but by page ten, the audience is going to know what the story is all about and be riveted. You will tell them, by the end of Act I, why your character(s) is on this journey and the dilemma that they face.

You will also tell the audience what or who your characters are up against. By the end of Act I, you will also have a dramatic event occur (plot point) that will set your character(s) off on a journey that is different from where they were when the story started. Now start writing and let your screenplay hit the ground running…

DAY TWO PEP TALK

Good morning! I bet the wheels were turning in your head all night. You could hardly get to sleep, anxious to tell more of the story. Okay, first, let's talk about what happened yesterday. So you got your characters off and running and finished Act I, right? Okay, if you didn't, don't worry, you'll catch up. But, for those of you that finished Act I and started Act II, let's discuss what happened. Your character(s) embarked on their journey at the end of the act by taking action because of the event that occurred near the end. Their life or what they thought about their life has changed and a lot lay ahead of them. They are also probably aware that they are heading for confrontation and may or may not be prepared. There are those around them that may be able to help them, or that may be an illusion, as they are actually part of the problem. This they have to find out.

    A lot is going to happen to your characters today. You are going to find out that all is not what it seems. Your character thought he/she was up to doing what they needed to do, but are they having second thoughts, faltering, or are they unsure of themselves? Less than half way through today's writing, if you were able to get ten to fifteen pages into Act II yesterday, something is going to happen that will yet have a dramatic impact on the story and your characters. We knew it wasn't going to be easy for the characters and that things will go wrong. Well, it will happen. It will even cause the confrontations and conflict to intensify. This is the midpoint of your story. Your characters will forge forward either now more determined to reach their goal or will find resolution of their dilemma or will be set back. Hopefully, if you have built your characters right, they will lead you to the final resolution, Act III, by the end of the day. Wind 'em up and let's go!

DAY THREE PEP TALK

Good morning! You should be on page 70 (plus or minus 10 pages). If you hit the end of Act II, you should have noticed that something dramatic happened just before the end of the Act (plot point). It was not expected or was not what the character expected. Or, possibly it was unexpected and wonderful. However, you really put your characters through the mill yesterday and we got to see what they are made of. Today everything will be resolved, one way or the other. Depending on the type of story you are writing, your character is entering his/her final battle or has finally figured that the girl with that angelic smile who supported him through all of the horrible or selfish things that he has done is the girl he wants to spend his life with. This is when the character gets what they are after... or doesn't... and all of the loose ends get tied up. ALL of them. Depending on the type of ending, it will be a happy one, or a not-so-happy one. Either the character has learned something about themselves or the world, or they have not. Finish the story. You and the characters deserve it.

POLISHING AND REWRITES

CONGRATULATIONS! YOU HAVE COMPLETED the first draft in 3 days. Take a break from the screenplay for about a week. We want it to get cold. After a week or so, pick it up and read it like it's the first time. You are going to find lots of problems. Some will be grammatical, some will be story problems, etc. I'd suggest that you read it all the way through, envisioning it on the screen, and get a feel for how it plays out. Don't worry about grammar at this point (if you hit something, use a red pen to highlight it) just focus on the story.

Remember what I said about story buddies to bounce your story off of? Well, people around you and others in the business can offer their opinion or comments on your first draft as well. When I was writing a screenplay for Oprah about working women in a corporate environment (no she hasn't bought it, YET), I asked women to read the script and provide feedback. I got some excellent advice from them. One point that they brought up was they didn't feel that they had gotten closure on the story. I went back and fixed the problem and had the girls re-read it. They liked the rewrite and felt that I hit it on the head. Thanks to them, I was able to improve the screenplay. You MUST be open to criticism from those whom you ask to review your work.

Sometimes, you are so close to the problem that you can't see it. For example, my mentor, who is a far better writer than I am, was told that her screenplay was way too long and was told to cut about twenty pages. Ouch! Writers hate that word. Nonetheless, she couldn't see what scenes needed to be removed. Of course, being the writer, she thought that ALL of the scenes were needed. So she asked me to help her cut the nonessential material out. It's a painful process for a writer to remove scenes that they put their heart into, but sometimes it must be done.

Making painful decisions about your work is part of the polishing process. How many movies have you watched that just seem to drag and you thought to yourself (or like me, out loud) somebody should have done some cutting. Whether we like it or not, this process improves the story flow and keeps it from dragging. So let people read your screenplay, and try to find those that are knowledgeable, so they can help you identify areas that need rewriting or, yes, cutting.

Also, look for ways to make the dialogue more crisp and clean. Sometimes writers get wordy and add extraneous words or dialogue that isn't needed. Remove extraneous words like "well" or "you know" that we sometimes use to begin sentences. Look for words that don't add to the dialogue and ways to shorten it and get to the point.

You'll be surprised how many times you can go through your "final" screenplay and STILL find things that are wrong (word misuse or misspellings) every time. Review it and polish it. Put it away for a while or have someone review it, again. Go back and reread it. You'll find more. Screenwriters don't usually consider a screenplay a final until it's had at least a half a dozen rewrites or versions. Some of mine have at least ten to fifteen versions before I consider it a "Final". DO NOT send your first cut to any producer or director! NO! Take the time to review it multiple times and get it read by lots of people before doing this. I don't know how many times I have sent out a screenplay to find out afterwards that I have sent it with a mistake. Ouch! You really regret not having reviewed it one more time.

SELLING YOUR SCREENPLAY

How do you get your screenplay sold in the marketplace?

Usually, studios and large film production companies deal only with agencies and agents. Good agents are hard to find. I chose an agent because he lived in my hometown. However, my hometown happened to be in Illinois and having an agent in the Midwest doesn't work very well. For a writer to have representation, the agent should be positioned on the east or west coast where the large film producers are located. If your agent doesn't have the connections or can't do lunch with the insiders, then they're not very effective.

However, getting an agent on the coast is harder than it sounds. Today, unless someone recommends you to someone they know in the business, they take on writers by the project. This means if the current project you are working on doesn't interest them, they won't represent you. You can get a list of agencies and signatory agents from the Writers Guild of America (WGA). It identifies agencies and agents that are open to new writers. Most want you to write a query letter and to send a synopsis of the screenplay. They will use this to determine if you have a project worth representing. Many so-called agencies out there say they have connections and can get you read by studios. The most they will do is place your project on a list or in a database where no one will find it. Be careful. They will also ask you to spend hundreds of dollars with no results. If anyone you approach wants money for ANYTHING, then bail and say no thank you. A legit agency won't ask for money.

Can I get read if I don't have an agent?

Some film companies do solicit from time to time, and by making connections on the Internet, you may find someone that knows someone, etc. Most studios don't accept unsolicited materials. This means that if they don't ask for it, then they won't accept it.

Your best hope is to find an agent or agency that is accepting new writers, and you'll want to send them your very best story idea. Otherwise, you will be left having to shop your project to independent film production companies. Many film production companies DO accept solicitations via email and some require snail mail submissions. Look up film production companies on the Internet and find their submission requirements. Just follow their submission guidelines. Also check your local area for film production companies; most states have several small companies. It's a good idea to call them up before you go as most are very busy. After you've set up an appointment to discuss your projects with them, prepare some pitches and a clean screenplay to take with you. Sit down and talk about their needs. They could be looking for a screenwriter for a project.

To market your screenplay, just about everyone will ask for a synopsis first. I usually send them logline first to see they are interested. Some will accept screenplays. Spend some time writing a good synopsis that captures the essence of your story. Keep the synopsis to one page at the max. If they want more information, they'll ask for it. The synopsis is one of the most important selling tools a screenwriter has. It's what sells them on reading the screenplay. The Internet Movie Database (IMDB) has synopses on movies and provides a good example of summing up your screenplay. You'll find numerous websites that discuss how to write a synopsis.

An unlikely place that you may find help with your pitch is at film festivals. While attending the Great Plains Film Festival in Nebraska, Lew Hunter asked the screenwriters in the audience to come up with a quick pitch and throw them out. He listened as we all pitched and then he gave us feedback on the pitch. It was great. A lot of film festivals (in most states) have screenwriting contests with workshops for screenwriters. Check them out in your local area and bring some pitches. You never know...

How much do screenplays sell for?

The WGA minimum is around $30,000 to $40,000 (story and screenplay are priced separately but total around $40,000). However, they can sell for up to six figures. Typically, studios pay anywhere in the low six figures to the mid six figures. Hot screenplays, on the other hand, can sell in the millions. The biggest payoff was to Shane Black and Joe Eszterhas at around $4 million. If you get hooked up with an independent film company, they will probably ask you to "defer" payment. This means that they want to pay you when they finally make money on the film. I wouldn't go out and buy a new car on that speculation. Indie films don't have large budgets and they figure that the writing credit is worth something to you.

I hear people mention Options. What does that mean?

This is where a film production company has an intent to make your screenplay into a movie and wants to secure the rights to it for a period of time. This could be anywhere from six months to a year or longer. They will pay you a sum of money, usually $5,000 to $10,000, to have the rights for that period to try to get it into production. If they fail, the rights revert back to you. However, during that period, you can't shop it around to other producers. Some writers actually make a living from their options.

I've heard about the Writers Guild of America (WGA). How can I join the Writers' Guild to be considered for film projects?

Actually, you don't get to join unless you are produced and have been paid the minimum wages set by the Writers Guild of America. The Guild has minimums (see the WGA site) that a writer MUST be paid to be accepted into the Guild. You must receive credit in the titles as screenwriter of the film and must have been paid the minimum. The minimum, the last time I looked, was $38,000 for both story and screenplay. This is important, because when dealing with an independent film company, make sure you are clear that you need the minimum so you can qualify to join the Guild. The Guild provides services to non-guild members such as screenplay registration services, agent/agency listings, etc. See the WGA site for a complete list of their services.

PROTECTING YOUR SCREENPLAY

THERE ARE TWO WAYS to protect your screenplay and they offer different levels of protection. You can copyright the screenplay with the U.S. Copyright Office or you can register it with the WGA. The protection by the WGA is not recognized in a court of law if you should ever file a lawsuit, if someone steals it, for example. The copyright, however, is recognized by the court. The WGA registration can be used in an arbitration case by the guild and is only good for five years. You would have to renew it every five years at a price of $20 (http://www.wgawregistry.org/webrss/). Remember that screenplay ideas cannot be copyrighted and if you throw your pitch out on the Internet, anybody can use it. However, if they take specific ideas and elements from your screenplay, it is grounds for legal action.

Also, be careful when selling screenplays to production companies. Make sure you understand the rights that are transferred to them. When you sell a screenplay to a production company, they will ask you to sign a document that transfers rights to the film. If rights aren't transferred, the film company will have a hard time selling their film. A film company needs to show that all elements of the film (screenplay, actors, music, etc.) have rights secured properly. Most companies will use a Work for Hire Contract since it is the simplest without any obligation other than being paid for your work. If you don't understand the rights in the contract, get a lawyer to review it. However, there should be a copyright transfer of the screenplay and it should explain all of the rights involved.

RESOURCES

Screenplay (1979) Syd Field

The Screenwriter's Workbook (Revised Edition - Delta; Rev Upd edition (October 31, 2006) Syd Field

The Power of Myth (Doubleday, 1988) Joseph Campbell with Bill Moyers

Screenwriting 434, (Perigee Trade. Revised edition, 2004) Lew Hunter

Writers Guild of America http://www.wga.org/

Internet Movie Database (IMDB) http://www.imdb.com/

RECOMMENDED SCREENPLAYS/FILMS

Unforgiven (The William Munny Killings), screenplay by David Webb Peoples
China Town, screenplay by Robert Towne
Gothika, screenplay by Sebastian Gutierrez
Memento, screenplay by Christopher Nolan

Drama/Action: *Get Carter* (with Stallone), *CopTown*, *The Color Purple*, *Catch 22*, *Casablanca*, *Bullet* (Steve McQueen), *Deliverance*, *The Man Who Would Be King*, *Fargo*, *Reservoir Dogs*, *Mystic River*, *Stand by Me*, *Magic*

Sci-Fi: *Robocop* (the first), *The Time Machine* (both), *Planet of the Apes* (the first original), *Predator* (the first), *The Terminator* (the first), *The Thing* (Both, with Arness and Kurt Russell), *Bladerunner*, *Outland*, *Soldier*, *War of the Worlds* (the original), *Journey to the Center of the Earth* (the original), *Forbidden Planet*, *The Body Snatchers*, *The Abyss*, *The Day the Earth Stood Still*.

Comedies: *Overboard*, all Pink Panther films in original version, *Blazing Saddles*, *Young Frankenstein* (okay, all Mel Brooks stuff), *The Producers* (original), *The Bird Cage*, *Flubber* (the original with Fred McMurray), all Abbot and Costello films, all Cheech and Chong films, *Scrooged*, *Caddyshack*, all Chevy Chase *Vacation* films, *Dumb & Dumber*, *The Majestic*, *The Mask*, *Liar Liar*, *School of Rock*, *100 Kisses*, *Mr. Deeds*, *Father Goose*.

Horror: *Alien*, *Evil Dead* (the first and second), *Return of the Living Dead* (first and second), *Psycho* (the original), *Lost Boys* (the first), *Halloween* (the first), *Hellraiser* (the first), *Pet Cemetery*, *The Shining* (the original), *Hellboy* (the first).

Westerns: *Shane*, *McCabe and Mrs. Miller*, *Rio Bravo*, *Sons of Katy Elder*, *Little Big Man*, *Dancing with Wolves*

To name a few....

HOW TO WRITE A SCREENPLAY IN 3-DAYS

```
            "IN YOUR DREAMS"

        A Screenplay by Jackie L. Young
```

IN BLACK... ...a police siren WAILS, wheels SQUEAL on a city street followed by a volley of GUNSHOTS.

"...for all those who dare to dream".

1) EXT. CITY STREETS - DAY

A police car is in hot pursuit of an old sedan. The CRIMINAL hangs out of the speeding car's driver's side window and fires a large caliber gun back at the police car blowing the exterior mirror into pieces.

2) INT. POLICE CAR - DAY

From the back seat, we watch as HARRY, 30s, the policeman riding shotgun, hangs his weapon out the window and fires several rounds with no success.

A small hand (of a child) holds a very large caliber gun out the window and firing. A direct hit takes the fleeing car's back window out. Harry is impressed.

                    HARRY
         Good shooting Officer Morris.

CLOSEUP: On MORRIS, 6 years old, driving the police car, dressed in full policeman gear and uniform, his hat brim pulled down to the top of his eyes. He peers out determined as he cuts a corner.

                    MORRIS
         Thanks Harry. It's nothing.

Another perfect shot by Morris takes both the back and front tires out.

                    HARRY
         Wow! Two tires with one shot!

The bad guy's car squeals around the corner on the rims and flips, rolling down the street of the rundown part of town.

3) EXT. CITY STREET - DAY

The police car slides sideways to halt and the driver's door swings open.

The small shiny policeman shoes stroll up to the overturned bay guy's car. It's smoking and hissing, The back tires lopsidedly spinning. The driver of the car, a hardened and tough looking criminal, is sprawled beneath the overturned car wreckage. He sits up on his side as the tiny feet approach him.

The camera PANS UP to reveals our little officer, Morris, sneering down. He raises his large gun and aims it at the criminal.

>   MORRIS
>   (In his best Dirty Harry voice)
>   I know that in all of the confusion,
>   I may have lost count of how many
>   bullets I fired. Seeing that this is
>   the most powerful handgun ever made,
>   and holds six bullets, you have to
>   ask yourself one question, punk. How
>   many bullets did he fire? Five or six?

Morris cocks the gun and moves it towards the criminal. The criminal draws back in fear as Harry approaches the scene.

>   HARRY (O.S.)
>   Moe?

>   MORRIS
>   Well, do you feel lucky..punk?

>   HARRY (O.S.)
>   Moe?

Morris looks back at Harry.

>   MORRIS
>   Just a minute partner.

>   MORRIS
>   (To Criminal)
>   Well, do you-

That of Morris' Mother replaces Harry's voice.

>   MOTHER (O.S.)
>   Moe?

Morris turns to look at Harry. Harry has been replaced by Morris' Mother, ANN HILL, 25, now wearing Harry's police uniform. Morris looks at her strange wondering why she's dressed like a cop.

>   MORRIS
>   Ah, Mom..

As Morris turns back to his criminal we go to.

4) INT. HILL HOUSE - DAY

From Morris' POINT OF VIEW we are now looking at a teddy bear lying under an overturned large plastic car. Morris disappointedly looks at the plastic gun that is now pointed at the bear. His police uniform now replaced with his school clothes. Behind him, a large cardboard box cutout to look like a police car has replaced his squad car. Morris drops his gun in defeat.

                    MORRIS
        Ah, Mom, I had the bad guy
        and you ruined it.

His Mother approaches with his lunch. She hands it to him and pats him on the head. She kneels down, wets one of her fingers and makes a curly "Q" on the front of his hair. She smiles.

                    MOTHER
        Sorry. You'll just have to
        chase them down after school.

She puts her hand between her eyes and waits.

                    MOTHER
        Come on..

Morris hesitates, and then a smile grows on his face. Suddenly, Morris goes into his 3-Stooges routine, playing Moe. With his two fingers making a "V", he jabs towards his Mother's eyes. Of course, her hand blocks it. They laugh. Then with a little push, he's guided towards the door as his father, WALTER HILL, 29, a REAL policeman, rounds the corner.

                    FATHER
        Ready, sport?

Morris lays his toy gun down and accompanies his dad towards the door.

                    MORRIS
           (Not pleased)
        Bye Mom.

                    MOTHER
        Bye dear.

The door closes as we FADE TO BLACK:

                PIRATE CAPTAIN'S (V.O.)
        Remove the blindfold

FADE IN TO:

5) CLOSEUP: on a beautiful blond girl's face, 17, ANGELA, who's bound to the mast with thick ropes. She looks out of place in this time. Her hair is styled for current day, but she's on this pirate ship.

Go WIDE to reveal that we're now on a pirate ship on the high seas some time in the 1600s. Everything, but the girl, is authentic.

The pirate CAPTAIN, hobbles towards her on his peg leg, a parrot is perched on his shoulder (we're going for the comic book version here). As he reaches the Angela, he raises his sword to her throat as the other PIRATES move in closer.

                    PIRATE CAPTAIN
               (In overdone pirate voice)
          You'll tell me where to find
          Captain Morris or else yee'll
          walk the plank my dearie.

                        ANGELA
               (In Valley Girl)
          I don't know where he is. So
          give me a freakin' break.

CUT TO:

6) Morris, now 16 yrs old, in full swashbuckling gear, high above up on the mast, stands with his hand on his hip.

                        MORRIS
          I'm here, Captain One Leg.

Morris draws his sword and with his free hand grabs the line leading down to the ship.

                        MORRIS
         Release her or suffer my wrath!

CUT TO:

7) The Ship Deck on Captain One Leg:

Captain One Leg raises his sword and points it at Captain Morris.

                    PIRATE CAPTAIN
          Suffer you will captain Morris
          when I cut off her head and feed
          her to the sharks!

                        ANGELA
          Uueeee. That is totally gross.

8) Back to Morris.

He swings down, sword in his other hand and upon arriving on deck, kicks two of the PIRATES over the railing and into the water.

9) CLOSEUP: On sharks immediately devouring the two PIRATES. They SCREAM.

Morris goes for Captain One Leg. Captain One Leg thrust his sword towards Morris. Morris easily fends it off with his sword.

> PIRATE CAPTAIN
> You are as good as they say ye are. But, I'm better.

The fencing continues as Angela looks on.

> PIRATE CAPTAIN
> I only have one question for ye, Captain Morris..

The Parrot speaks up.

> PARROT
> (Parrot voice)
> Where's your homework.

Morris stops mid swing with his sword and looks at the Parrot strangely.

> MORRIS
> What?

> TEACHER (O.S.)
> (Male voice)
> I said where is your homework?

10) INT. HIGH SCHOOL CLASSROOM - DAY

Morris is standing at his desk, his arm stretched out. His sword now gone and replaced with a pencil. He still has that little curly "Q" that his Mother does to his hair. The entire class breaks into LAUGHTER.

11) CLOSEUP: On one of the classmates, BEN HARRIS, 16 and the lead school jock, who doesn't like Morris and is really enjoy--ing this.

The TEACHER is still waiting for the homework. Morris, embarrassed, sits down. As he does, Angela, the girl from the pirate daydream is seated in front of him. She rolls her eyes as Morris digs in his backpack for his homework. She's embarrassed just to be seated in front of Morris.

Finding it, Morris hands it over her shoulder. She handles it like it has cooties and passes it up to the awaiting Teacher.

The bell RINGS. The STUDENTS rush for the door. The Teacher organizes the homework papers as they depart. He reminds them.

                    TEACHER
         Don't forget about the Pep
         Rally. Show your support by
         being there..please.

Some of the Students moan at the thought as they depart.

12) EXT. HIGH SCHOOL HALLWAY - DAY

On Ben as he's joined by his other football BUDDIES.

                    BEN
         What a momo.

His Buddies LAUGH. Ben checks over his shoulder for Morris.

                    BEN
         Come on, let's get to the locker
         room. We'll show everybody what
         an idiot he is.

One of his Buddies does a high five with Ben.

                    BUDDY
         Yeah!

13) INT. LOCKER ROOM - DAY

Ben and his buddies enter and bully a couple of FRESHMAN out of the locker room. Ben looks around for witnesses then opens Morris' locker. An article about Angela being nominated as head cheerleader has been cut from the school newspaper and taped onto the inside of the locker door. One of Ben's football buddies spots the picture of Angela.

                    BUDDY
         Look, dummy has the hots
         for Angela.

Ben spots Morris' jockstrap hanging from a hook. He reaches into his school jacket and removes a small bottle of itching powder.

                    BEN
               (To Buddy)
          Take it out.

                    BUDDY
          No way. I'm not touching his
          jock strap.

Ben turns and slaps him on the back of the head.

                    BEN
          Do it before someone comes.

His Buddy reaches in and lifts it out carefully with two fingers. Ben opens the bottle and dumps the contents into the jock strap. His Buddy gently places it back on the hook. The door slams as we CUT TO:

Morris slams the door. He's now dressed in his cheerleader outfit (yes, he's a male cheerleader). He trots away to the Pep Rally unsuspecting as we FOLLOW him.

14) INT. GYM ROOM - DAY

Morris bursts through the door into the gym, revealing a full gym, crowd noises, and a band out of tune practicing. Morris takes his place next to the other cheerleaders who are warming up.

Ben and his football buddies are lined up on the gym floor for display and keeping an eye on Morris waiting for the powder to kick in.

Morris' Parents: His Mother, now 35, and his Dad, the Police Chief, now 39 years old, are in the audience. His Dad is in uniform. They spot Morris and proudly wave, trying to get his attention.

The PRINCIPAL approaches the microphone and stand. He taps on it, causing a SQUELCH. Everyone moans. He tries again and it's normal. He begins.

                    PRINCIPAL
          As you are all aware, we
          are eleven and "0"-

Audience breaks into CHEERS and applause. The Principal raises his hands to settle them down.

                    PRINCIPAL
          But we have a tough game ahead
          of us. Westside is no pushover.

The Audience "Boos" Westside.

> PRINCIPAL
> So we're counting on our
> star quarterback..
> > (Looks to Ben and his Buddies)
> Ben Harris to lead us to victory.

The audience stands and applauds. The school band immediately goes into the school fight song.

To Ben and his football buddies. Ben and his buddies raise their fists in victory. The audience loves it.

To Morris: The itching powder is kicking in. Morris feels something strange going on in his pants. He repositions his legs, then crosses them not sure what to make of it. Then the leader of the Cheerleaders, Angela, runs and flips across the floor to lead the Cheerleaders out. The Audience CHEERS. Some of the guys whistle.

The Cheerleaders run out to follow her. Morris awkwardly follows, the itching powder getting worse.

To Ben and his buddies: Ben nudges one of his buddies to check out Morris who's walking very strange.

To Morris' Parents. They too, notice that Morris is walking strange.

The Cheerleaders line up to form the standard cheerleading pyramid. Morris is in the middle on the bottom as the others climb up.

As Angela climbs up to the top of the pyramid, Morris is trying his hardest to resist scratching his privates. As Angela gets to the top, she thrusts her arms out in pride. The Audience CHEERS as Morris gives in and tries to reach down.

The human pyramid rumbles and collapses. Everyone in the gym stands, shocked.

CLOSEUP: on the pile of Cheerleaders as they recover and begin standing. As they do, in the middle of the floor lying outstretched is Morris. He has his hand down the front of his pants and is vigorously scratching and massaging his privates. As they all step back in shock, the scene is revealed to the whole gym.

To Morris' Mom: She covers her eyes in embarrassment.

Suddenly the Audience bursts into laughter as Morris begins thrusting his pelvis into the air and kicking his feet as he scratches.

To Ben: He and his buddies are laughing so hard they're in tears.

15) CLOSEUP: on Morris: He stops and sits up. Everyone stops laughing and waits for his reaction. Morris jumps up and runs out of the gym. They burst into laughter at the sight of Morris scurrying while trying to scratch himself.

16) INT. LOCKER ROOM-SHOWERS - DAY

Morris is vigorously lathering up in soap, trying to get the powder off.

17) INT. LOCKER ROOM - DAY

Ben and the other football players laugh and do a high five but immediately stop and begin dressing for practice upon noticing Morris' Father, Walter, Chief of Police, standing with his arms crossed in the doorway. Walter adjusts his gun-belt and approaches Ben. Ben starts to open his locker but Walter slams it shut.

>   WALTER
>   That was a funny stunt you
>   boys pulled. Why don't you
>   tell me who set it up. I'd
>   like to talk to him.

Ben ignores him and tries to open his locker. Again, Walter slams it shut.

>   WALTER
>   Maybe it was you.

Morris rounds the corner of the locker room just as his Father, Walter, grabs Ben and violently throws him up against his locker. Morris is seeing a side of his Father he's never seen before.

Back to Walter:

Walter gets in Ben's face. Ben struggles to get free.

>   BEN
>   Come on, man. Let me
>   go. You're hurting me.

>   WALTER
>   I'm the law around here. Know
>   what that means?

>   BEN
>   No. What?

                    WALTER
          Means I can do what I want and
          It would be my word against yours.
          Who do you think they'll believe?

                    BEN
               (Struggles)
          What's your problem?

                    WALTER
          You. You're my problem. If
          you know what's good for you,
          you'll keep away from my son.

Walter releases him, turns and sees Morris watching. He walks away.

Back to Morris:

Morris looks down disturbed by his Father's actions. The pristine image of the father that he'd held so highly has just been permanently tarnished.

19) INT. MORRIS' BASEMENT BEDROOM - MORNING

The objects in Morris' room tell us what he likes and has been up to over the years.

There are several posters on the walls. One is a "*TJ Hooker*" poster and one is a Stallone "*Cobra*" Movie poster. The other is a "*Dirty Harry*" Movie Poster. A framed photograph has Morris at age 6 dressed in his toy policeman gear and standing next to his younger Father who's dressed in his formal Police Chief uniform, proudly smiling.

A framed degree "Hopeville Community College Associate Degree in Criminology" issued to Morris M. Hill in 1994 hangs on the wall.

INSERT: Current Day, 20 Years Later

The alarm SOUNDS. The clock shows 7:00 AM. A body buried under the covers slowly comes to life. A hand reaches out from under the covers and smacks the top of the Alarm clock shutting it off. The arm retracts. After a moment of stillness, the covers are thrown back and Morris, now early thirties, slides up to a sitting position. Morris' hair is standing straight up his eyes are still closed. He slowly parts his mouth and lets out a small breath of air as if he'd just come back from the dead. It's followed by an award-winning yawn. His eyelids flicker open as he stands half bent over, with his butt protruding outward. Morris awkwardly straightens and scratches his unruly hair.

20) INT. KITCHEN - MORNING

Morris enters the kitchen dressed in a blue uniform. His Mother, ANN, now 56 years old, jumps from Walter's lap and straightens her hair and house robe. Morris, almost repulsed by the thought of what may have been going on, looks at his father, Walter, who's now 60 years old. Walter clears his throat and takes a sip of coffee. To distract from just happened, his Mother quickly pours a cup of coffee for Morris and places it on the table.

Morris scans his watch and then slumps his shoulders. He lets out a exasperating breath.

                    MORRIS
         Mom, you know I have coffee at
         the café every morning.

She approaches Morris and straightens his unturned collar. Licking her finger she makes a little curly "Q" of several strands of his hair. Morris rolls his eyes until she finishes. She smiles.

                    ANN
         There, Moe.

Hs Mother puts her hand to her eyes waiting for Morris to do their 3-Stooges ritual gag. He unenthusiastically obliges as if it's a chore. Then she steps back as Morris lifts his blue military style hat from the coat rack hook in the kitchen and puts it on. Morris scans his watch again impatiently, pecks his Mother on the cheek and dashes out.

Walter stands and walks to the window. He sips his coffee as he watches Morris walk down the sidewalk.

21) EXT. HOUSE - MORNING

We join Morris as he walks down the sidewalk. The insignia on the back of Morris' blue shirt reads "Hopeville Animal Shelter."

As he hits the end of the sidewalk, he notices that MR. CRIMSHAW, 65 years old and bald, is holding the leash to his dog SKIPPY, who's taking a crap on Morris' front lawn. Morris tries to handle it professionally.

                    MORRIS
         You know Mr. Crimshaw, you
         should let Skippy do that in
         your own yard or else carry..

Morris digs out a little scooper from his back pocket.

                    MORRIS Continues
            A pooper scooper with you so
            you can clean-

Skippy finishes as Mr. Crimshaw drags him away.

                    MR. CRIMSHAW
            Bite me, dog boy.

Morris is left standing alone with the scooper extended.

                    MORRIS
                (Trying to recover)
            Okay. See ya.

Morris shoves the scooper back into his pocket and climbs into his white van with "Hopeville Animal Shelter" painted on the side. The van pulls away.

22) INT. HILL HOUSE - MORNING

Walter is still at the window, having watched the whole episode. He shakes his head in disappointment as his Wife Ann looks over his shoulder. She puts her hand on his shoulder to comfort him.

                    WALTER
            Where'd we go wrong, Annie?

                    ANN
            Who says we went wrong, Walter?

                    WALTER
            Three generations of law officers,
            and then.. Morris.

                    ANN
            It's his life..

                    WALTER
            He was meant to be the police chief
            just like my Father and me.

Walter reaches up and clasps her hands in his.

                    ANN
            Things change.

                    WALTER
            Why can't they change with some-
            one else?

She puts her head on his shoulder and smiles a devious smile.

                    ANN
          I feel frisky.

                    WALTER
          Oh, boy.

23) EXT. HOPEVILLE TOWN STREET - MORNING

Morris' truck enters the town limits. He passes the town
sign, "Entering Hopeville, Town of Hopes and Dreams,
Population 849"

Small shops decorate the conservative town's square.
Morris' truck parks on the side of the street near the
Hopeville Café.

On Morris.

As he walks down the street, he passes his reflection in a
shop window. Stopping, he turns to face his reflection. He
quickly messes up the front of his hair to kill his Mother's
curl then brushes his hair back.

As he turns around, he almost bumps into one of Hopeville's
elderly citizens, the owner of the Antique shop, MRS. AVERY,
60 yrs old.

                    MORRIS
          Good morning Mrs. Avery.

She fumbles with her keys to open the door.

                    MRS. AVERY
          What's so good about it? Fudge
          off.

She enters and closes the shop door. Morris shakes it off,
checks his watch, and heads towards the restaurant.

24) INT. HOPEVILLE CAFÉ - MORNING

Morris enters. The café is already busy with the morning
customers. A single stool at the counter is empty (Morris'
stool). Sitting at the first counter seat is Ben, his
archenemy, now in his 30s also, wearing the police Chief's
uniform. He's chatting with JENNY, late 20s and attractive
with short dark hair, who's holding a full coffee pot.
Morris makes it a point not to make eye contact with Ben as
he passes. Jenny spots Morris and smiles.

Morris makes his way through the busy café to his seat. Jenny tears herself away from Ben to grab Morris' morning Danish and a clean cup.

Morris compares his watch with the café clock as Jenny places his Danish in front of him and pours his coffee. It shows 7:50.

                    MORRIS
          Morning, Jenny. How are things?

                    JENNY
          It's Monday. What can I say?

The cook, DELORIS, 50 and a large woman who could easily be mistaken for a trucker, works the grill. She puts another order up.

                    DELORIS
                (To Jenny)
          Order's up!

Jenny puts the coffee back on the burner and grabs the order. Morris prepares his coffee as he keeps an eye on the clock. Taking a bite of the Danish, he watches Jenny service the customers in the Café. Ben pinches her on the behind as she passes by him. She turns and swats at his hand. He laughs. Some of the other men also laugh but she isn't finding it funny. She looks at Morris, her eyes almost pleading for him to do something. Morris breaks eye contact ashamed that he's not man enough to do something about it. The clock hand reaches 7:59 and the Bank Alarm Bell SOUNDS its weekly test.

Morris turns to see two BANK ROBBERS run out of the bank and head for a getaway car. A PATRON in the café yells.

                    PATRON
          Someone is robbing the bank!

Morris slowly and calmly stands and walks to stand by Ben, the Chief of Police, without taking his eyes off of the Robbers. The bank president, MR. HODGES, a large man in his 60s, runs out from the bank.

                  MR. HODGES
          Help! They've robbed the bank!

Jenny steps to the counter where Ben's seated.

                    JENNY
          For Gods' sakes, Ben, do
          something.

Ben looks struck with fear.

                    BEN
          But they have guns.

Morris hands Jenny his half-eaten roll, and still chewing a mouthful of roll, unfastens Ben's holster and takes his gun.

                    MORRIS
               (To Jenny)
          Hold this. I'll be right back.

Morris steps calmly from the café, the large gun dangling at his side.

25) EXT. TOWN STREET - MORNING

Morris calmly steps out onto the street while watching the two Bank Robbers climbing into their getaway car. They see Morris with the gun and fire a couple of random shots. The glass of the café shatters. Morris calmly looks back at the shattered glass and shakes his head. Stepping forward towards the now moving car, he aims the huge gun.

                    MORRIS
          Halt!

The car speeds wildly towards Morris.

At the Café: A crowd of patrons gathers at the café windows to watch.

Back to Morris:

Morris calmly takes aim at the car quickly that's approaching him and fires. The windshield is blown out. The car veers away just missing Morris and careens out of control. It slams into a dumpster. The driver slams against the steering wheel and is knocked out. The HORN is stuck on. The passenger door flies open and a bloodied Bank Robber staggers out with a shotgun. Morris turns and slowly walks towards the crashed vehicle. The Bank Robber fires and misses. Morris aims and fires. The Bank robber is hit. He falls over.

26) INT. HOPEVILLE CAFÉ - MORNING

Morris enters dragging the two Bank Robbers. He deposits them at Ben's feet. Ben, still shook by fear, looks down at them. Morris puts the gun back into Ben's holster and buttons it.

                    BEN
          Might want to lock up these
          fellas when you get time.

The Marathon Method

He grabs Ben by his collar and pulls him up to his face.

                    MORRIS
          And if you ever pinch or
          touch Jenny again, I'll
          break your fingers.

Morris releases him. Ben thinks about it, then.

                    BEN
          Yes, sir, Mr. Hill.

Morris steps to Jenny.

                    MORRIS
          You have something for me?

Jenny lunges into his arms and passionately kisses him.
Everyone in the Café CHEERS. She steps back and smiles.

                    MORRIS
          I meant the Danish, honey.

He holds out his hand. She lays the sticky Danish back into
his open palm. He takes the Danish with his other hand and
looks at the icy mess on his palm. Jenny sees it.

                    JENNY
          Oh, I'm so sorry.

Jenny takes his hand and licks the icing. She licks again
and begins licking it aggressively to the point where she's
lapping it like a dog. Morris is starting to experience
something wonderful. He lets it out.

                    MORRIS
          Oooohhh Yeah!

A burst of LAUGHTER takes us to.

Morris is seated at the counter with his arms at his side
engrossed in his daydream. A PATRON'S Dog is lapping at the
icing on Morris' hand that's hanging to his side. Another
PATRON (one of Ben's friends) quickly finishes tying Morris'
shoelaces together and scurries away.

Morris looks up at the clock. It shows 8:00. Slowly he
looks around. Everyone behind the counter has stopped in
their tracks and is staring at Morris. Ben is leaning
forward at the counter staring at Morris. Slowly they go
about their business. Morris stands and starts to walk
away. He falls over flat onto his face. Everyone LAUGHS.

Morris pulls his face from the floor and looks down. His
shoes are tied together. Ben nearly gags on his coffee, then
holds it out for a refill. Jenny refreshes it.

                JENNY
     That wasn't funny.

Ben tries not to smile, but can't help it.

                BEN
     Yeah. You're right. It wasn't
     funny... It was hilarious!

Everyone laughs again as Morris quickly fixes his laces. He
stands and turns to face Ben. Everyone becomes quiet as Ben
swivels around in his seat. Morris looks at the badge that
says "Sheriff."

                BEN
       (Now serious)
     Yeah, Morris? What can I do
     for you?

Morris looks over at Jenny. She looks down, embarrassed for
Morris.

                BEN
     That's what I thought.

Ben spins around as Morris contemplates some kind of gesture
that would prove he's a man. His fists tighten then relax
and open. He can't find it. He turns and walks out.

Ben and the other patrons set their watch for 8:00. Jenny
leans against the counter during a lull in orders. She sips
a cup of coffee. Ben looks up after adjusting his watch.

                BEN
     If it weren't for Mr. Hodges
     testing that old Bank Alarm
     every Monday mornin', none
     of us would have the right
     time.

Ben stands and stretches. He takes out a five and holds it
out to Jenny. She starts to take it, but he doesn't let go.

                BEN
     You know, if I get reelected
     it'll mean a raise.

She tries to pull the money away. He finally lets go.

                    JENNY
                (Not impressed)
            Yeah, that's great.

Ben moves around the end of the counter towards her as she
goes to the register and gets his change. She holds it out.
He folds her hand around it.

                    BEN
            A man shouldn't be alone.
            A woman either.

Jenny waits for him to release her hand then puts the change
in her tip jar.

                    JENNY
                (Cold)
            Thanks Sheriff.

Ben exits. Jenny watches him leave and the door close.
Maybe he was right. She didn't know but it made her think.

                    DELORIS (O.S.)
            He may not be the man of
            your dreams but you could do
            worse.

Jenny turns to pickup another order while giving Deloris a
dirty look.

                    DELORIS
            Just trying to help.

                    JENNY
            Don't.

Jenny shoots her a half smile as she steps away with the
order.

27) INT. MORRIS' TRUCK - MORNING

Morris is sitting silently in his truck staring at himself
in the mirror, not happy with what he sees.

                    MORRIS
            What a loser.

He starts the truck and drives away.

28) INT. HOPEVILLE ANIMAL SHELTER - DAY

Morris enters the back door of the shelter. Half of the
cages are filled with cats and dogs. ALICE, 30s, and plain

looking with glasses, is just closing up one of the cages she's just cleaned. Morris says hi to the animals.

> MORRIS
> (To a gray Cockapoo)
> Hey boy.

Morris backs up to one of the cages. The Cockapoo doesn't respond but remains lying on the cage floor. Alice approaches.

> ALICE
> Hey, Morris.

Morris is preoccupied with the somewhat depressed Cockapoo.

> MORRIS
> Oh, hi Alice. No claim on him yet?

> ALICE
> Nope. I posted his picture on the web with the others. Nothing.

> MORRIS
> Poor guy.

Alice hands him a list.

> ALICE
> Got some strays to pick up in Anderson.

> MORRIS
> Geesh, that's forty-five minutes.

> ALICE
> It's s big county. Swing by Lewisville. Got a call from a lady
> (She hands him another slip)
> Says some strays are getting into her trash.

Morris takes it, still preoccupied with the Cockapoo.

> MORRIS
> Too bad you couldn't just tell us where you came from fella.

> ALICE
> Yeah, If I had a talking dog, think I'd hang around this dump?

                    MORRIS
          You love this job and you
          know it.

                    ALICE
          The job's fine. It's the
          town that sucks.

He turns.

                    MORRIS
          What's wrong with it?

She opens a cage and removes the empty water bowl. She closes the door and bumps into Morris who's trailing her. She steps around him and heads for the faucet.

                    ALICE
          Yeah, right. You know why they
          call it Hopeville?

Morris starts to comment. She continues.

                    ALICE
          People come here when there's
          no hope left. It's the end of
          the road. They should call it
          HopelessVille.

She fills the water bowl, steps around Morris and takes the bowl back. She puts the bowl in the cage. The puppy springs to the bowl and laps it up. Morris stares at the dog lapping the water. He's glazed over for a minute being reminded of the earlier incident. He snaps out of it and starts to comment. Alice is gone. He spots her at another cage and approaches.

                    MORRIS
          Well, now that you've brightened
          my day, I'm gonna go hang myself.

29) INT. MORRIS' TRUCK - DAY

Morris climbs into the truck and starts it. He stares at an old weathered sign that says "Welcome to Hopeville, Town of Hopes and Dreams." He shakes his head and drives away.

30) EXT. HIGHWAY - AFTERNOON

Morris's truck drives along the desolate highway.

31) INT. MORRIS' TRUCK - AFTERNOON

Morris is deep in thought as he spots two Indians along side the road. One has his thumb out.

Morris slows down the truck and pulls over to the shoulder. He turns around to back up to them and suddenly they are at the door. He's alarmed as to how they got there so fast. One Indian, in his 30s, JOHN SON-OF-LITTLE BEAR JOHNSON (John John), opens the passenger and pokes his head in. He has long black hair and is dressed in a suit jacket that's too small and a black tie that's wrinkled.

> JOHN JOHN
> Hi.

> MORRIS
> (Uncomfortable)
> Hi. Where are you heading?

> JOHN JOHN
> Anderson. My sister is getting married there.

> MORRIS
> Hop in. I'm going by there.

John John backs up and helps his grandfather, Cherokee Shaman JACK LITTLE BEAR JOHNSON, 80s, into the truck. Jack is also wearing a suit jacket that's bear brown and a couple sizes too large and a plaid bow tie. Jack slides over next to Morris. John John tosses a couple of backpacks onto the floorboard and climbs in. Morris curiously watches them, having never met a real Indian before. John John and Jack settle in but notice that they aren't moving. They both slowly turn to look at Morris. Morris turns forward and throws it into gear.

LATER: Morris tries to break the awkward silence with conversation.

> MORRIS
> My name is Morris Hill.

> John John
> I am John Son-of-Little Bear Johnson. People call me by John John. This is my Grandfather Jack Little Bear Johnson. You can call him Jack. Grandfather is a Cherokee Shaman.

Morris nods and looks out the window, no idea what a Shaman is.

32) CUT TO:

The Old West: Morris dressed as a Indian Scout with buffalo Bill goatee and buckskin jacket stands beside the Calvary Captain. They're inside a circle of wagons. Civilian bodies and dead soldiers are strewn everywhere, arrows protruding from their bodies. The Captain is surveying the hills for reinforcements with his binoculars. He drops them to his side.

      CAPTAIN
  Well, scout Morris, looks
  like we may not get out of
  this Indian fight alive.

Morris takes a breath and checks his gun chamber. The Captain breaks down crying.

      MORRIS
  What's wrong, Captain?

      CAPTAIN
  We don't have a prayer. They've
  got Shamans with them.

Morris scans the mob of Indians sitting on the hill.

      MORRIS
  (Not wanting to sound stupid)
  I've been meaning to ask you about
  those..Shamans. Exactly what kind
  are these?

      CAPTAIN
  (Shakes his head)
  The worst kind...cannibals.

Morris is stricken with fear, then.

      JACK (V.O.)
  na na-s-gi u-do-hi-yu

Morris turns to find himself facing Jack the Indian from the car. The Captain is gone. The subtext "That is not true" hangs out in the middle of the air. Morris touches the block letters, then.

33) Back to the car. Morris jerks as he comes back from the daydream and swerves the truck.

      MORRIS
  Jesus. How'd he do that?

                    JOHN JOHN
            Grandfather can see dreams. He's
            a medicine man.

Jack leans towards Morris. He waves his arms towards the top
of Morris' head. Morris ducks.

                    JACK
            tsa-gi ha-ni-gi gv-do-di
            ni-hi ni-go-hi-lv—I

                    JOHN JOHN
            Grandfather says that dreams
            follow you.

                    JACK Continues
            ni-hi a-s-gi-ti-s-di u-tsa-ti

                    JOHN JOHN
            He says you dream too much..

                    JACK
            ni-hi na-s-gi a-li-he-li-s-di

                    JOHN JOHN
            ...and are not happy.

Morris is stunned by his wisdom. He looks at Jack. Jack
smiles then motions to John John for his bag. John John
hands him the bag. After some digging, Jack comes out with
his Shaman bag.

                    MORRIS
            What's he doing?

John John smiles, then.

                    JOHN JOHN
            He's going to help you.

LATER:

34) Morris is trying to drive and see through the smoke in
the car. He has an Indian necklace on and is coughing.
Jack is busy CHANTING and swishing feathers across Morris'
face.

35) EXT. HIGHWAY - AFTERNOON

The car zooms down the Interstate, the occupants totally
obscured by the smoke filled car.

36) EXT. ANDERSON-STREET

Morris' truck pulls up and parks. John John and Jack exit the truck with a big cloud of smoke that rolls out with them. John John removes the bags and escorts his Grandfather away. They wave as the truck, still bellowing smoke, pulls away. We hear Morris COUGHING.

37) INT. MORRIS' TRUCK - AFTERNOON

Morris heads back from his rounds. The cages in the truck are half full of dogs and cats. He whistles as he drives.

38) CLOSEUP: on one of the stray cats in a cage. He lies down and as it does, a dream cloud forms above it. In the cat's daydream, it is chasing a huge dog.

39) CUT TO Morris as he glances up in the mirror. He does a double take when he spots the dream cloud and nearly drives off the road. Pulling over, he jumps out leaving the driver's door open.

40) EXT. TRUCK - AFTERNOON

Morris apprehensively swings the back door open.

AT THE SAME TIME the stray Cat awakes from his dream. The dream is gone. Morris studies the interior of the truck, not sure what he's looking for. Climbing in, he searches on top of the cages and around them for the weird cloud that he saw.

He climbs back out and closes the door as we TRANSITION TO:

41) EXT. HOPEVILLE ANIMAL SHELTER-LATE AFTERNOON

Morris has the back doors open and is unloading the cages. As he turns towards the building, he notices another strange dream cloud above the building. This one is bigger and brighter that the one before and involves Alice. Alice is dressed in a very skimpy outfit and is dancing on a stage to a room full of cheering men.

As Morris stares at the dream cloud, he starts getting into the music and starts swaying, then he's really getting into the action...thrusting his pelvis. As he swings around, he's surprised to find himself facing the Janitor, WILLARD, 65 and black, who's staring at him.

Morris makes one last move and stops. Morris looks back up at the dream cloud. Willard looks up to see what he's looking at then gives Morris a strange look.

                    WILLARD
          You feeling alright, Morris?

Morris turns and finishes unloading the cages and slams the door. The dream vanishes. He turns to notice it's gone. Willard looks up again.

                    WILLARD
          You ain't having one of them
          close encounters like I saw
          on TV. They say ten percent
          of the people have one.

Morris thinks about it.

                    MORRIS
          No. I'm not seeing little
          green men.
              (To himself)
          Wish I were.

Willard picks up a couple of the cages.

                    WILLARD
          They's ain't green. They's
          gray. Gray with big black eyes.

Morris picks up a couple of the cages.

                    MORRIS
          Ohhhkay..I stand corrected.

They enter with the cages.

42) INT. HOPEVILLE ANIMAL SHELTER - AFTERNOON

Morris fills out some paperwork as Alice finishes caging up the strays. Willard is busy mopping the floor and whistling.

As Morris puts the paperwork away and stands from his desk, a dream cloud appears over Willard. Morris, intrigued, steps forward a couple of steps and sits on the edge of the desk.

Willard is at a High School Graduation ceremony. Smiling, he walks up the aisle in his graduation garb and steps up onto the stage. He's handed a diploma. The audience applauds.

Curious as to how this dream stuff works, Morris lifts an animal encyclopedia from his desk and drops it intentionally hard. Willard looks towards Morris as the dream vanishes. Morris thinks about the cause and effect, then turns to leave.

>   MORRIS
>   Night Alice..Willard.

>   ALICE (O.S.)
>   Night.

>   WILLARD
>   (Still mopping)
>   Good night, Morris.

Morris exits.

43) INT. MORRIS- BEDROOM - NIGHT

Morris, wearing his pajamas, jumps into bed. He snuggles up for a well-deserved sleep. A dream forms and looms over Morris. He doesn't realize it's there until he hears APPLAUSE.

Rolling over, flat on his back, he finds himself facing his Father's dream of Morris accepting the Police Chief position.

In the center of the dream, Morris, dressed in Officer blues, approaches the podium. Morris sits up on his elbows.

>   MORRIS
>   What the-

Suddenly, a supernatural force from the dream begins pulling at Morris. His legs are being lifted up towards the dream. Turning, he grabs for anything he can to hold onto. Desperately, he flails about trying to grab something... anything. Morris is pulled into the dream, his hand clinging to a pillow.

44) INT. WALTER'S DREAM

Well, there he is, Morris, standing at the podium, looking good in his dress blues...but he's still holding the pillow. He smiles and tosses it over his shoulder. His dad, Walter and his Mother Ann, look at each other strange, not sure where the pillow came from. They shrug it off and settle in for Morris' acceptance speech.

27

Back To Morris: Morris, not quite sure what to do or say notices his written speech sitting on the podium in front of him. He lifts it and starts to read.

                      MORRIS
                 (Reading)
          For generations our family has
          been part of a tradition here
          in Hopeville. By accepting your
          nomination as Police Chief, I
          will be upholding a long-

Morris stops reading and lays the speech down. He looks at his Father and Mother.

                      MORRIS
          I'm sorry Dad. I can't accept.

The MURMUR comes over the audience as Morris fumbles for words.

                    MORRIS Continues
                 (To Audience)
          Thank you all for nominating
          me, but I'm not the man for the
          job. I wish I were.

Morris steps down and as he walks away, he's met by his Father and Mother.

                    WALTER
                 (Upset)
          What are you doing, Morris?
          You can't turn this down.

                      ANN
          Your Father is right. You can't
          do this.

                      MORRIS
          I can and have.

                    WALTER
          I don't understand. I don't
          get it. Ever since you were
          a boy that's all you've dreamed of
          is being a cop like your old
          man.

                      MORRIS
          That's right, Dad. It was
          a dream.

                    WALTER
          Fine. Do what you want.
          But do it somewhere else. I
          want you out of my house.

                    ANN
               (To Morris)
          He doesn't mean it.

                    WALTER
          Yes, I do.

45) EXT. HILL'S HOUSE-DREAM

Morris loads his truck with his belongings.

46) INT. ANIMAL SHELTER-DREAM

Morris is sitting at his desk drinking a mixed drink and smoking a cigarette. He looks like Hell. He's unshaven and his clothes are dirty and wrinkled. Alice approaches with an envelope.

                    ALICE
          Sorry, Morris. We have to let
          you go. You're a dirty drunk
          and all of the animals hate you.

Morris takes the envelope.

                    MORRIS
          Who cares what the stinking
          animals think?

He gets up and leaves.

47) EXT. TOWN ALLEY - NIGHT-DREAM

Morris, looking even worse than before, fights with an Alley Cat over scraps in a trash can. Grabbing the cat by the tail he slings him around his head and slings him through the air.

48) CUT TO: Morris strangles a MAN for his bag of food. The man falls over dead. Morris rips open the bag and devours the food.

49) AS WE GO TO: A mob of angry townspeople is gathered with torches and shotguns (dark, like a scene from Frankenstein).

50) CLOSEUP: on Morris's face as it steps out of the shadows, looking drawn and evil. Ben, in the crowd, spots him.

                    BEN
          There he is. Get him.

The Crowd races after him.

51) EXT. PRISON-YARD - NIGHT-DREAM

Now in a prison uniform, that's reminiscent of the 1950s prison movies, Morris runs out to the middle of the yard trying to make a break for it as the prison ALARM sounds. The Guards on the towers spot him and throw the spotlight on him.

                    MORRIS
               (James Cagney voice)
          Come and get me you dirty coppers!

They riddle him with bullets as we TRANSITION TO:
52) EXT. GRAVEYARD - DAY-DREAM

Walter and Ann stand with a few other townspeople at Morris' gravesite. Ann sobs.

                    WALTER
          Where did we go wrong?

53) INT. MORRIS' BEDROOM- NIGHT

Morris is catapulted back out of the dream and lands on his bed. He hits it so hard that he bounces right off and onto his head.

Rolling up to a sitting position, he rubs his head and looks up for the dream. It's gone. As he looks over at the clock, it shows 5:30 AM. Collapsing back onto the floor, he looks up.

Another dream begins to form over him. It's a chorus line of bulging male strippers that all look like Barry Mantilow. His Mother, Ann, is slapping one of them on the butt.

                    MOTHER
          Shake that booty baby.

He looks up.

                    MORRIS
                 (Grossed out)
              Oh, God.

He's sucked up into the dream.

54) INT. KITCHEN - DAY

Morris drags himself into the kitchen looking like he hadn't gotten any sleep. His Mother, Ann, sips a cup of coffee at the kitchen table.

                    MOTHER
              Morning, dear.

Morris stumbles to the coffeepot and pours a cup of coffee. He guzzles it black as he turns around. She's startled with how terrible he looks.

                    MOTHER
              You look terrible, Moe.

                    MORRIS
                 (Sarcastic)
              How'd you sleep, Mom?
              Any interesting dreams?

                    MOTHER
              No. Why?

                    MORRIS
              Ohhhh, No reason.

Morris fakes a cough and rolls the words "Barry Mantilow" in his cough. His Mother doesn't get it. Morris' Dad isn't in his usual chair.

                    MORRIS
              Where's Dad?

                    MOTHER
              He didn't sleep very well
              last night. He's on the patio.

Morris wanders off towards the patio.

55) EXT. HILL HOUSE-PATIO - DAY

Morris exits and sits down at the patio table with his dad, Walter. Walter is deep in thought about his dream gone bad.

MORRIS
              Dad, I've got to move out.

Walters snaps out of it.

                    FATHER
              Why? Something we did?

                    MORRIS
              No. It's not you. Something
              I need to do.

                    FATHER
              I see.

Morris stands and turns to leave. He turns back.

                    MORRIS
              I'm sorry If I let you
              down, Dad.

Walter looks down then up and starts to speak. Morris is gone. His wife, Ann, is standing in the doorway, having heard. She turns and goes in.

56) INT. HILL HOUSE-KITCHEN - DAY

Morris grabs his hat and starts to leave. His Mother, Ann catches up with him. She kisses him on the cheek. He smiles as she reaches up to do his curl. He gently takes her hand, stopping her.

                    MORRIS
              Mom, you don't have to do
              that anymore.

She lowers her hand.

                    MORRIS
                 (Trying to be cheerful)
              I'd just undo it in the truck
              anyway.

                    MOTHER
              I see.

Morris kisses her on the cheek and leaves. Ann slowly sits at the table, not sure what to think.

57) INT. HOPEVILLE CAFÉ - MORNING

Morris enters. The café is filled with its usual crowd. Morris makes his way past Ben and to his usual chair. Jenny is on the spot with his coffee and Danish. She notes his somewhat disheveled look on this morning.

              JENNY
       You okay?

Morris takes a gulp of the coffee black.

              MORRIS
           (putting on his game face)
       Yeah, sure.

              JENNY
       Anything I can do?

              MORRIS
       Not unless you know where I
       can find an apartment.

              JENNY
       So happens that I do.

              MORRIS
       Really?

              JENNY
       Really. The apartment above
       mine is vacant.

              DELORIS (O.S.)
       Orders up.

              JENNY
       Stop by after work. I'll
       show it to you.

              MORRIS
       Thanks.

Jenny goes back to work. Morris looks around and sees that Ben has been watching them. He stares for a minute then goes back to his breakfast. Morris glances up at the clock. It shows 7:59. He prepares for his usual Monday daydream. He closes his eyes.

The Bank Bell alarm GOES OFF.

58) CLOSEUP: of Morris' closed eyelids. The Bell ends and Morris opens his eyes. He looks around. Nothing had happened. Ben and the other patrons are setting their watches by the clock.

Morris clinches his eyes closed and tries even harder. He opens them... Still nothing. He looks at the clock again. It shows 8:02. Something's wrong. He's becoming panicked.

Suddenly, he sees a small daydream cloud floating above Deloris, the cook. It's close enough to touch. Inside the dream cloud, Deloris (remember that she's a "butchy" woman) is dressed in S&M gear (black leather and skimpy). Morris can't believe his eyes. As he leans forward, the PATRON on the left side asks for the salt.

> PATRON
> Morris could you-

Morris is sucked up into the dream. The Patron looks around for Morris as Jenny steps up to refill his cup.

> JENNY
> Where'd he go?

The Patron shrugs his shoulders and reaches for the salt.

59) INT. DELORIS' DREAM - DAY

Morris, dressed in black S&M gear with a black leather head mask is hung up by his arms. His feet are spread and bound. He tries to look back behind him, where Deloris is standing. He notices that the seat of his black leather bottoms is missing. She raises her little black whip with tassels and swats him across the butt.

> MORRIS
> Oh nooooooooo.

WHAC! WHAC!

On the CRASHING sound of dishes hitting the floor, we CUT to:

Morris is thrown back into his seat so hard he nearly falls backwards. The Patron next to him, looks at him with a mouthful of food stunned. The Patron hands the salt back without chewing. Morris puts the salt down and notices Jenny cleaning up some broken dishes. Morris reaches down and rubs his butt. The Patron still not chewing watches him and looks down at Morris' butt. Morris leans over.

> MORRIS
> Hemorrhoids.

The Patron leans towards him and chews.

                    PATRON
          Me too. Mine are so big,
          you could tie knots in 'em.

Morris is grossed out.

                    MORRIS
          Whoaaaaa. Okay. Gotta go.

Morris stands and walks to the end of the counter to pay.
He hands Jenny three dollars as Ben watches on.

                    MORRIS
          So I'll see you when you
          get off. Right?

She hands Morris back his change. He puts it into her tip
jar.

                    JENNY
          Sure, Morris.

Morris exits. Ben turns and watches him leave then turns to
Jenny.

                    BEN
          Thought you said you'd go
          to dinner with me tonight?

                    JENNY
          I did. Morris wants to look
          at the apartment above me
          that's available.

Slightly jealous, Ben turns to watch Morris get into his
truck and drive away. Jenny smiles and goes back to work.

60) INT. ANIMAL SHELTER - MORNING

Morris opens the door to the back room, where the cages are
located. He stops cold in his tracks. Every animal in the
place is having a dream. The room is filled with dreams of
the pets humping other animals. He spots one of a dog
humping a squirrel. Morris feels his breakfast coming up.

                    MORRIS
          Uhhh.oh..ah...eeeeh

He jumps back outside the door, slams it, and throws his
body against it.

Alice steps up, just having arrived for work. She looks at him odd.

> ALICE
> What's wrong?

Morris fumbles for words.

> MORRIS
> It's a humpfest!

He makes like a squirrel with his fingers.

> MORRIS
> Eeee..Eeeee

...and then like he's humping. Alice's mouth drops open. She's speechless.

> MORRIS
> Dogs doing cats, cats doing mice, dogs and squirrels..

Alice pushes him out of the way and opens the door expecting the worst. Nothing. Not sure if Morris has lost his mind or not, she cautiously enters. Morris peeks in then follows. She looks back.

> ALICE
> Are you taking medication for something?

62) INT. ANIMAL SHELTER - DAY

LATER: Morris goes over his pickup list.

> MORRIS
> I'm telling you all animals think about is humping something.

Over Alice's shoulder, he sees that Max (the Cockapoo) is having a daydream and it's not about humping. He steps around her without taking the ticket. She follows. Morris approaches the cage and is in awe. Above Max's cage is a fairytale scene of a beautiful farm cottage and an apple orchard. Alice doesn't see what he's in awe of. The phone RINGS. She turns to get it just as Morris reaches towards the dream. He's gone. As she's talking on the phone, she notices that Morris is gone.

63) INT. MAX'S DREAM - DAY

Morris runs along side of Max as he races towards the house, BARKING (I'm home!). Morris stops at the end of the sidewalk by the mailbox as Max races up to the door and scratches at it.

Morris looks at the name on the mailbox. It reads like Greek. He studies it as the front door opens. Max races up to greet them.

The owners ELMER, 70s, and ELEANOR, 70s, step out. Max jumps up, trying to give them a kiss. They both scratch and pet him. Morris smiles.

                    MORRIS
          Hi. I guess he's yours, huh?

                    ELMER
               (Most words are Garble)
          Garble Garble Garble Max good boy.

Morris looks at him strange. Then he understands. It's Max's dream and Dogs have a limited vocabulary. Morris nods in agreement.

Morris looks at the address of the house and it too is Greek. Dogs don't know numbers either. Scanning the surrounding community for landmarks, he spots several large white irrigation windmills. The SLAMMING of a cage takes us back to:

64) INT. ANIMAL SHELTER - DAY

Morris arrives back from the dream unprepared and lands on the floor on his face. As he slowly looks up, and sees Alice looking down at him.

                    ALICE
          You've got some real explaining to
          do.

LATER we join them after Morris has just finished telling her his incredible tale. She's staring at him, considering whether to believe or not.

                    ALICE
          You had to know that a Shaman
          is the tribal medicine man. For
          God sakes you had two years of
          community college, Morris.

                    MORRIS
               Well, I think I missed Indian
               Medicine men 101.

                    ALICE
               Ha Ha. Funny.

She stands.

                    ALICE
               It's still hard to believe.

Morris stands.

                    MORRIS
                  (Gyrates)
               Okay, how did I know about you
               wanting to you know..(Pelvic thrust)

                    ALICE
               Okay, okay.

Morris walks to Max's cage and opens it. Taking a leash
from a wall hook, he takes him out.

                    ALICE
               I thought you said that you
               didn't know the address?

                    MORRIS
               All I have to do is look for
               those windmills.

                    ALICE
               That's all you have to go
               on?

                    MORRIS
               And apple orchards.

                    ALICE
               Okay.

She turns and sits down at the desk. She takes out the
phone book and starts thumbing. She scribbles down the
addresses on a piece of paper.

65) INT. MORRIS' TRUCK - AFTERNOON

Max is seated on the passenger seat as they drive by some
apple orchards. Morris eyes the surroundings and then drives
away.

66) EXT. HIGHWAY - AFTERNOON

Morris' truck drives down the interstate towards some irrigation windmills.

67) INT. MORRIS' TRUCK - AFTERNOON

Morris pulls up to a crossroad and looks both ways.

                    MORRIS
          I hope we find it soon Max.
          We're running out of orchards.

Max BARKS.

                    MORRIS
          That way, boy?

Max BARKS again. Morris turns and drives.

68) EXT. FARM-LATE AFTERNOON

The truck pulls up and parks. It's the same farm from the dream. Morris climbs out and Max jumps from the cab and runs towards the house. Morris beams a smile then follows.

AT the farmhouse: Morris knocks on the door. No one answers, so he tries to look inside.

A farmer's truck pulls up and stops. Morris turns to look. The FARMER turns off his truck, rolls down his window, and motions Morris over. Morris approaches the truck. The Farmer, 60s, dressed in coveralls, rests his arm on the window.

                    FARMER
          Can I help you, son.

                    MORRIS
          I'm looking for the people
          who live here.

                    FARMER
          I'm sorry to say but Elmer
          Willowby passed couple 'o
          months back. Right after his
          wife, Eleanor. Maybe I can help.

Morris looks at Max, who's scratching at the door trying to get in.

                    MORRIS
               That's their dog.

The Farmer studies him for a second.

                    FARMER
               Well, I'll be. He does
               look familiar. Elmer was sick
               about that dog disappearing
               like he did.

The Farmer starts the truck up and puts it in gear.

                    MORRIS
               What should I do with him?

                    FARMER
               Guess he's yours now, son.

He drives away as dust and rocks kick up. Morris slowly walks through the dust to reach the house. He sits down on the steps. Max walks over and sits beside him. Morris pets his head.

                    MORRIS
               Sorry, boy.

69) EXT. HOPEVILLE CAFÉ - EVENING

As Jenny exits the Café after a hard day's work, she locks the door and turns to find Morris and Max waiting.

                    JENNY
               Morris..

Upon seeing Max, she kneels down and pets him. He wags his tail.

                    JENNY
                    (To Max)
               And what's your name?

                    MORRIS
               Max.

                    JENNY
               Hi Max.
                    (To Morris)
               Is he yours?

Morris kneels down and strokes Max's mane back, to reveal his eyes.

The Marathon Method

                    MORRIS
          I think he is now.

MEANWHILE:

70) INT. HOPEVILLE SHERIFF'S OFFICE - EVENING

Ben pulls a blind down to get a better view of Morris and
Jenny in front of the restaurant. He watches them walk away
together with Max, then lets the blind flip back up.

71) EXT. HOPEVILLE MAIN STREET - EVENING

Morris and Jenny stroll down the sidewalk with Max towards
her house.

72) INT. VACANT APARTMENT - EVENING

The door is unlocked. Jenny leads Morris and Max into the
sparsely furnished apartment. Max sprints away joyously for
his own tour of the apartment.

                    JENNY
          Looks like Max likes it.

                    MORRIS
          So the landlord doesn't mind
          pets?

                    JENNY
          I guess I'd better not, or I'll
          have to get rid of my dog, Butch.

                    MORRIS
          You're the landlord?

                    JENNY
          What's the matter? A girl
          can't own property?

                    MORRIS
          Oh no. I didn't mean that.

                    JENNY
          It's okay. It was a steal. I
          live downstairs and rent this
          one out. It helps pay the bills.

She turns.

                         JENNY
                 Come on. I'll give you the
                 nickel tour.

Morris follows.

73) EXT. MORRIS' APARTMENT-BALCONY - EVENING

Morris and Jenny exit the apartment through a couple of aged
French doors onto the balcony as the tour finishes up.
Jenny steps to the balcony that looks out over the small
older homes that populate the town landscape.

                         JENNY
                 Not exactly a view of the French
                 Riviera, but I like it. So what
                 do you think?

Morris lifts Max for a look at the scenery.

                         MORRIS
                    (To Max)
                 So Max? (Max licks him)
                    (To Jenny)
                 I think we'll take it.
                 When can we move in?

                         JENNY
                 Is immediately okay?

                         MORRIS
                 Immediately is great! I'll
                 write you a check.

Morris takes out his checkbook.

74) INT. MORRIS' TRUCK - EVENING

Morris drives with Max sitting in his lap. Jenny is in the
passenger seat.

                         MORRIS
                 You really don't have to
                 help me move in.

Jenny smiles.

                         JENNY
                 I want to.

                         MORRIS
                    (Smiles)
                 Okay then.

75) INT. MORRIS' TRUCK - EVENING

Morris parks in the drive of his house. As he climbs out, he puts Max in the driver's seat. Jenny climbs out. Max climbs up on the steering wheel and barks that he wants to come too. Morris removes several folded boxes and puts them under his arm. They approach his parent's house.

76) INT. HILL HOUSE-LIVING ROOM - EVENING

Morris enters the living room with Jenny.

> MORRIS
> Mom..Dad..I'm home.

> MOTHER (O.S.)
> In the kitchen, Moe.

Jenny looks at Morris and mouths the name "Moe?" Morris tries to smile.

> MORRIS
> (hushed voice)
> My middle name is Moe.

> JENNY
> Your name is Morris Moe Hill?

> MORRIS
> Morris was my Great Grandfather
> and Moe was ..oh never mind. My
> name sucks. Just follow me.

Morris slumps his shoulders and enters the kitchen. Jenny laughs and follows.

77) INT. HILL HOUSE-KITCHEN - EVENING

Morris enters. His Mother, wearing an apron, and doing dishes, starts in before she realizes that he has company.

> MOTHER
> Moe, you weren't here, and you
> didn't call, so supper's in the-

She turns to find herself looking at a female, something that's never happened in the house before. Mom is stopped dead in her tracks and speechless. Dad who's reading a CD box takes over. Racing over, he turns his wife, who's now in a stupor, and from behind pushes her forward by the shoulders.

                    MOTHER
                (She finishes)
            ..the fridge.

                    MORRIS
            Mom, this is Jenny.

                    FATHER
            She's pleased to -

Morris's Mother snaps out of it. She turns and whacks her
husband on the shoulder. He looks down at the suds on his
shoulder.

                    MOTHER
                (To Husband)
            I can speak for myself.

She offers her hand.

                    MOTHER
            I'm pleased to meet you.

As they shake hands, Morris' Father wipes off the suds with
a kitchen towel and retrieves his video from the table. He
returns like a kid with a new toy.

                    FATHER
                (To Morris)
            Moe, I got the last season of
            NYPD Blue…and it's on DVD!

His Mother rolls her eyes.

                    MOTHER
                (Not impressed)
            Everything's on DVD today,
            Walter.

Morris is becoming embarrassed that his Father hasn't said
anything to Jenny.

                    MORRIS
                (Motions with head)
            Dad..Dad..

                    FATHER
            Oh..sorry. Hi. I'm Moe..rris'
            Father.

                    JENNY
            Hello.

Morris' Mother already has the fridge open and removing the
leftover bowl of spaghetti. Morris notices.

                    MORRIS
          Mom, that's okay. We're not going
          to stay. I'm moving out.

Both parents freeze. His Mother, holding the bowl of
Spaghetti, looks to Walter for help.

                    MORRIS
          Dad, remember? I told you.

Morris exits. Jenny gives them a sympathetic smile then
follows.

                    FATHER
          Who knows? I thought he was
          kidding.

His Mother starts to tear up. Walter approaches and puts his
hand on her shoulder.

                    FATHER
          Dear?

                    MOTHER
              (Through teary eyes)
          Yes?

                    FATHER
          You're crying on the spaghetti.

Walter gently takes the bowl of spaghetti from his Wife's
hands. She looks down at her empty hands and cries.

78) INT. MORRIS' BEDROOM - EVENING

As Morris packs his belongings into a box, Jenny lifts a
picture from his dresser. It's one of his Father and him
when he was a boy. His Father's dressed in Police Blues and
Morris is dressed in his toy cop gear. She then lifts the
Associate Degree from the wall and examines it.

                    JENNY
          I remember when your Dad was
          the police chief.

She walks over and hands the pictures to Morris. Morris
takes them and studies them for a moment.

                    JENNY
          We use to see him on our
          bikes. He always waved to us.
          My Dad said he was the best
          Sheriff we'd ever had.

Morris packs the pictures and diploma.

                    JENNY
          In that picture, you look like
          you're standing with your hero. You
          wanted to be like him didn't you?

                    MORRIS
          I suppose.

                    JENNY
          Can I ask what happened?

Morris moves to the wall and removes a Dirty Harry poster.

                    MORRIS
          Yeah, but I'm not sure I have
          an answer.

Jenny is puzzled by his remark and starts to inquire when Morris' Mother enters the room carrying a bag of his toiletries. His Dad follows but stops at the doorway and watches. She lays it on the bed.

                    MOTHER
          I brought your toiletries.

                    MORRIS
          Thanks, Mom.

She sniffs and waits. Morris puts the poster into a box and approaches his Mother. Gently putting his hands on her shoulders he kisses her on the cheek.

                    MORRIS
          It's just across town, Mom.

                    MOTHER
          Could we...you know?

Morris steps back and rubs his hands together like he's going to do a magic feat.

                    MORRIS
          Okay.

Jenny is curiously watching, not quite sure where all of this is leading.

                    MOTHER
          Your Father too?

Morris sighs.

                        MORRIS
              I guess.

His Father beams a smile and quickly joins them. He messes
up his hair so it's stretched in every direction as Morris'
Mother comes to life and quickly grabs the pillow stuffing
it under her blouse, creating a fake stomach.

Jenny oddly studies them.

Morris checks himself in the dresser mirror. Using a comb
from the dresser, he combs his hair down in the front so he
resembles Moe Howard as his Mother and Father move together
side-by-side. As Morris moves to the bedroom door for his
entrance, he sees that Jenny has a confused look on her
face.

                        MORRIS
                   (To Jenny)
              You might want to cover your
              eyes. This could be scary.

                        JENNY
              I'm fine. Pretend I'm not here.

Here we go with their 3-Stooges routine...Morris steps up
and pushes his Mother and Father aside.

                        MORRIS
              Spread out.

His Mother, doing her imitation of Curley, wipes her hands
across her face and shoves her stomach out towards Morris.

                        MOTHER
              Mmmmmmmm.

His Father turns to him to do his Larry impression.

                        FATHER
              Hey, what gives?

Morris bops him in the forehead with the palm of his hand
then slaps him on the back of the head.

                        MORRIS
              How about that?

His Father rubs his head.

                        FATHER
              Okay...okay.

His Mother does the Curley routine with the wavering hand that moves past Morris' face. Morris watches the hand go up and down.

      MOTHER
   Knuck knuck knuck.

Morris holds out his two fingers to his Mother.

      MORRIS
   See dat?

      MOTHER
    (In Curley voice)
   Yeah. So what?

Morris tries to jab her in the eyes. She blocks it with her hand.

      MOTHER
   Knuck knuck knuck.

Jenny bursts out laughing (Loud) at their antics. The three stop and look at her. Morris' Mother wraps her arms around him and hugs him tight. Jenny stops when she sees that it's turned emotional. His Father looks down and tries to smooth down his hair.

79) EXT. HILL-HOUSE - EVENING

Morris and Jenny finish loading boxes into the truck. Morris and Jenny climb in.

80) INT. MORRIS' TRUCK - EVENING

Morris starts the truck as Max climbs into his lap. His Mother and Father wave from the window.

      MORRIS
   Sorry about that.

      JENNY
   Oh no. It was very..interesting.
   I've never seen a family do the
   3-Stooges before. It's not
   something you see everyday.

      MORRIS
   My Mom loved them and with a name
   like Moe, she's always loved to-

                    JENNY
                (Interrupting)
          Morris, you don't have to explain.
          It was very touching.

                    MORRIS
          Oh. Okay.

Morris puts the truck in gear and pulls away.

81) INT. MORRIS APARTMENT-BEDROOM - EVENING

Morris is putting away his belongings while Jenny is putting his toiletries in the bathroom cabinet when there's a knock on the front door.

82) EXT. MORRIS' APARTMENT - EVENING

Ben is waiting at the door, dressed in a casual jacket and holding a bouquet of flowers. The door opens to reveal Morris. Ben steps in past Morris without an invitation.

                    BEN
          I'm looking for Jenny. Is
          she here?

                    MORRIS
                (Sarcastically)
          Sure..come in.

The door closes.

83) INT. MORRIS APARTMENT-BEDROOM - EVENING

As Ben, unimpressed by the apartment, surveys it, Jenny enters with several pair of Morris' underwear not realizing that Ben's in the room.

                    JENNY
          Your Mother must have put these
          in with your toiletries-

Jenny is caught off guard by Ben's appearance then she recalls the date.

                    JENNY
          Oh ..our date.

Ben silently looks at the underwear she's holding, then approaches her. He holds out the flowers.

                    BEN
            I got you flowers.

She starts to take them, but realizes she's holding the underwear. Morris quickly grabs the underwear so she can take the flowers. She examines the flowers then smells them.

                    JENNY
            They're beautiful.

As Morris helplessly looks on, he sees Ben eyes roaming Jenny's body. A dream cloud begins forming over Ben.

84) INT. DREAM CLOUD

Ben, dressed in a robe, has Jenny on the couch of his apartment. The lights are low and a Sinatra song is playing. Ben caresses her shoulder and then kisses it romantically. Jenny throws her head back.

                    JENNY
                  (Sexy)
            Take me, you big stud.

Ben pulls her dress strap down to reveal-

Morris CLEARS his throat extremely LOUD. The dream vanishes as Jenny and Ben both look at him. Morris grabs his throat and does a couple of pretend throat clears.

                    JENNY
            I think there's a couple of
            old vases under your sink. You
            mind?

                    MORRIS
            NO.

Jenny enters the kitchen and digs under the sink. Ben steps to the doorway and eyes Jenny's body bent over. The dream cloud reappears.

85) INT. DREAM CLOUD

Now Ben is in bed, undressed, his hairy chest exposed above the covers. Jenny sexily steps into the frame and undoes her sexy nightgown straps and it falls revealing-

Morris CLEARS his throat LOUDLY again. The dream cloud vanishes. Ben looks at him strangely again.

Jenny fills a vase with water and puts the flowers into it, then exits the kitchen.

                    JENNY
              Okay, I'm ready.

Ben leads her towards the door and opens it. Morris follows and closes the door after them. A moment later, there's a knock at the door. He opens it to reveal Jenny holding a house key.

                    JENNY
            Almost forgot...your key.

                    MORRIS
            Thanks for everything.

                    JENNY
            Thank you. I enjoyed meeting
            your family. It was fun.

She turns and leaves. Morris hangs on the door watching her leave; regretful that he doesn't have the guts to stop her, then slowly closes the door.

86) INT. MORRIS' APARTMENT - NIGHT

Morris has fallen asleep on the couch with Max. A car door SLAM wakes him from his sleep. The local news is on the Television. He clicks it off, groggily stumbles to the balcony, and looks out over the parking lot. It's Ben bringing Jenny home from the date.

Max trots up and sits next to Morris. He cocks his head, trying to figure out what Morris is doing. Morris lifts him so he can see. Max growls.

                    MORRIS
            Yeah, I don't like him either.

Jenny quickly climbs out of the car. Ben exits and tries to cut her off. Grabbing her arm, he tries to pull her to him. Max growls again as Morris watches intensely. Jenny looks up at Morris then hastily makes her way towards the apartment. Ben is obviously frustrated with how the date went and slams the door when he climbs back in. He speeds away.

Morris turns with Max to go inside, then stops, something out of the ordinary having caught the edge of his vision. With Max still in his arms, he slowly turns back around to face the night landscape of the small town.

His mouth drops at the sight of hundreds and hundreds of dreams floating above the houses in the town. Creeping slowly towards the balcony railing, he gapes in wonder.

> MORRIS
> Look boy. Look at all of the dreams. What's wrong with me? Why am I seeing all of this?

Max whimpers.

> MORRIS
> Yeah, maybe I'm crazy, huh?

Morris turns with Max.

> MORRIS
> Maybe we should get a closer look.

87) EXT. RESIDENTIAL STREET - NIGHT

Morris walks Max down the sidewalk as he observes a montage of dreams hovering above the house's rooftops of Hopeville.

Morris is attracted to the dream that's floating above MR. LACASTA's house. Although it's maybe not the most unusual, it's the loudest. The dream is blaring out with a symphony of horn instruments. Mr. Lacasta had been the High School's musical directory and teacher and loved music.

As Morris is drawn closer and closer by the wonderful music, a dancing figure in the center comes into focus. It's actually Marylyn Monroe, doing her popular stand over the grate that blows up her dress. That's odd…

WHOOSH…Morris has gotten too close. He's gone. The leash drops to the ground. Max cocks his head and looks around as we go to:

88) CLOSEUP: On lush red lips of Marylyn.

As we pull back, the face becomes familiar. It's Morris dressed as Marilyn...the blond wig, the white dress. Morris struggles to keep the dress from being blown up into the air.

Then Mr. Lacasta, in his 80s, appears out of nowhere.

> MR LACASTA
> How about a kiss, baby?

89) CLOSEUP: On Morris' face as he screams in horror...then runs from the old man...as we pull back to watch the dream from a distance. Max is still oblivious to the strange dream as he sits quietly on the ground waiting for Morris...as we FADE TO:

90) INT. HOPEVILLE CAFÉ - MORNING

Morris drags his body into the café. He looks like crap. Jenny takes note as he finds his seat and melts into it. Ben is in his usual seat, but Morris is so worn out he doesn't even notice him today or Jenny approach with his usual Danish and coffee.

                    JENNY (O.S.)
         Rough night?

Morris jumps then collects himself enough to get his hands around the coffee and find his mouth. After a sip, he looks up at Jenny.

                    MORRIS
         If you consider being chased
         by a horny old geezer with no teeth
         aaaall niiiiight bad, yeah it was-

It dawns on Morris of what just came out of his mouth. He wasn't in a dream. He was in reality and that may have been a little TOO MUCH.

As he turns to face the jeering crowd in the café, he notices that nobody's paying attention. It's just Jenny who's still standing in front of him.

                    JENNY
         I see. That sounds a little
         strange, Morris.

                    MORRIS
              (Over confident)
         And I was dressed like Marylyn
         Monroe. Yeah.

THAT DID IT! Every dull conversation in the place comes to a screeching halt on that note. Forget about hearing a pin drop, you could hear a dust mite flossing. Morris notices this and turns to face his fear. Yep, everyone has their eyes on Morris, including Ben.

                    MORRIS
         Costume party.

And with that, as suddenly as it had stopped, it starts again...the murmur, the chatter. But Jenny is not satisfied. She's concerned.

                    JENNY
            Are you alright?

Morris takes a big gulp of coffee to wash his stupidity away.

                    MORRIS
            Yeah. Sure.

                    JENNY
            Good. Then maybe you'd like
            to follow me.

Jenny puts the coffeepot down and walks back towards the stock room. Morris follows. Jenny swings open the stockroom door to reveal Max, who is lying on the floor. A small dream cloud floats over him, showing him in the arms of Morris. Morris smiles.

                    MORRIS
            Oh, Max.

Max perks up. The dream disappears as he rushes to Morris' arms. Morris stands.

                    JENNY
            I found him outside my door this
            morning on the way to work. What
            happened to you last night? For
            real.

                    MORRIS
            If I told you, you wouldn't
            believe me.

                    JENNY
            Trust me. You hear some whoppers
            as a waitress.

Morris looks around for witnesses within ear range.

                    MORRIS
            I can see dreams.

It takes a minute for her to digest it.

                    JENNY
            You mean you have visions?

                    MORRIS
            No. I mean DREAMS. You know when
            you sleep or daydream?

                    JENNY
          You can read people's minds? I
          don't understand.

                    BEN (O.S.)
          Then read mine. Let me help
          you. I'd like to pay my tab
          so I can leave.

They both turn to find Ben leaning against the doorway with
his arms crossed.

                    MORRIS
          I have to go. I'll be late
          for work.

Morris approaches the doorway. Ben doesn't make any effort
to move out of the way.

                    MORRIS
               (Looking down)
          Excuse me.

Ben leans forward towards him.

                    BEN
               (Hushed voice)
          You need help Morris. Stop by
          my office and I'll make some
          phone calls to reserve you a
          nice little padded room.

Morris finally looks up at Ben. Reaching up, he puts his
hand on Ben's arm.

                    MORRIS
          I said excuse me. That means
          move out of my way.

Ben looks down at Morris' hand, then steps aside. Ben turns
to watch him leave not sure what to think of Morris' sudden
possession of guts. Jenny steps up beside him.

                    BEN
          Did you see the way he talked to
          me?

                    JENNY
          Yep. It's about time.

She walks away. Ben shakes his head and follows.

91) INT. HOPEVILLE-ANIMAL SHELTER-OFFICE - MORNING

Morris enters with Max. Alice, at the desk is doing paperwork.

>   ALICE
> What happened yesterday? Did
> you find his owners?

>   MORRIS
> Yeah, we found his home. But
> his owners had passed.

He bends down to pet Max.

>   ALICE
> Want me to lock him up?

>   MORRIS
> No. He's sort of claimed me.
> And I like it.

She smiles.

>   ALICE
> Your parents don't mind?

>   MORRIS
> He's gonna live with me in
> my new apartment.

>   ALICE
> Congratulations. Good for you,
> Morris.

Alice leans back and observes him and Max together.

>   ALICE
> The kennel is getting crowded.
> Think you could do that again?

Morris stands and looks at the closed kennel door, wondering what dreams lurk behind it. He turns to her.

>   MORRIS
> Sure.

92) INT. KENNEL - MORNING

The door of the darkened kennel slowly creaks open. Morris and Alice peek around the edge of the door. They pull back and the door closes.

93) INT. HOPEVILLE-ANIMAL SHELTER-OFFICE - MORNING

Morris motions her away from the door.

> MORRIS
> We've got a problem.

> ALICE
> What is it?

> MORRIS
> I'm gonna need your help. I spent the other night dressed as Marilyn Monroe being chased by an old geezer with no teeth.

> ALICE
> Wow. I didn't even want to hear that. I'm a visual person. Ouch.

> MORRIS
> What I mean is that I can only get out if they wake up. You'll have to make noise to wake them.

> ALICE
> Won't it wake up all of them?

> MORRIS
> Yeah, you're right.

Alice hands him her cell phone. He studies it.

> ALICE
> ET phone home.

94) INT. KENNEL - MORNING

The door slowly creeps open. They poke their heads around the edge of the door again.

> ALICE
> (Whispers)
> Call me when you want out. I'll poke him with a stick to wake him up.

Morris rolls his eyes to her and gives her a strange look for the absurdity of her comment.

CUT TO:

95) Morris and Alice crawl on all fours across the darkened kennel. Morris puts his hand over his eyes as he passes one cage.

>   ALICE
>   (Whispers)
>   Is it bad?

>   MORRIS
>   You don't want to know.

Morris stops.

>   MORRIS
>   (Whispers)
>   Good. Here's one.

Morris puts the cell phone into his pocket and quietly moves closer to the cage. Whoosh. He's gone. Alice's eyes slowly rotate around looking for Morris. She feels the floor where he was kneeling.

>   ALICE
>   (Whispers)
>   Wow.

Alice creeps backwards towards the exit.

96) INT. HOPEVILLE-ANIMAL SHELTER-OFFICE - MORNING

As Alice backs out of the door on all fours, she bumps into Willard, the janitor, who's waiting with his mop and mop bucket. She looks at his work shoes and bucket then quickly springs to her feet. He starts to move past her with his bucket into the kennel.

>   ALICE
>   Uh, where are you going, Willard?

>   WILLARD
>   To mop the kennel. Why?

>   ALICE
>   Uh..you can't.

>   WILLARD
>   Why?

>   ALICE
>   I don't know.

>   WILLARD
>   Okay.

He turns and pushes the mop bucket away as she scurries to her desk and checks her phone for dial tone. She hangs it up and sits, tapping her fingers on the desk.

Willard collects the trash as he keeps an eye on her because of her strange behavior. She gives him an "I'm normal" smile as she acts as if she's doing paperwork.

There's a knock on the front door glass. Willard unlocks the door and talks to someone briefly. He closes it and approaches Alice.

                WILLARD
There's a lady at the door.
Said she lost a cat. I told her
we weren't open. She wants to talk
with you.

Alice stands, looks at the phone then steps away. Every few steps, she turns and looks back at the phone. Willard looks at the phone, then at Alice. He takes off his hat and scratches his head.

97) EXT. HOPEVILLE-ANIMAL SHELTER - MORNING

Alice steps out and closes the door behind her.

                ALICE
Can I help you?

A robust woman, MRS. WHITE, 50s, starts in.

                MRS. WHITE
I hope so, dear. Missy, my
precious and darling cat was
outside last night..

98) INT. HOPEVILLE-ANIMAL SHELTER-OFFICE - MORNING

The phone rings. Willard picks it up, holds it up, and listens.

                MORRIS (V.O.)
You got get me out of here. Hurry.
I've got a pit bull on my ass.

                WILLARD
Hello. Is this Morris?

                MORRIS (V.O.)
Who's this?

                    WILLARD
          Willard, sir.

                    MORRIS (V.O.)
          Oh. Is Alice there-Ouch!

Willard pulls the phone away and looks at it weird then puts
it back.

                    WILLARD
          You at home, sir?

                    MORRIS (V.O.)
          No. I'm stuck in this crappin'
          dream! Get Alice please. I need
          to get out. Ouch!..you little shit!

                    WILLARD
          Just a minute.

Willard lays the phone down and walks to the front door.

99) EXT. HOPEVILLE-ANIMAL SHELTER - MORNING

Willard sticks his head out the front door. Alice is busy
writing down information from the woman.

                    MRS. WHITE
          And if you can't reach me on
          that cell phone number-

                    ALICE
          No that's fine ma'am.

                    WILLARD
          Excuse me.

They both look at Willard.

                    WILLARD
          It's Mr. Hill. He's having a
          nightmare or something weird.

Alice moves towards the door.

                    ALICE
          Okay Mrs. White, we'll see
          what we can do.

Alice and Willard quickly disappear. Mrs. White stares at
the door for a minute then walks away as we go to:

100) INT. HOPEVILLE-ANIMAL SHELTER-OFFICE - MORNING

Alice rushes to the phone and almost knocks it off the desk answering it. Willard follows, curious as to what the Hell is going on. Alice turns away from him.

> MORRIS (V.O.)
> Get me the hell out of here!

> ALICE
> Have you got it?

> MORRIS (V.O.)
> Yeah. yeah. I got it. Ouch!

Alice throws the phone down and runs around the room looking for something she can poke the dog with to wake it. She grabs several things but they won't do. She tosses them over her shoulder as Willard watches her puzzled. Finally, she spots the mop bucket and grabs the mop from it. Dropping to all fours, she crawls through the kennel door. Willard follows.

INT. KENNEL - MORNING

Alice crawls along the floor pulling the mop behind her. The door slowly creeps open. Willard peeks around the corner to see what she's doing. There she is, in front of the cage, poking a sleeping dog with the mop handle. He scratches his head. With a whoosh, Morris falls out of nowhere and rolls across the floor. Willard's eyes widen then he disappears.

101) INT. HOPEVILLE-ANIMAL SHELTER-OFFICE - MORNING

Alice and Morris work on descriptions of the homes of the dogs. Morris is busy writing out the descriptions on a long list.

> ALICE
> You think that's enough to
> go on?

> MORRIS
> It'd be nice if animals could
> read and write in English. Then
> I could just write down the addresses.
> Everything in their dreams is in
> some sort of weird language.

Alice lifts the list and examines it.

                    ALICE
          Some of these don't make sense.
          They're just a list of toys and
          stuff.

                    MORRIS
          Not all of them had dreams of
          home. Happiness for some of
          them is just a chewy or stuffed
          animal away.

Then they suddenly realize that Willard has stopped mopping
and is staring at them. They both look up, realizing how
weird it must sound. Willard guards his mop as if they
might want it back. He quickly looks away and whistles.

102) EXT. HOPEVILLE-ANIMAL SHELTER - MORNING

Morris and Alice load up the pets destined for their homes.

Morris makes a series of stops to homes delivering the
animals. Glad and happy owners shake his hand and hug their
animals.

103) INT. ANIMAL TOY STORE - AFTERNOON

Morris rolls up with a cart of chewies and toys. The
CLERK's mouth drops open at the sight of all of them.

104) EXT. HOPEVILLE STREET-LATE AFTERNOON

Morris' truck moves down the street. In front of the
HopeVille Beauty Salon, Mr. Lacasta is escorting his wife
BETTY, 70s, into the salon. Morris' truck stops and backs
up.

105) INT. MORRIS' TRUCK-LATE AFTERNOON

Morris watches them enter the beauty salon. Moments later,
Mr. Lacasta exits and drives away. Morris looks at Max.

                    MORRIS
          Are you thinking what I'm
          thinking?

Max barks.

106) INT. BEAUTY SALON - AFTERNOON

Morris and the BEAUTICIAN, 20s, stand behind Betty having an animated discussion about a great hairdo for Betty. The Beautician nods in agreement. As the Beautician begins, Morris spots a dress shop across the street through the salon window.

107) INT. DRESS SHOP - AFTERNOON

Morris lays a Marilyn Monroe look-a-like dress on the counter.

108) INT. SALON - AFTERNOON

Morris and the Beautician impatiently wait at the bathroom door. Finally, the door swings open and Betty steps out. She looks like a Marilyn Monroe look-a-like (except older) with her blond hair, red lips, and white dress.

109) INT. MORRIS TRUCK-LATE AFTERNOON

Morris watches as Mr. Lacasta, like a boy in love, carries his wife in his arms from the salon as he smooches on her. He puts her in the car. The car speeds away. Morris puts his hand up for a high five from Max. Max doesn't get it. With his free hand, Morris gives him some help with the high five. Morris throws it in gear and drives away.

110) INT. SHERIFF'S CAR- LATE AFTERNOON

The Sheriff, Ben, has been watching. He doesn't know what to make of it.

111) INT. EDUCATION CENTER-LATE AFTERNOON

Morris waits at the counter. A YOUNG WOMAN returns and lays a package on the counter. It reads "GED" on the front.

> MORRIS
> So this is as good as getting a real high school diploma?

> YOUNG WOMAN
> Yes sir, it's recognized by the state.

Morris lifts the package and tucks it under his arm.

112) INT. KENNEL-LATE AFTERNOON

Morris and Alice hand out chewies and toys to the animals using the list they made up.

113) INT. ANIMAL SHELTER-LATE AFTERNOON

Morris and Alice are seated on the edge of her desk with their arms crossed. Willard moseys up to them.

                    WILLARD
        You wanted to see me 'for I went
        home?

                    MORRIS
        Yes, we did Willard. We have
        something very important to
        discuss with you.

                    WILLARD
        I'm not fired cause I seen
        something I wasn't supposed to
        see?

Morris has to think about it a second.

                    MORRIS
        No.

They slide apart revealing the GED package behind them. Willard is not sure what it is but approaches anyway.

                    MORRIS
        Go ahead.

Willard picks it up and reads the letters.

                    WILLARD
        G E D

                    ALICE
        General Education Diploma.

Willard looks at her, not sure what that means.

                    MORRIS
        It's a high school equivalency
        diploma, Willard.

                    WILLARD
        High School diploma?

                         ALICE
            Yes. You study the materials
            and then take the tests. That's
            it.

Willard turns the package over examining it.

                         WILLARD
            All that in this little package?

Morris stands.

                         MORRIS
                  (Points to Willard's head)
            The package is up here, Willard.

Morris puts his hand on the package.

                         MORRIS
            That's just the paperwork
            to prove it.

                         WILLARD
            How do you know I can do
            it?

                         MORRIS
            Because I know that you want
            it.

Willard nods.

                         WILLARD
            I do.

Willard turns and starts to leave. He turns.

                         WILLARD
            Thank you. Even if the aliens
            are involved, I still thank you.

He leaves. Morris and Alice look at each other.

                         ALICE
            Aliens?

114) INT. MORRIS' APARTMENT-BEDROOM - NIGHT

Morris is asleep, when he rolls over to find himself inches
from Jenny's dog, Butch's dream. Butch is humping a fire
hydrant and making god-awful slobbering noise.

Realizing the importance of getting away from THIS dream,
Morris immediately lunges backwards and lands on the floor

with a loud THUD. Trying to maintain his distance from the dream cloud, he crawls across the floor and pulls his robe from the chair. Dragging it, he makes his way out of the room.

115) EXT. MORRIS BALCONY - NIGHT

Morris sips on a cup of tea. There's a slight KNOCKING at his door. He enters from the balcony and answers it. It's Jenny in her robe. She looks half-asleep.

>   JENNY
>   Are you okay? I heard this loud
>   noise and-
>
>   MORRIS
>   Everything is fine. I'm sorry
>   I woke you.
>
>   JENNY
>   What are you drinking?
>
>   MORRIS
>   Tea. Want some?
>
>   JENNY
>   Sure.

She enters.

116) EXT. MORRIS BALCONY - NIGHT

As Jenny and Morris sip their tea, Morris is busy studying the dreams that hover above the sleeping citizens' homes. He takes out a black notebook and takes notes then puts it away.

>   JENNY
>   Something's happening to you
>   Morris.
>
>   MORRIS
>   It is?
>
>   JENNY
>   I mean a good something.
>
>   MORRIS
>   Oh. Thanks.

Morris puts his cup down and turns to her.

                    MORRIS
          Do you believe in dreams?

Jenny searches for an answer, then.

                    JENNY
          I don't think I have dreams.
          I mean, I don't remember them.
          I don't know why. I suppose
          we just lower our expectations
          and finally get to the point
          where there are none anymore. If
          you don't expect, you won't be
          let down.

                    MORRIS
          Wow. I guess that's safe. But
          isn't it lonely?

                    JENNY
          Sometimes. But you can always
          count on men like Ben, who has
          more hands than an octopus to
          keep things lively.

                    MORRIS
          Ever since I was a boy, I had
          these expectations of myself
          that were really so out there..
          that they couldn't even happen
          ..in the real world, anyway. I
          wanted to be like my Dad so bad
          that I created this world in my
          head where I could. It was real
          to me.

                    JENNY
          What happened?

Morris turns and looks off in the distance.

                    MORRIS
          Nothing. Nothing at all.

Jenny looks down.

                    MORRIS
          But, in my mind, everything
          could happen..and everything
          did..until.

                    JENNY
          Until what?

> MORRIS
> I'm not sure. But now it's
> gone.

> JENNY
> I'm sorry.

> MORRIS
> Oh, no. It's okay. Because
> now I see that there's a lot
> of dreams out there besides
> mine. Hopeville is still a
> town of hopes and dreams.
> They're just not being realized,
> that's all.

He shifts and leans against the railing.

> MORRIS
> Am I crazy or insane?

> JENNY
> No. I think it's wonderful.

Morris slides towards her.

> MORRIS
> You do?

> JENNY
> I think that it's great that
> you would spend the time
> to talk with people about their
> dreams and-

Morris moves closer.

> MORRIS
> Oh no. I can see them as
> clear as day. That's what I was
> trying to tell you the other
> day. I really see them.

Now he's starting to scare her.

> JENNY
> Oh. You can really see them?

Morris stands and points.

> MORRIS
> (Excited)
> Yeah, old Mr. Lacasta the
> music teacher always dreams
> of Marilyn Monroe.

                    JENNY
                (Unbelieving)
            He does?

                    MORRIS Continuing
            ..and my Mother dreams of these
            Barry Mantilow strippers..
            and the pets in the kennel dream
            of home and chewies and -

Jenny puts her cup of tea down. She's becoming frightened.

                    MORRIS
            and- what's wrong?

Jenny pulls her robe tight.

                    JENNY
            I really should be going.
            It's late and I have to open
            at five. Goodnight, Morris.

                    MORRIS
            You're afraid.

                    JENNY
            Afraid? Afraid of what?

                    MORRIS
            Afraid to hope...to dream.

                    JENNY
            What's the point? I'm a waitress
            with bills. I hope for tips.

                    MORRIS
            That's sad.

                    JENNY
            I'm sad? You just moved out your
            parent's house and chase dogs and
            cats for a living. Goodnight.

She exits. Morris is deflated. He leans forward on the balcony and looks out. Max plops down beside his leg.

EXT. MORRIS' APARTMENT - NIGHT

Jenny slams the door to Morris' apartment and leans back against it, regretting her remarks. Pulling her robe together, she steps away into the night.

INT. MORRIS' BEDROOM - NIGHT

Morris enters. The dream cloud is still next to his bed of Butch the Bulldog humping the hydrant. Morris sneaks close and whips the covers off of the bed. He looks down at Max.

                    MORRIS
           That dog has taken humping to
           a new level.

He turns and leaves.

117) INT. HOPEVILLE CAFÉ - MORNING

The café is bustling. Jenny is trying to keep up with the crowd as she passes the seat where Morris sits every day. It's empty. She looks back at the clock. It shows 8:35. She takes a breath and moves on with her business.

118) INT. ANIMAL SHELTER-KENNEL - MORNING

The door slowly creaks open. Alice and Morris slide their heads around the edge of the door.

                    ALICE
                  (Whispers)
           How's it look?

Morris nods his approval, until he spots the one remaining dream of the dog humping the squirrel. Morris slides a stuff squirrel from behind his back and shows Alice. She gives him the thumbs up.

119) INT. ANIMAL SHELTER-LATE MORNING

Alice goes over her pickup list and hands it to Morris.

120) INT. MORRIS' TRUCK - MORNING

As Morris drives out of town, he notices that Ben is putting up a re-election poster on a telephone pole.

121) CLOSEUP: On poster to re-elect Ben for Sheriff. Morris' truck passes in the background.

SERIES OF SCENES:

1) Morris rounds up some stray cats.
2) Morris chases a stray dog.

122) INT. MORRIS' TRUCK - AFTERNOON

As Morris drives towards town with the strays, he passes a bookstore. He turns around the truck and parks in the bookstore parking lot. Pulling out his black book of dreams he scans it with his finger, stopping on one.

                     MORRIS
                  (To Max)
          Mr. Henderson's wife is dreaming
          of a new kitchen. Think they might
          have some remodeling books?

Max barks.

                     MORRIS
          While I'm in there I'll see if
          they have anything for Ms Jansen
          who's dreaming of writing the
          great romantic novel.

Max barks again.

123) EXT. STREET - LATE AFTERNOON

Morris' truck pulls up to a mailbox with the name "Hendersons" on it. He leans out the window and shoves the book into the mailbox.

124) INT. APARTMENT BUILDING - LATE AFTERNOON

Morris examines a book titled "Writing the Great American Novel" then puts it into a mailbox with the name "Jansen" on it.

125) EXT. MAIN STREET - LATE AFTERNOON

Morris and Max approach Mrs. Avery's Antique Shop. Morris takes a book from under his arm. It's titled, "Selling Antiques on the Internet"

                     MORRIS
                  (To Max)
          You know Max, antiques are a
          hot commodity on the Web.

Max barks as he puts the book into her business mailbox.

                     MORRIS
          I think Mrs. Avery will be a
          lot happier when her sales
          pick up.

126) INT. MORRIS' TRUCK - LATE AFTERNOON

Morris crosses out more names. He taps the pen on Dick Randal's name. He ponders Dick's dream.

                    MORRIS
                   (To Max)
          Dick's always dreams of being
          a fireman. Instead, he works in
          a shoe store. Big difference.

Max barks. Morris looks up at the fire station through the window.

                    MORRIS
          You think being a volunteer
          fireman would make him happy?

Max barks twice.

                    MORRIS
          Me too.

Morris climbs out.

127) INT. FIRE HOUSE - LATE AFTERNOON

A FIRE CHIEF nods in agreement and hands some forms to Morris. Morris shakes his hand and leaves.

128) INT. SHOE STORE - LATE AFTERNOON

While DICK, 30s, is fitting a shoe on a customer, Morris writes a note to him on the counter.

CLOSEUP: on note:

Dear Dick,

The firehouse is glad to have volunteers. Fill out this form and you're on your way. Good luck.

Morris slides the forms under the note and walks out.

129) EXT. SHOE STORE - LATE AFTERNOON

Morris stops on the sidewalk, takes out his black notebook, and crosses Dick's name off. Climbing into his truck, he drives away.

130) MEANWHILE: Just down the street, Ben is writing out a ticket and putting it on a car as he watches Morris with interest.

131) EXT. AL'S FANCY LADIES STRIP CLUB - LATE AFTERNOON

Morris stares at a small sign in the window "Part Time Help Needed- Free Costumes"

>   MORRIS
> I wish I could take you
> in with me boy.

Max lays his head down and whimpers.

>   MORRIS
> You're not going to miss much,
> just voluptuous big breasted
> woman in very tiny revealing-

Morris quickly opens the door.

>   MORRIS
> Be right back.

Max jumps up and barks.

132) INT. AL'S FANCY LADIES STRIP CLUB - LATE AFTERNOON

Morris talks with the MANAGER while surrounded by several beautiful DANCERS. He gyrates and does several pelvic thrusts. The Manager nods his approval and writes down info on a piece of paper.

133) INT. HOPEVILLE CAFÉ - MORNING

Jenny serves the customers at the counter. As she pours Ben a refill, she spots Morris' truck drive by and over fills his cup.

>   JENNY
> Sorry.

She cleans up the mess as Ben turns to see what caught her eye.

                    BEN
          If I were you, I'd stay away
          from Morris. There's something
          really wrong with him. I saw
          him the other night just
          walking the streets, pointing
          up in the air, writing in that
          book of his, and talking with
          that mutt like it was a person.
          I tell you he's getting ready
          to go to pieces.. and when he
          does, I'm gonna be there to pick
          'em up.

She turns and goes back to work.

                    BEN
          What's wrong with you? You don't
          like him?

                    JENNY (O.S.)
          Butch makes noise all night. I
          just need a good night's sleep.

Ben takes a sip of coffee.

                    BEN
          Oh...Who's Butch?

134) INT. ANIMAL SHELTER - DAY

Morris helps Alice bathe the animals. Willard is at Alice's
desk working on his GED homework. The phone RINGS. He
answers it and waves her to the phone. Morris continues to
bathe a long-haired dog as he watches her response to the
call. She jumps and down with joy at the offer of an
audition to dance. As she returns, she scoops up a handful
of soap and douses Morris with it.

                    ALICE
          You set that up, didn't you?

                    MORRIS
          I don't know what you're talking
          about.

Morris scoops up a handful and returns the favor. It hits
her in the face.

                    MORRIS
          You're going to try it, right?

                    ALICE
              (Wiping away suds)
          I'll audition. They may not like
          my dancing.

She does a little hip movement.

                    MORRIS
          They'll love it.

Willard looks up at them and smiles.

135) EXT. HOUSE - AFTERNOON

Morris crawls under a porch and comes out with a cat. He hands the cat up to the awaiting owner, a large MAN. He cuddles the cat and smiles.

136) INT. JOHN'S HAIR CLINIC - DAY

A man, JOHN, 30s, with a bad toupee shows Morris hair options with several brochures.

137) EXT. JOHN'S HAIR CLINIC - DAY

Morris exits John's Hair Clinic and climbs into his truck.

138) INT. MORRIS' TRUCK - DAY

Morris takes out his black book and opens it.

139) CLOSEUP: On list of names, most crossed out. He scans down to Mr. Crimshaw. Next to Mr. Crimshaw's name are the words "Dreams of hair." He draws a line through it.

140) INT. POLICE CAR - SAMETIME

POV - Through binoculars of Morris drawing line through name. Ben lowers the binoculars as he watches Morris' truck pull away. Ben starts the car and follows.

141) INT. MUSIC STORE - DAY

Morris studies a Music CD in his hand titled *"Barry Mantilow's Greatest Hits"*

142) INT. MEN'S STORE - DAY

Morris holds up a pair of men's leopard briefs.

143) EXT. STREET - DAY

Morris' truck pulls up next to Mr. Crimshaw's mailbox. Morris leans out and puts the literature into the mailbox.

144) INT. POLICE CAR - SAMETIME

POV - Through binoculars of Morris pulling away from the mailbox. Ben lowers the binoculars as he watches Morris' truck pull into his Father's driveway.

145) INT. HILL'S GARAGE - DAY

Morris enters with a small package under his arm. His Father is under the car changing the oil. His legs protrude out from under the car.

>MORRIS
>Where's Mom?

>FATHER (O.S.)
>Shopping.
>>(Realizes it's Morris)
>Oh, is that you Morris?

Suddenly he slides out on the coaster, his hands and face oily. He struggles to get to his feet. Morris helps to pull him up. Walter wipes his hands and then leans over the engine.

>FATHER
>So how are things going, Mr. Bachelor?

Morris leans over to see what he's doing.

>MORRIS
>Dad, did you ever daydream?

>FATHER
>Are you kidding? I was the king.

>MORRIS
>You were? What kind did you have?

Walter straightens up.

                    FATHER
          Oh boy, I was Flash Gordon and
          Buck Rogers zooming through the
          universe. Saving gorgeous damsels
          in distress, of course.

                    MORRIS
          Of course.

Walter begins to stroll the garage, his imagination taking
over. Morris follows, intrigued.

                    FATHER
          I was John Wayne with my six guns
          blazing.

Walter pretends to draw his guns on Morris.

                    FATHER
          Blam, Blam, Blam!

Morris pretends to be shot and staggers against the car.

                    MORRIS
          You dirty coward, I thought
          we were partners..ooohhhh

                    FATHER
              (Blows smoke from barrel)
          Now you're partners with the grave.

Morris stands having gotten over his own death.

                    MORRIS
          And what else?

Walter begins a smooth dance.

                    FATHER
          I was Fred Astair dancing with
          the lovely ladies all night. They
          couldn't get enough of my fancy
          dancing.

Morris steps up.

                    MORRIS
          May I have this dance Mr. Astair?

Walter takes the lead.

                    FATHER
          Be my pleasure Miss Rogers.

As they dance around the garage, Walter twirls Morris away. Morris curtseys and Walter bows. Walter then rejoins the real world and grabs several quarts of oil from the shelf.

                    MORRIS
          What about being a policeman?
          Was that one of your dreams?

Walter opens a quart and pours it in the engine.

                    FATHER
          That was the one that got me.
          That's why I did it for thirty
          years.

                    MORRIS
          So I got it from you?

                    FATHER
          I guess so.

                    MORRIS
          Do you still daydream?

                    FATHER
          Right now, I'm getting my
          car ready for the NASCAR 500.

                    MORRIS
          I love you, dad.

Walter stops, wipes his hands and hugs Morris.

                    FATHER
          I love you too.

Morris hands him the present.

                    MORRIS
          I got you something.

Walter takes it and looks at it.

                    FATHER
          It's not my birthday. What is
          it?

                    MORRIS
          It's really for you and Mom.

                    FATHER
          Oh, thanks.

Morris turns to leave.

MORRIS
I'll see you later.

FATHER
Morris?

Morris turns back around.

MORRIS
Yeah?

FATHER
I'm happy. Maybe I wasn't an
astronaut or a big star like
Fred Astair, but I have you and
your Mother. That makes me happy.
Only you know what your dream is.
Go be happy. Do what you have to
do.

MORRIS
Thanks, Dad.

Morris exits the garage. Walter goes back to work.

146) GARAGE - DAY

Morris peeks in the window of the garage. Above his Father
is a dream cloud. Walter is in the pit stop of a racetrack.
Racecars ROAR by as he works quickly on a racecar. Morris
smiles and departs.

147) PET SUPPLY STORE - DAY

Morris loads up a cart with half a dozen large bags of dog
and cat food. As he's pushing the cart towards the counter,
he passes the pet toy aisle. Slowly he backs up. A foot-
high yellow toy hydrant comes into view.

148) EXT. PET SHOP - DAY

As Morris exits the pet shop, he gets stuck behind two OLD
WOMEN, 80s, who are moving very slow and jabbering. They're
both reading the re-election poster of Ben's.

OLD WOMAN # 1
Why does he put those up?

OLD WOMAN # 2
Yeah, it isn't like there's
anybody running against him.

                    OLD WOMAN # 1
               Right man for the job. Hah.

As they move on, Morris finds himself staring at the poster.
The poster boasts "The Right man for the job." The smile
disappears. Morris takes out his pen and draws buggers
hanging from his nose and blacks out several of his teeth. A
CUSTOMER enters and Morris quickly departs the scene.

149) INT. HILL HOUSE-KITCHEN

Walter is sitting at the kitchen table. The Barry Mantilow
CD sits on the table in front of him. He holds up the skimpy
leopard underwear and examines them. His wife, Ann enters
the kitchen from a trip to the store. She places two bags
of groceries on the counter and puts her purse down.
Turning to go for more groceries, she steps from the
kitchen.

                    ANN (O.S.)
               Dear, could you help me
               with the rest of the-

Okay, it just hit her that her husband is holding up a pair
of leopard underwear. She slowly backs into the room, her
eyes now locked on the underwear he's holding. Walter looks
at her odd.

                    WALTER
               Now isn't that strange? Morris
               came by and gave these to me.

Walter then picks up the CD and shows it to her.

                    WALTER
                 (Puzzled)
               And a Barry somebody CD.

As he looks at his wife, there's this strange animal lust
look coming over her face. She throws off her coat, grabs
the CD and Walter by his arm. She pulls him straight up from
the chair.

                    ANN
               Screw the groceries!

150) INT. ANIMAL SHELTER - AFTERNOON

Morris unloads the pet food and is storing it away when
Alice approaches him.

                    ALICE
          I've got good news and I've got
          bad news.

Morris stacks the food.

                    MORRIS
          Good news first.

                    ALICE
          I got homes for three of the
          dogs on a farm from the website.

Still working.

                    MORRIS
          That's great..and the bad news?

                    ALICE
          It's a ten-hour drive from here.

Morris stands and stretches.

                    MORRIS
          That's fine.

Alice is perplexed.

                    ALICE
          You complain when it's a half
          hour drive. What gives?

Morris removes his gloves.

                    MORRIS
          I'm gonna run for Sheriff.

Alice is in shock.

                    ALICE
          What?

                    MORRIS
          I'm gonna run for-

                    ALICE
          I heard that part. Why?

                    MORRIS
          If you can go after your dream,
          why can't I?

She slides over and puts her arm around his shoulder.

ALICE
Do you know how long we've been waiting for you to say that?

MORRIS
About as long as I've been wanting to say it.

ALICE
And since we're sharing good news, I took off an hour this morning and went over for an audition.

She beams a smile.

MORRIS
Well?

ALICE
I blew them away!

Morris embraces her and twirls with her.

MORRIS
I knew you could do it.

She kisses him on the cheek.

ALICE
Thanks.

MORRIS
I've got to go. I have to stop by City Hall before I leave town. There is money in the budget for a motel room?

Alice squeezes her two fingers together.

ALICE
A little bit.

MORRIS
Great, roach motel, here I come.

151) EXT. ANIMAL SHELTER - AFTERNOON

Morris loads the three dogs into cages and climbs into the truck.

152) INT. MORRIS' TRUCK - AFTERNOON

Morris climbs in and sees the fire hydrant. He smiles and starts the truck.

153) EXT. JENNY'S APARTMENT - AFTERNOON

Morris places the hydrant in front of the door. The note attached reads "To Butch from Moe"

154) INT. HOPEVILLE-CAFÉ - AFTERNOON

Jenny serves a table. At the table are seated Mr. Lacasta and his now blond wife, Betty. They're jovial and romantic. There's a couple of suitcases next to the table.

      JENNY
   Going on a trip, Mr. Lacasta?

      MR. LACASTA
   A weekend getaway. (He winks)

      JENNY
   Okaaaaaay.

She turns to bump into Mrs. Avery.

      MRS. AVERY
   Oh, my. Excuse me, dear.

Jenny starts to step around her.

      MRS. AVERY
   Dear, could you do me a
   favor?

Jenny turns. Mrs. Avery is holding out a stack of fliers for her Web site.

      MRS. AVERY
   Could I leave some of these here?
   They're fliers for my new antique
   web site.

Jenny takes them.

      JENNY
   Sure. I guess.

Mrs. Avery casually puts her hand on Jenny's forearm.

                    MRS. AVERY
              Ain't technology great!
              Thank you, dear.

She waddles away, cordially greeting other patrons as she
leaves. Jenny looks around and suddenly realizes that
everyone is smiling and laughing and being ever so nice to
each other. Something is off. As she makes her way back to
the counter, she feels her head to see if she has a fever.
The cook, Deloris, approaches and stands next to her,
spatula in her hand.

                    DELORIS
              It ain't you, honey. I see it
              too. Very strange.

Deloris goes back to work, as Jenny tries to make sense of
it. She opens a beer for Ben and places it in front of him.
Willard, the janitor, is seated a couple of seats down and
is reading a book and taking notes.

In another seat, eating lunch is Mr. Henderson and his Wife.
Mr. Henderson is dressed in painting clothes and they are in
a very enjoyable discussion about how they are going to
remodel the kitchen.

                    JENNY
                 (To Ben)
              What's going on?

Ben, naturally, is oblivious to the people.

                    BEN
                 (While eating)
              Maybe it's a virus. Who knows?

                    JENNY
              They're not sick. They're
              alive.

155) INT. CITY HALL - LATE AFTERNOON

Morris enters the lobby, which is currently being remodeled,
and checks the room listing on the wall for city offices. An
old man, RUPUS, 70s, dressed in white coveralls and speckled
with paint, is removing a series of portraits from the wall
and placing them into a box. The last one that Rupus takes
down is of Morris' father, Walter, as Sheriff.

Morris walks to the box and looks down. He lifts his
Father's portrait out of the box. Rupus sees him at the box
and approaches.

The Marathon Method

                    RUPUS
            Can I help you, son?

                    MORRIS
            This is my Father.

Rupus moves around to get a better look at him.

                    RUPUS
            So you're Morris? You
            probably don't remember me.

Rupus offers his hand likes it's an honor. Morris looks up at him and studies his wrinkled face.

                    MORRIS
            I don't think so.

                    RUPUS
            Rupus Smith. Folks call me
            Smitty. I knew your Father,
            Walter, when he were Sheriff.
            I knew your Grandfather too,
            Moe. I was a little bit of
            a troublemaker back then.

                    MORRIS
            I see.

Morris puts the portrait back and lifts another. It's his Grandfather "Moe Hill", also a previous Sheriff. Another portrait is of his Great Grandfather "Morris Hill".

                    RUPUS
            It's a real honor, Mr. Hill.
            And I mean that with all my
            heart. Your father was a good
            man. He put me up many a cold
            night when I had no place to
            go.

Morris gently puts the portrait back and wipes the dust from his hands.

                    RUPUS
            I quit drinking and carrying
            on years ago. Even got back
            with my family. My wife
            passed a few years back, but
            I've got some great boys.

Rupus takes out his wallet and shows a picture of him and his two SONS.

MORRIS
They look nice. I'm glad
things worked out for you.

Rupus puts his wallet away. He notices that Morris is still focused on the portraits.

RUPUS
The Sheriff's idea. Said he's
gonna change things around here.
I just cleanup 'round here and
take orders.

MORRIS
So these aren't going back up?

RUPUS
Said to put them into storage. We're
starting a new era, is what he
said.

Morris turns and walks away.

MORRIS (O.S.)
We'll see about that.

A big grin comes over Rupus' face. He quickly follows Morris.

INT. CITY CLERK'S OFFICE - LATE AFTERNOON

Morris waits patiently as the Clerk, DIANA, 30s, finishes some filing work. She then turns her attention to Morris.

DIANA
How may I help you, sir?

Rupus sneaks up to see what's going on. Diana looks at him, wondering what he's doing. Rupus looks around as if he's looking for something.

MORRIS
I'd like to officially run
for office.

DIANA
I see. What office, sir?

MORRIS
Sheriff.

Several of the other OFFICE WORKERS all perk up and look. Rupus smiles a big smile. Diana is a little shook by it. She obviously hasn't had a request like this for a while.

She searches though her paperwork and finally finds the forms. She takes out a pen.

                DIANA
          Your name?

                MORRIS
          Morris Hill. No, make that
          Morris Moe Hill.

She stares at him, her mouth parted.

                MORRIS
          Something wrong?

She snaps away from her stupor and begins writing.

                DIANA
          No.

Diana looks back over her shoulder at the other Girls. They all smile. She smiles and turns back to finish the form.

TRANSITION TO:

Diana finishes the form and turns it around for his signature. Morris signs.

                MORRIS
          Is that it?

                DIANA
          Yeah. We'll just attach the
          signatures when you bring them
          in. But we'll need them by close
          of business Monday since the
          election is Tuesday. You're
          cutting it short by-

                MORRIS
          What signatures?

                DIANA
          The two hundred you need to
          get on the ballot. I thought
          you knew.

                MORRIS
          I need two hundred signatures?

                DIANA
          Yes. Why?

                    MORRIS
          Because, I don't have them.

                    DIANA
          Oh. I'm sorry. Maybe you can-

                    MORRIS
          I'm going out of town. Besides
          I couldn't get that many signatures
          by Monday.

Diana puts the form under the counter.

                    DIANA
          Maybe next election?

                    MORRIS
          Yeah. Thanks anyway.

Morris turns and almost bumps into Rupus. He tries to smile.

                    RUPUS
          Tell your pops that I said
          hello.

Morris offers his hand to Rupus. They shake.

                    MORRIS
          I will. Take care Rup- Smitty.

Morris exits. Rupus scratches his unshaven face then looks at Diana. He approaches the counter.

156) EXT. CITY HALL - LATE AFTERNOON

Morris walks out onto the steps and looks out. A dream, a destiny, an era, has just slipped away. It was too little too late. He walks to the truck, climbs in and drives away. Max climbs up into his lap.

157) INT. MORRIS' TRUCK - LATE AFTERNOON

A very somber and depressed Morris drives down the highway. Max is lying in the passenger seat.

158) EXT. HILL'S HOUSE - LATE AFTERNOON

Rupus steps to the door and rings the doorbell. He waits and waits. Then he moves his head closer to the door. He can hear faint "Barry Mantilow" music.

                    ANN (O.S.)
                  (Faint)
               Shake that booty baby!

He draws his head back.

                    RUPUS
               Booty?

He turns and starts to leave, then realizing the importance
of his mission, he turns back around and pushes the doorbell
with determination. Then the door swings open. Walter is
wearing a robe. Some of his leopard underwear is showing.
Rupus stares at it. Walter quickly covers it then recognizes
him.

                    WALTER
               Smitty!? What are you doing
               here?

                    RUPUS
               Could I could in? I need
               to talk to you about your son.

                    WALTER
               Come in.

The door closes.

159) EXT. HOPEVILLE CAFÉ - EVENING

Jenny locks up the café and heads home.

160) EXT. JENNY'S APARTMENT - EVENING

Jenny steps up and looks down at the fire hydrant. She
reaches down and picks it up.

She reads the note as she opens the door. Butch rushes to
greet her.

                    JENNY
               Hey, boy. Someone left you
               a present.

She closes the door.

161) EXT. MORRIS' APARTMENT - EVENING

Jenny knocks on his door.

                    JENNY
          Morris?

She waits and listens, then walks away.

162) EXT. CHEAP MOTEL - NIGHT

As the Sun sets, Morris climbs wearily from the truck. Max
follows as he walks towards the desolate motel in the
disappearing sunlight.

163) INT. JENNY'S APARTMENT - NIGHT

Jenny lays in bed, motionless, staring at the ceiling. A
love for Morris is growing to the point of bursting out.
She rolls over and looks down at Butch. He's cuddling the
toy hydrant like a lover. Throwing back the covers, she
springs to her feet, grabs her robe and rushes out.

164) INT. ALICE'S APARTMENT - LATE NIGHT

Alice covers her head to hide from whoever is POUNDING on
her door. From underneath the covers, she bellows.

                    ALICE
          Go away. I don't do pets at home.

                    JENNY (O.S.)
          It's about Morris.

That registers with her. Slowly, she comes around and slumps
up to a stand, her eyes still closed.

                    ALICE
          Coming..

165) EXT. ALICE APARTMENT - LATE NIGHT

The door swings open to reveal the half-asleep Alice.

                    ALICE
          This better be good.

                    JENNY
          I think I love him.

                    ALICE
          That'll do. Come in.

Alice tries to focus on her as she passes by. She slams the door closed.

166) EXT. MOTEL - LATE NIGHT

Morris and Max walk out on a deserted landscape with a few straggling trees. The stars and moon are bright and near. Morris stops and looks up at the full, large moon.

> MORRIS
> You know what sucks, Max? I can't even dream of her.

Morris takes a few steps but notices that Max isn't following. Max has decided to take a break and is lying on the ground. Morris walks back to join him and sits. A small dream cloud appears over Max. It's Jenny and she's bending down and petting Max.

> MORRIS
> Thanks, Max.

Morris props his elbow on his knee and rests his chin on his fist. The dream plays like a personal movie, magically glowing, lighting the night sky and Morris' smiling face.

167) INT. JENNY'S APARTMENT - NIGHT

Jenny lies on her side, watching Butch cuddle the hydrant. She rolls over on her back and stares at the ceiling.

168) EXT. MOTEL - LATE NIGHT

Morris lies on his side watching the dream of Jenny play over Max.

169) EXT. COUNTY JAIL-NOT FAR AWAY - DAY

Two inmates, LARRY (the leader) and ALBERT (the dummy), both in their late thirties and wearing jumpsuits, are on a work detail, unloading a truck at the back of the jail. As the Guard, BILL, 40s, turns his attention to a car that speeds by, Larry and Albert overpower him, knocking him out. Larry, the leader, takes his gun. They make their break over a six-foot wire fence. As the other Guard, KEVIN, 30s, runs over to help Bill up, he looks up to see that the cons are gone.

> BILL
> Damn it. They got my gun!

170) EXT. FARM - DAY

We watch from a distance as Morris unloads several dogs at a farm. The dogs take off playing and running (finally free- and home) The FARMER shakes Morris' hand. Morris climbs into the truck and drives away. A cloud of dust spits up as the Farmer runs to join the dogs.

171) EXT. MOTEL - DAY

Morris has the hood of the truck open. Max is sitting nearby, watching. Morris bends down and looks under the truck. There's a pool of antifreeze under the truck. Morris stands, puts his hands up on the hood, and stares at the motor.

172) INT. HOPEVILLE ANIMAL SHELTER - DAY

The phone rings and rings and rings until.

                 MORRIS (V.O.)
     Alice. You must not be into
     work yet. I'm stuck at the
     motel. The truck is broke
     down. I think it's the
     water pump. The Motel manager
     said the nearest garage is
     an hour or so from here. He's
     not sure when they open. I'll
     call when I know more. Bye.

173) EXT. GAS STATION-LATE SATURDAY AFTERNOON

In a one-horse town with a single small and rundown gas station, a dirty mechanic, HOWIE, has the hood of Morris' truck open and is examining the water pump. The tow truck is parked nearby, the DRIVER waiting. Morris and Max look on.

                 HOWIE
     Yep, it's your water pump.

Howie closes the hood.

                 MORRIS
     Can you fix it?

                 HOWIE
     Sure. I can have it for you
     tomorrow mornin'

                    MORRIS
          No chance of getting it today?

Howie looks back at his full garage.

                    HOWIE
          Got a full garage today. Sorry.

                    MORRIS
          Tomorrow's fine. Thanks.

Morris climbs into the tow truck. It drives away.

174) INT. HOPEVILLE ANIMAL SHELTER - LATE SATURDAY AFTERNOON

Alice finishes feeding the dogs and leaves. As the door closes, the phone rings, and rings, and rings.

                    MORRIS (V.O.)
          Alice. I'm stuck here until
          tomorrow. Sorry. I'll be back
          early Monday morning. Take care.

175) EXT. HIGHWAY-LATE SATURDAY AFTERNOON

Larry and Albert emerge from the brush and step up onto the highway. A sign along the highway reads "Hopeville 80 Miles." Albert steps to the edge and puts out his thumb. Larry steps up to him and looks down the highway then looks the other way.

                    LARRY
          What are you doing?

                    ALBERT
          I'm getting us a ride.

Larry can't believe his ears. He grabs Albert's shirt and pulls it out for him to see.

                    LARRY
          You think this might be
          a dead giveaway that..
               (Raises voice)
          WE'RE ESCAPES CONVICTS!

Albert looks down at the shirt.

                    ALBERT
          Oh.

Larry pulls him by his shirt.

                         LARRY
               Come on. There's gotta be a
               car on one of these farms.

176) EXT. GARAGE - LATE AFTERNOON SUNDAY

Morris shakes Howie's hand, climbs into his truck, starts it and takes off. Howie waves as he drives away.

177) EXT. HIGHWAY - NIGHT

Morris' truck drives down the dark highway towards home.

178) INT. FARMHOUSE KITCHEN - LATE SUNDAY NIGHT

Larry finishes tying and gagging a FARMER into his kitchen chair while Albert holds the gun. Larry goes through the Farmer's wallet and takes out a few bills, then tosses it over his shoulder. Then he turns and grabs the car keys from a hook on the wall and exits.

179) EXT. FARMHOUSE - LATE SUNDAY NIGHT

Larry steps out of the front door with the keys. Larry doesn't realize that Albert is not with him.

                         LARRY
                  Okay, give me the-

Larry stops and looks around. Furious, he stomps back into the house.

180) INT. FARMHOUSE KITCHEN - LATE SUNDAY NIGHT

CLOSEUP: on Albert as he looks through the food in the refrigerator.

                       LARRY (O.S.)
                     (Nonchalantly)
                See anything you like?

                         ALBERT
                     (Nonchalantly)
                Yeah, the meatloaf looks tasty-

Suddenly, Albert is jerked out of the refrigerator and the door slammed. Larry pulls Albert close to his face.

                    LARRY
          Do you understand that we're on
          the lamb?

                    ALBERT
          The lamb? I don't get it.

                    LARRY
               (Raises voice)
          ON THE RUN! ON THE RUN!
               (Normal)
          When you're on the run, you're
          on the Lamb. And you don't
          hang out with the hostage
          or in their refrigerator. It's
          how you get caught.

Larry releases him.

                    LARRY
          Now give me the gun and let's go.

Albert puts the gun behind his back.

                    ALBERT
          I want a gun too.

                    LARRY
          We only have one. So give it
          to me.

                    ALBERT
          Why do you get the gun?

Larry tries to reach behind him to get it, but Albert moves away. Finally having had enough, Larry grabs Albert by his collar and throws him against the wall. He then takes the gun away.

                    ALBERT
          What am I suppose to use?

Larry heads for the door.

                    LARRY
          I don't know. Find something
          'cause I'm leaving, with or
          without you.

As Larry exits, Albert panics and searches the kitchen drawers for a weapon.   Finally, out of time, he grabs a small knife and runs out.

181) EXT. FARMHOUSE-LATE SUNDAY NIGHT

Larry climbs into the Farmer's old truck and starts it. Albert runs out of the house and jumps into the truck just as it takes off.

>   ALBERT (O.S.)
>   Where we going now, Larry?

>   LARRY (O.S.)
>   To find some cash. One of these
>   hick towns has got to have a
>   bank.

182) EXT. HIGHWAY - NIGHT

As Morris drives, the two Indians, John John and his Grandfather appear out of nowhere. John John has his thumb out. Morris pulls over and stops. As before, they somehow appear next to the truck. John John opens the passenger door and sticks his head in.

>   JOHN JOHN
>   Hello again. We're going home.

>   MORRIS
>   Climb in. I can take you as
>   as far as the Hopeville exit.

John John holds the door open as his Grandfather, Jack climbs in. John John follows.

183) INT. MORRIS TRUCK - NIGHT

Morris drives as John John and his Grandfather are having a quite conversation.

>   MORRIS
>   How was your sister's wedding?

>   JOHN JOHN
>   We stayed at her house
>   a while. Grandfather had too
>   much spirits at the wedding party.
>   He was not well for a while. He
>   is better now.

>   MORRIS
>   That's good.

Jack leans towards John John and whispers.

JOHN JOHN
               Grandfather says that you are
               much better now.

                    MORRIS
               Yeah. I'd like to talk to you
               about that. I'm seeing-

Grandfather whispers again.

                    JOHN JOHN
               He says that you have learned a
               lot but you are not done.

                    MORRIS
               I'm not?

Grandfather motions for his bag from his Grandson. He hands
it to him.

                    MORRIS
               What's he doing?

                    JOHN JOHN
               He's going to help you.

                    MORRIS
               To do what?

                    JOHN JOHN
               You must learn to share.

                    MORRIS
               Share what?

                    JOHN JOHN
               Dreams.

                    MORRIS
               Oh, no…

LATER:

The Truck is stopped along the dark highway. The sun is
starting to come up. The "Hopeville" turnoff sign is just
down the road. The passenger door opens. As John John
helps his Grandfather out, smoke again rolls out. Morris
COUGHS. John John closes the door and waves goodbye. The
truck pulls away.

184) INT. MORRIS' TRUCK - EARLY MORNING

Morris coughs and looks in the mirror at the two Indians. They wave as he drives away. Morris puts on his blinker and looks again. They're gone. Morris slows down and looks over his shoulder to be sure.

185) EXT. HIGHWAY-TURNOFF TO HOPEVILLE - EARLY MORNING

Morris' truck pulls over and stops. Morris climbs out and stands in the deserted highway looking both ways. They are nowhere in sight. Morris looks down and then climbs back into the truck.

186) INT. MORRIS' TRUCK - EARLY MORNING

Morris continues driving as the Sun rises. Morris passes the "Entering Hopeville" sign" and the farmer's stolen pickup, which is parked along side the road.

187) INT. FARMER'S STOLEN TRUCK - MORNING

Larry checks his gun and looks out the windshield at the small bank in town.

188) EXT. HOPEVILLE STREET - MORNING

Morris parks the van and walks down the sidewalk towards the café. He passes a storefront without noticing the new poster that is now replacing Ben's reelection poster.

CLOSEUP: On "Elect Morris Moe Hill as Sheriff" poster.

189) EXT. HOPEVILLE BANK-BACK - MORNING

As Mr. Hodges unlocks the back exterior bank door, Larry and Albert rush him and push him in.

190) INT. HOPEVILLE BANK - MORNING

Larry has the gun against Mr. Hodges backside and forces him towards the safe. Albert follows.

                      LARRY
            Get it open!

                      MR. HODGES
      I can't. It's on a timer.

                    LARRY
          What's it set for?

                    MR. HODGES
          Eight O'clock.

Larry looks up at the clock. It shows 7:55

                    LARRY
          Okay. We wait.
               (To Albert)
          Get the truck and be ready
          to split.

Albert runs out.

191) INT. HOPEVILLE CAFÉ - MORNING

Morris enters and doesn't notice that everyone is watching him and smiling. Jenny smiles as Morris sits down at the counter. Jenny quickly attends to him.

                    JENNY
          Welcome back..Moe. How was your
          trip?

Morris looks up and smiles.

                    MORRIS
          The van broke down.

                    JENNY
               (Still smiling)
          I heard.

                    MORRIS
          Jenny, there's something that-

Suddenly Ben stands and steps to the center of the café. He adjusts his gun belt (tough guy).

                    BEN
          Okay, everybody listen up.

Everybody stops talking and looks. Morris turns in his chair.

                    BEN Continues
          I know what you've all been
          up to this weekend. I'm very
          disappointed in all of you.

Ben steps over to Morris.

                    BEN
          And you don't have a chance of
          beating me for Sheriff. You'll
          find that out.

Puzzled, Morris looks around at everyone then Jenny. She
smiles. He turns to Ben.

                    MORRIS
          I don't know what you're talking
          about. I'm not running against
          you.

                    BEN
          Oh, no?

Ben walks out the front door and to a nearby pole. He takes
down a poster and walks back in. He steps to Morris and
hands it to him.

CLOSEUP: Of Morris holding a poster with "Elect Morris Moe
Hill as Hopeville Sheriff." The picture has Morris with the
little curly "Q" in his hair.

                    BEN
          Then explain that?

                    MORRIS
          Oh God, not that picture. Tell
          me you didn't use that one?

Jenny smiles.

                    JENNY
          Sorry. It's the only one your Mother
          had and -

Alarmed, a PATRON stands and points at the clock:

                    PATRON
          Hey it's eight O'clock! What
          happened to the bank alarm?

Everyone starts talking and agreeing that something is
wrong. As they turn to look at the bank, the stolen
farmer's truck slowly pulls up and parks in front of the
bank. Ben steps up to the window.

                    BEN
          What the-?

Just then, Larry rushes out of the bank and rushes for the
awaiting truck. Immediately Ben draws his gun and heads out
the door.

192) EXT. MAIN STREET - DAY

Larry steps up to the door of the truck as Ben runs towards them with his gun raised. Larry takes aim and fires. Ben is struck and tumbles to the ground. The truck starts pulling away as Ben struggles to get to his feet. As the truck passes, Ben leaps forward and hangs onto the door of the truck bed door. He's dragged as the truck keeps moving.

193) INT. HOPEVILLE CAFÉ - DAY

Morris instinctively runs out the door. Everyone GASPS.

194) EXT. MAIN STREET - DAY

Morris lunges up into the air as the truck passes the café and lands on its hood. Albert wildly drives, trying to throw off the unwanted passengers. Morris and Ben hang on for dear life.

AT THE CAFÉ: Everyone rushes outside.

195) INT. FARMER'S TRUCK - DAY

Albert wildly drives as Morris is flung back and forth.

                LARRY
          GET RID OF THEM!

               ALBERT
          I'm trying.

As Morris is flung, he pulls off one of the windshield wipers. Using it as a weapon, he starts whacking Albert in the shoulder through the open window.

196) INT. FARMER'S TRUCK - DAY

Albert flinches with every whack.

               ALBERT
         Ouch! Hey stop that!

The truck careens and crashes into a telephone booth. Morris and Ben are thrown free from the truck.

TO BEN: As Ben comes to and looks up, Larry is standing over him with his gun aimed at him.

                    LARRY
          You stupid cop. You just
          couldn't stay out of it.
          Now it's gonna cost you.

Larry cocks the gun and aims it. Suddenly, his gun hand is
hit with a windshield wiper. The gun fires and drops, but
misses Ben. Ben ducks to the ground as Morris steps forward
with the wiper. Larry rubs his hand as he turns to see his
aggressor. Just then, Albert staggers up to them. He pulls
his knife from his back pocket.

                    LARRY
          Kill these Mayberry hicks.

Albert looks at the knife then tosses it towards Larry. It
lands at his feet.

                    ALBERT
          You do it. I'm tired of you
          telling me what to do.

Larry sneers at Albert, then dives for the knife. Morris
dives at the same time. They collide and fight on the
ground, struggling over the knife. Larry jabs the knife
over and over towards Morris' mid section as they fight.
Finally, Morris grabs him, pulls him up to his feet and
punches him. Larry staggers back.

The café CROWD "Oooohhs" with the punch. Morris pulls him
back and aims his fist.

                    MORRIS
          We ain't hicks and this ain't
          Mayberry. It's Hopeville.

WHAM, he punches him out. Larry collapses onto the ground.
The crowd CHEERS and runs to gather around them. Albert
quickly raises his hands and collapses to his knees in
surrender. As the crowd surrounds them, Morris steps to Ben
and helps him up. Jenny pushes through the crowd to embrace
Morris. Jenny sees that Ben is bleeding.

                    JENNY
          Someone call an ambulance!

Jenny feels something strange on her hand that's around
Morris' waist. She lifts her hand and looks at the blood.

                    MORRIS
               (Oozy)
          I guess he got me.

Morris collapses.

197) INT. HOSPITAL ROOM - AFTERNOON

POV: Of Morris as he comes to. His Father, Mother, Jenny, and Alice come into focus. His Father leans towards him.

> FATHER
> Morris? Morris, are you okay?

> MORRIS
> (Sluggish)
> I'm fine. I just had this strange dream where I jumped on this truck and someone stabbed me and-

> FATHER
> It wasn't a dream, Morris. They were only flesh wounds but you needed stitches.

> MORRIS
> Oh, and the Sheriff part?

> FATHER
> That was Jenny's idea.

Jenny leans in.

> JENNY
> Everybody got together and-

Jenny digs into her bag and pulls out a stack of papers.

> JENNY Continues
> We get over three hundred signatures. More than enough to put you on the ballot for Sheriff. You're gonna be the next Sheriff of Hopeville, Morris.

She puts them back into her bag.

> JENNY
> (To Walter)
> I have to get these in today to get him on the ballot.

Morris tries to sit up. His Mother stops him.

> MOTHER
> You have to stay -

> MORRIS
> No, Mother. I want to do it.

198) EXT. CITY HALL BUILDING - AFTERNOON

Morris is helped up the steps to the front steps, his midsection covered with bandages, as the town is crowded on both sides of the steps watching. When he gets to the top at the entrance, he turns and looks back at the crowd. They cheer.

199) INT. CITY HALL - AFTERNOON

Morris enters the main doors and sees that the pictures of his past relatives who held office have been put back up. As Morris steps towards the office, Jenny steps up, hands him the signatures, and kisses him on the cheek. Before he can take another step, Ben steps up wearing an arm sling. He offers his hand. Morris shakes it.

>   BEN
> It might sound weird, but I
> wanted to wish you luck.

>   MORRIS
> Thanks. And thanks for hanging
> the portraits back up.

>   BEN
> They're heroes..like you. They
> belong there.

Ben steps back to allow Morris to continue.

200) INT. HOPEVILLE CAFÉ - MORNING

The café door opens. CLOSEUP: On the Sheriff badge and follow it as the guy wearing it moves to the counter and sits. We move up to reveal a smiling Morris. Jenny moves in close to his face, so close he can smell her breath.

>   JENNY
> Good morning...Sheriff.

>   MORRIS
> You can call me Morris or Moe.

>   JENNY
> Are you sure? How would that
> look? The Sheriff flirting
> with a waitress? You might
> get a reputation.

>   MORRIS
> You have a point there.

Just then, Ben enters, and yeah, guess what? He's wearing the dogcatcher uniform that Morris used to wear. Ben pats Morris on the shoulder as he passes.

                    BEN
          Morning, Moe.

                  MORRIS
          (Without taking eyes off Jenny)
          Morning Ben.
          (To Jenny)
          Maybe I can save my reputation.

                  JENNY
          You have an idea?

                  MORRIS
          Yeah, but I can't share it here.

                  JENNY
          Ohhhhh, I see. Maybe we should step into my office.

Jenny tries to poke Morris in the eyes. He blocks it.

                  MORRIS
          That would work.

Jenny turns and heads towards the storage room. She opens the door. Morris follows and steps into the room. She closes it. It's pitch dark. We can't see either one.

                  JENNY
          Maybe we should turn on the light.

                  MORRIS
          I have a better idea.

A dream cloud begins to form above their heads. It lights the closet and their faces. Jenny looks up at it. It's a beautiful beach with white sand and sky blue water.

                  JENNY
          Now maybe I'm crazy, but I think there's a dream above us.

                  MORRIS
          It's mine.

                  JENNY
          That's your dream?

Morris takes her hand and lifts it towards the dream. Whoosh, they're sucked into the dream.

201) INT. BEACH DREAM - DAY

There they are standing on that beautiful beach. Morris takes her hand.

> MORRIS
> It's my dream of our honeymoon.

> JENNY
> Honeymoon?

> MORRIS
> Only one problem.

> JENNY
> Yes...I will.

Jenny wraps her arms around his neck. They passionately kiss. She pulls back and looks at him.

> JENNY
> I only have one question.

> MORRIS
> What's that?

> JENNY
> How do we get back? Knuck Knuck.

> MORRIS
> Who cares?

They passionately kiss again.

Run Credits

Credit Scenes:

202) INT. AL'S FANCY LADIES STRIP-CLUB - NIGHT

The club is packed with Hopeville Townspeople. Alice, dressed in her skimpy cowboy outfit is gyrating and dancing to a steamy song. Everyone from the film is applauding and cheering, including Morris, Jenny, Ben, and Morris' parents.

203) INT. HIGH SCHOOL GYM - GRADUATION SCENE

Willard dressed in his high school gown and hat receives his GED diploma from a State Education representative as the whole town applauds.

Finish CREDITS:

                          The END

NOW YOU CAN FADE OUT:

A FINAL NOTE

REMEMBER TO WRITE what you know or love and that the words should make you laugh, cry, scare the hell out of you, or take you on a fantastic adventure... a rollercoaster ride. Write from your heart and gut, and if you need to take your kid gloves off to tell the story, do it! Be bold, be brave and try to be original. And most of all try to find that one thing that studios (including Spielberg) look for... a little magic. Good luck, and happy writing!

Jackie Lynn Young

AUTHOR BIO

JACKIE LYNN YOUNG earned a BA degree in Technical Management from Bellevue University with minor degrees in Commercial Art and Electronics Technology. Jack has managed Young Films, LLC since 2001, when he wrote, executive produced, and co-produced *Love Wine*, a romantic comedy. Additional credits include the short film, *Manimals*, which he wrote, produced, and executive produced. He also acted as manager on the Read-A-Movie™ series books and is author of many of the stories that appear in it. He has been the coordinator of Nebraskans for Film (a local screenwriting group) for over four years and has been a member of the Nebraska Writers Workshop (NWW), chaired by Sally Walker, for over five years. Jack has also appeared in *Screentalk Magazine* and is the author of over thirty original screenplays. Jack works full time as a Logistics Engineer Level III for a communications company and government contractor.

Visit our web site at www.readamovie.com

www.ingramcontent.com/pod-product-compliance
Lightning Source LLC
Chambersburg PA
CBHW071649090426
42738CB00009B/1473